IMAGES
of America

ALONG THE CHRISTINA RIVER

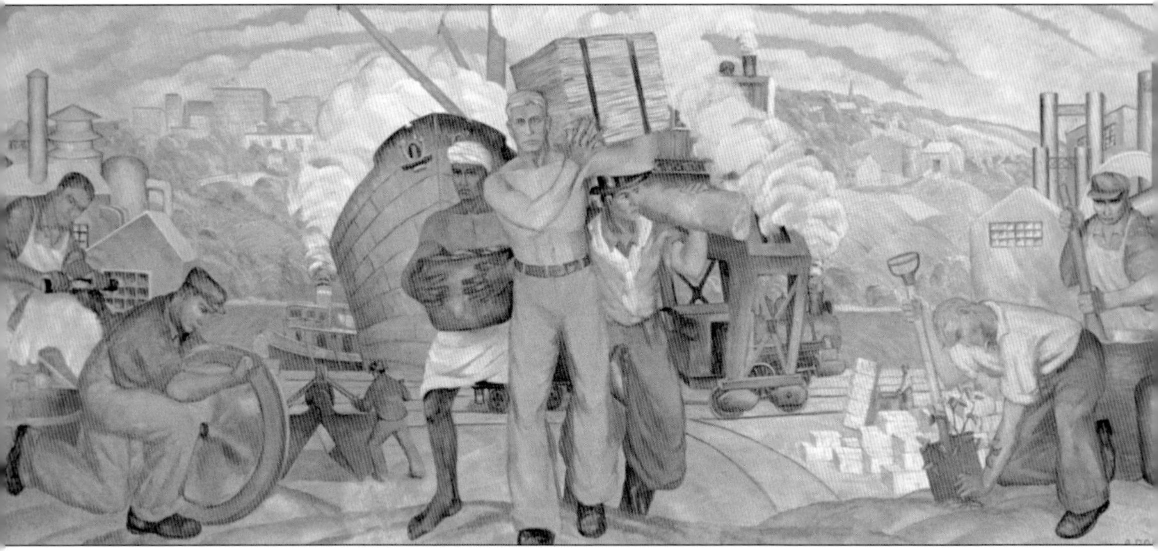

To honor the hardworking people and industry of Wilmington, native Delawarean Andrew Doragh (1897–1992) painted a mural in 1939 that hung in a building at the Port of Wilmington until 1995, when the city relinquished port operations to the state-owned Diamond State Port Corporation. The mural currently hangs in the lobby of the Louis L. Redding City/County Building. (Courtesy of Delaware Historical Society.)

On the Cover: Wilmington traces its founding to the colony of New Sweden, established when 24 Swedish and Finnish settlers arrived at "the Rocks" on the banks of the Christina River on March 29, 1638. The event is commemorated with Fort Christina Park at the foot of Seventh Street. The park was built by the Delaware State Highway Department (now DELDOT) in time to mark the colony's 300th anniversary in 1938. Swedish sculptor Carl Milles (1875–1955) created the granite monument topped with a representation of one of the settlers' two ships, the *Kalmar Nyckel* (meaning "Key of Kalmar"). (Courtesy of the Delaware Public Archives.)

IMAGES
of America

ALONG THE CHRISTINA RIVER

William Francis

ARCADIA
PUBLISHING

ISBN 978-1-4671-2043-2

Published by Arcadia Publishing
Charleston, South Carolina

Printed in the United States of America

Library of Congress Control Number: 2013935330

For all general information, please contact Arcadia Publishing:
Telephone 843-853-2070
Fax 843-853-0044
E-mail sales@arcadiapublishing.com
For customer service and orders:
Toll-Free 1-888-313-2665

Visit us on the Internet at www.arcadiapublishing.com

As always, to Michele

Contents

Acknowledgments

It is impossible to complete a work such as this alone. I am indebted to the great staffs at the Delaware Public Archives in Dover and the Delaware Historical Society in Wilmington. A big thank-you is extended for the assistance from the Newark Historical Society, Tom Zaleski and the City of Newark Parks & Recreation Department, Gerry Samson and the Minquas Fire Company of Newport, the Hagley Museum and Library, Bruce Knight, and Kenneth Baumgardt. I have a great appreciation to all the authors of the historical documents I viewed while compiling this book, from simple newspaper articles to printed volumes. I especially wish to thank DELDOT for its online archaeology reports and annual reports, which were instrumental in my research.

All images in this book, except where otherwise noted, are courtesy of the Delaware Public Archives, Dover, Delaware.

INTRODUCTION

Noted Delaware historian Clinton A. Weslager (1909–1994) calls the Christina River "Delaware's Forgotten River" in his 1947 history book with that nickname as its title. Another river in New Castle County, the Brandywine, is famous as the source of power for Wilmington's grain-milling industry and the DuPont Powder Works, but the Christina is the major river of New Castle County, and the Brandywine but one of its tributaries. Technically, the Christina is 15 miles long, starting about one half mile south of Kimblesville, Pennsylvania. It flows briefly in Cecil County, Maryland, and then crosses northern Delaware, passing Newark, Christiana, and Newport and emptying into the Delaware River at the Port of Wilmington. Along with the Brandywine, the White Clay Creek and the Red Clay Creek are major tributaries, flowing into the river's basin at Churchman's Marsh. The Christina River watershed encompasses 78 square miles and provides 100 million gallons of water a day for half a million people.

The Christina River was a major food source for native Lenni Lenape and Minquas tribes. In 1638, it welcomed European settlers from Sweden and Finland to what became Wilmington. The leader of this expedition, Peter Minuit (1580–1638), named the river after Sweden's child queen and called the colony Nya Sverige ("New Sweden"). The settlers had arrived on the Dutch-built *Kalmar Nyckel,* which made four trips to the New World, bringing more than 600 Scandinavians. However, Sweden's colonial efforts lacked support from home. In 1655, Dutch governor Peter Stuyvesant invaded with seven ships and 300 soldiers, and New Sweden surrendered without a shot fired. By 1664, the region fell under British control. New Sweden's legacy is the founding of Wilmington and the introduction of the log cabin to America.

Over the centuries, however, there has been confusion about the river's true name. Some old documents, maps, and school textbooks identify the waterway as the Christiana River. Under British rule, a variety of spellings were used, including Christianna, Christeen, Christiania, and Christinia. William Shipley of Wilmington called it the Christiana when he wrote and asked Thomas Penn (William Penn's son) for a charter, and Thomas Penn, in turn, called it as the Christiana. So, for many years, documents and Delawareans accepted the British interpretations and referred to the river as the Christiana. To end the confusion, Delaware state lawmakers, in preparation for the 300th anniversary of the Swedish colony that founded Wilmington, passed a law in 1937 that officially named the river Christina. The citizens in the village of Christiana, however, refused to change the town's name, and Christiana remains in the popular lexicon thanks in part to its attachment to a large shopping mall and hospital.

In Newark, the Christina River was part of the Welsh Tract of mining and milling operations and of the landscape during the only battle of the Revolutionary War fought on Delaware soil. At Christiana, the waterway played an important role in moving American troops and supplies throughout that conflict.

The Christina River was also instrumental in the founding and development of Christiana and Newport. The Christina was navigable inland to the town of Christiana, known through most of its early history as "Christiana's Bridge." It was more of an unofficial term than a name because shippers stopped their boats at the "bridge at Christiana," unloaded their shipments, and then used wagons to continue into Maryland and the Chesapeake Bay. This river-and-land course almost became a canal route, and some preliminary digging was done at Christiana before the idea was abandoned. Then, in 1829, the Chesapeake and Delaware Canal opened between Delaware City and Chesapeake City.

Newport joined Christiana as a thriving shipping center before the era of railroads. The town can also claim that one of its citizens, Oliver Evans—and not a du Pont—launched the American industrial revolution in Wilmington. In the 1780s, he created a new system of automated flour milling that, with an ingenious arrangement of water-driven wheels, gears, and shafts, almost eliminated the need for human labor in the process of turning wheat into flour. Evans's gristmills made Wilmington flour the most desired of the Colonial period and put Wilmington on the map before the first du Pont arrived.

Wilmington would develop from the Christina River around Front Street and up Market Street. Along the river's northern banks, heavy industry developed because of the arrival of the railroad in 1837. Tracks from the Philadelphia, Wilmington & Baltimore Railroad allowed for the shipping of heavy materials that would be used in railcar manufacturing and shipbuilding. During World War II, Wilmington was the largest shipbuilding city in the United States. On the Christina's south side, South Wilmington developed from marshland into a working-class neighborhood. South Wilmington streets are somewhat unusual in that, instead of numbers, letters designate east-west roads. For example, instead of Fourth Street, South Wilmington has D Street. With the heavy industry gone along the Christina River, South Wilmington has struggled to survive.

However, the world knows about the Port of Wilmington, which plays a vital role in global commerce as a full-service deepwater port and marine terminal that handles an average of 400 vessels per year. It is the nation's number one importer of fresh fruit and juice concentrates, among the many products it imports and exports.

The Christina River is not forgotten. Its role in the history and development of northern Delaware is well chronicled, and I am pleased to visually reiterate that history in the pages of this book.

One

Newark

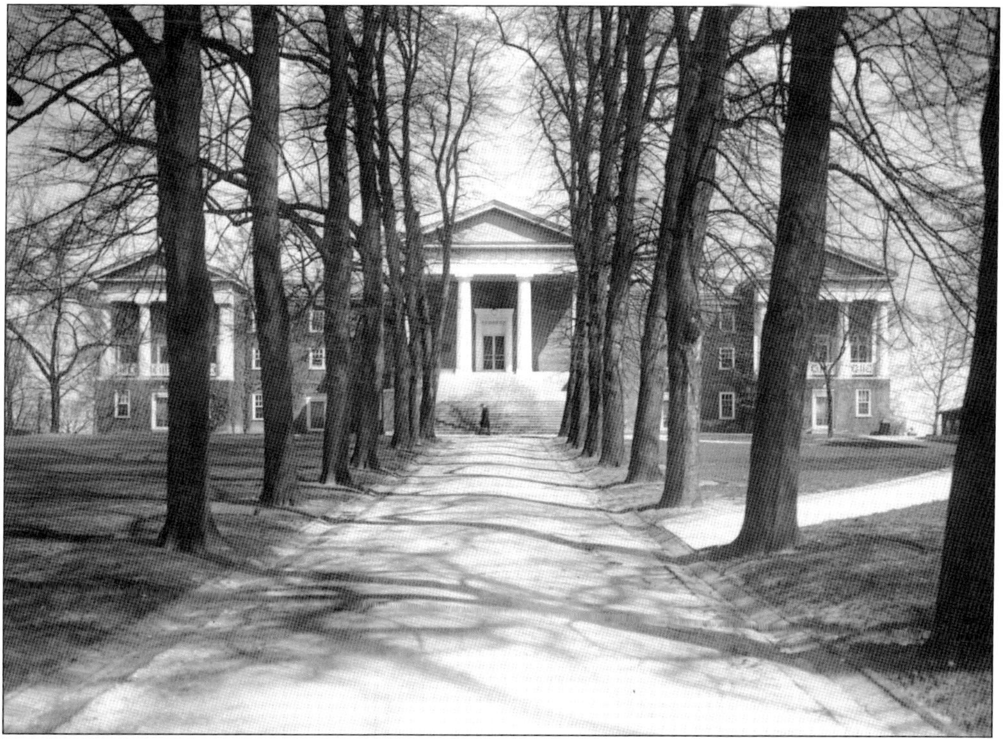

Among all the towns along the Christina River, Newark's founding and development was not as dependent upon the river as it was on the White Clay Creek, a tributary of the Christina. The Christina is more creek than river as it flows past the town's west and south sides, an area home to the University of Delaware. Pictured is Old College Hall on East Main Street in 1936. It opened as the all-male Newark College in 1834 and was renamed Delaware College in 1843.

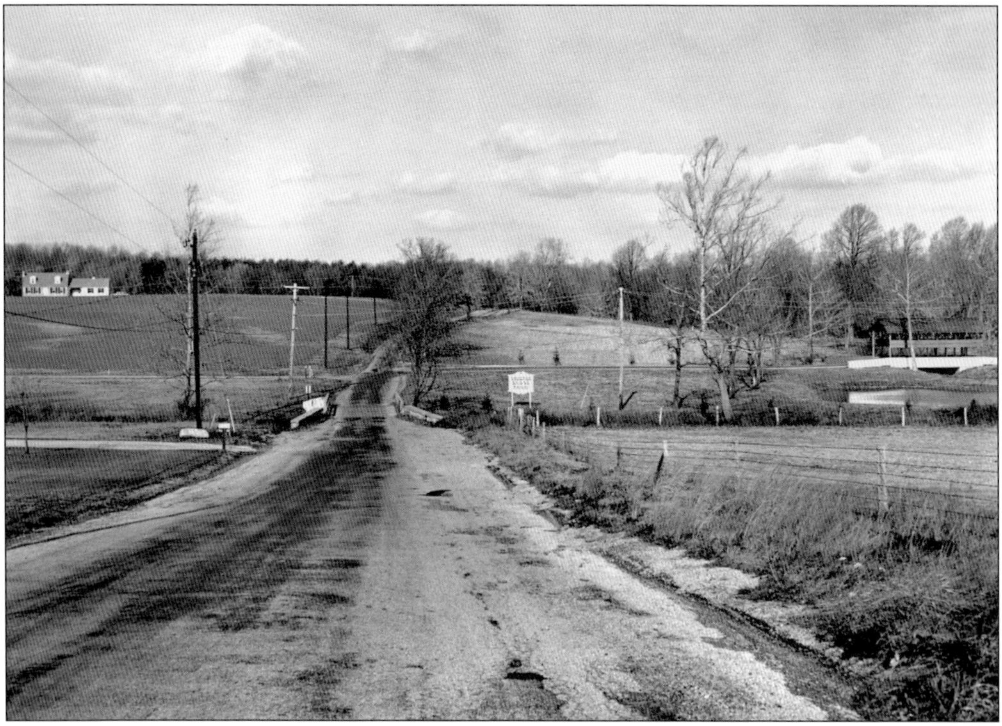

The Christina River (more of a creek at this point) enters Delaware west of Newark and flows beneath Wedgewood Road off Nottingham Road (Route 273). The east branch of the Christina flows under the covered bridge seen on the right, and the two waterways link near a housing development named Covered Bridge Farms.

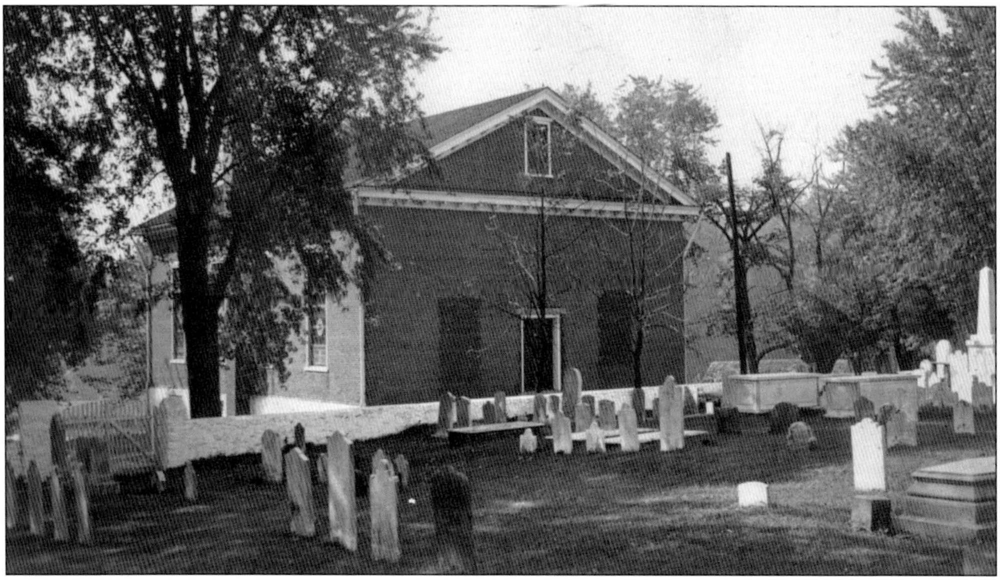

The Head of the Christiana Presbyterian Church at 1100 West Church Road is an example of the confusion over the river's true name. The church was founded in 1706. Its first, log building was replaced by a brick structure that burned down in 1858, and the present church was erected a year later. In 1983, it was listed in the National Register of Historic Places.

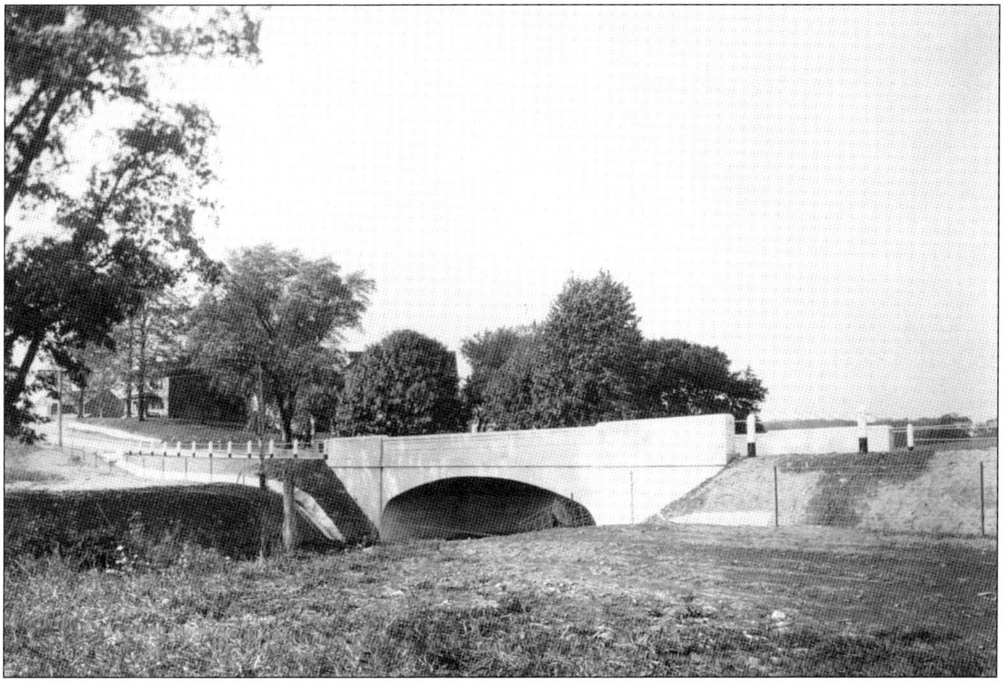

The Christina flows under Nottingham Road (Route 273) near its intersection with New Casho Mill Road. The arch bridge was photographed in 1930. From there, the river, or creek, continues south under Barksdale Road, then Elkton Road.

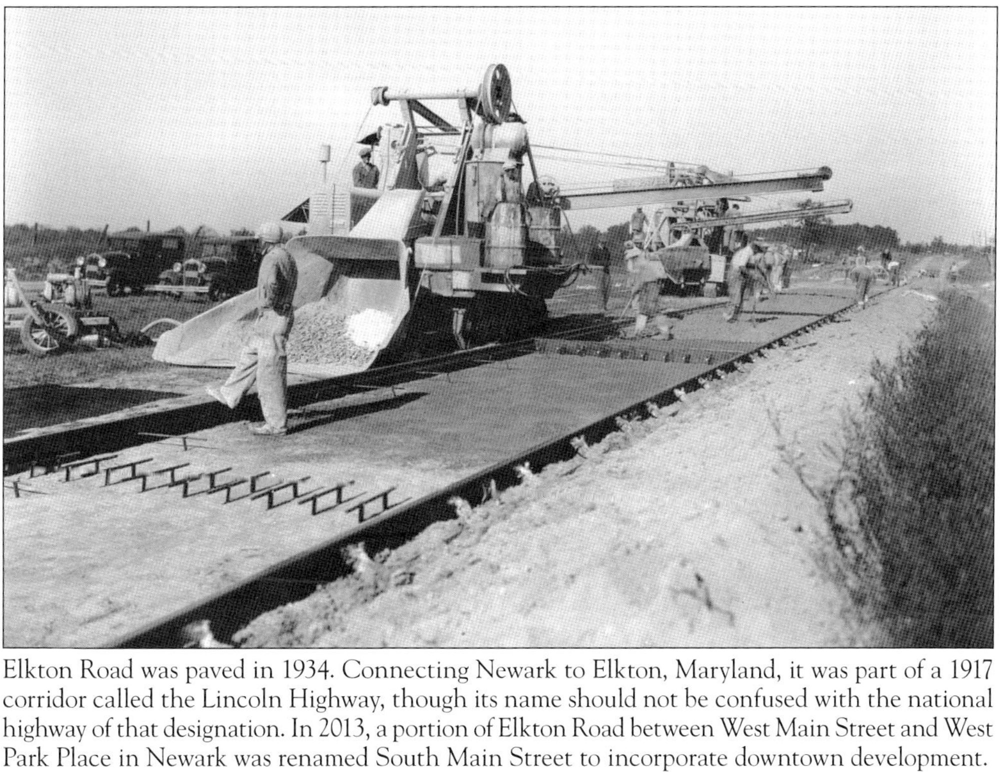

Elkton Road was paved in 1934. Connecting Newark to Elkton, Maryland, it was part of a 1917 corridor called the Lincoln Highway, though its name should not be confused with the national highway of that designation. In 2013, a portion of Elkton Road between West Main Street and West Park Place in Newark was renamed South Main Street to incorporate downtown development.

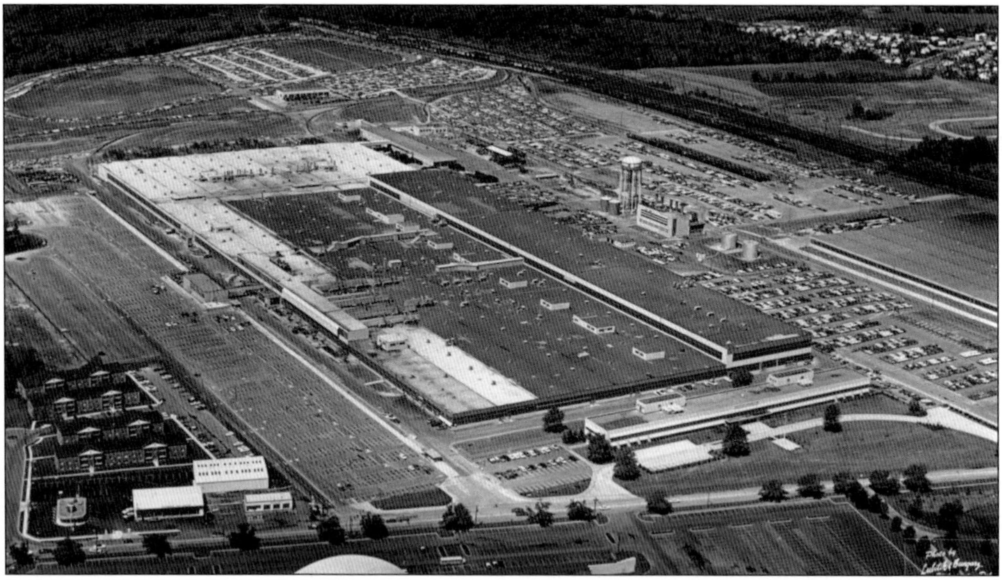

The Christina passes behind the former site of the Chrysler Automobile Assembly Plant on South College Avenue. Seen here in a 1969 aerial shot, the plant opened in 1952 and produced the Patton 48 medium tank. It converted to automobile production in 1957 but made its last car in 2008. (Courtesy of Delaware Historical Society.)

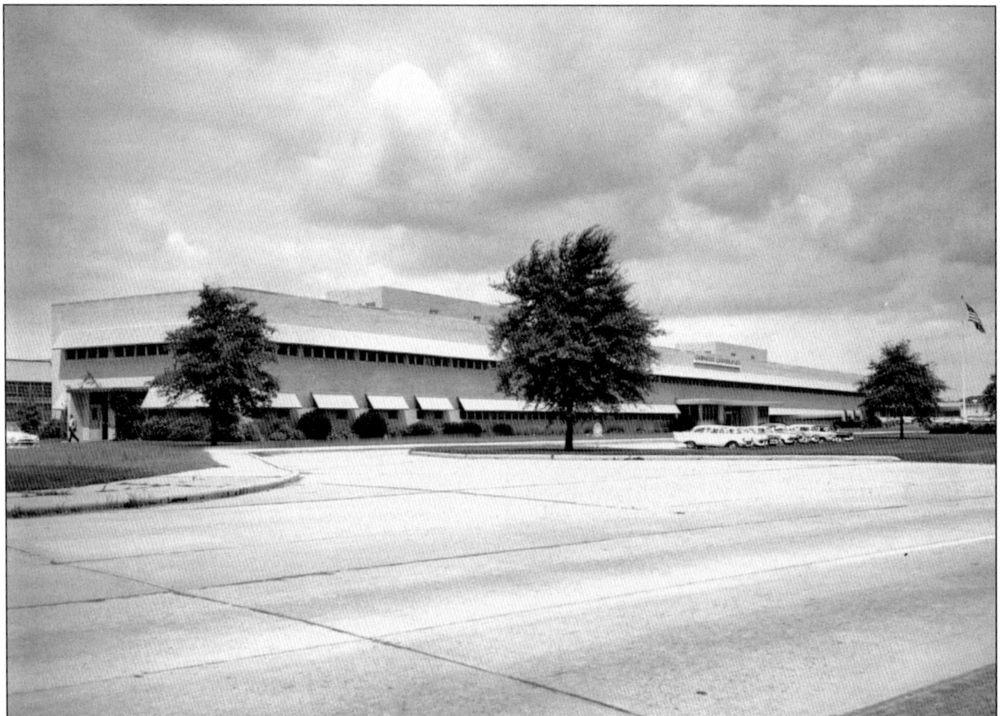

The University of Delaware bought the 272-acre property for $24.25 million and tore down the plant to convert the site into the STAR Campus—with facilities for science, technology, and advanced research.

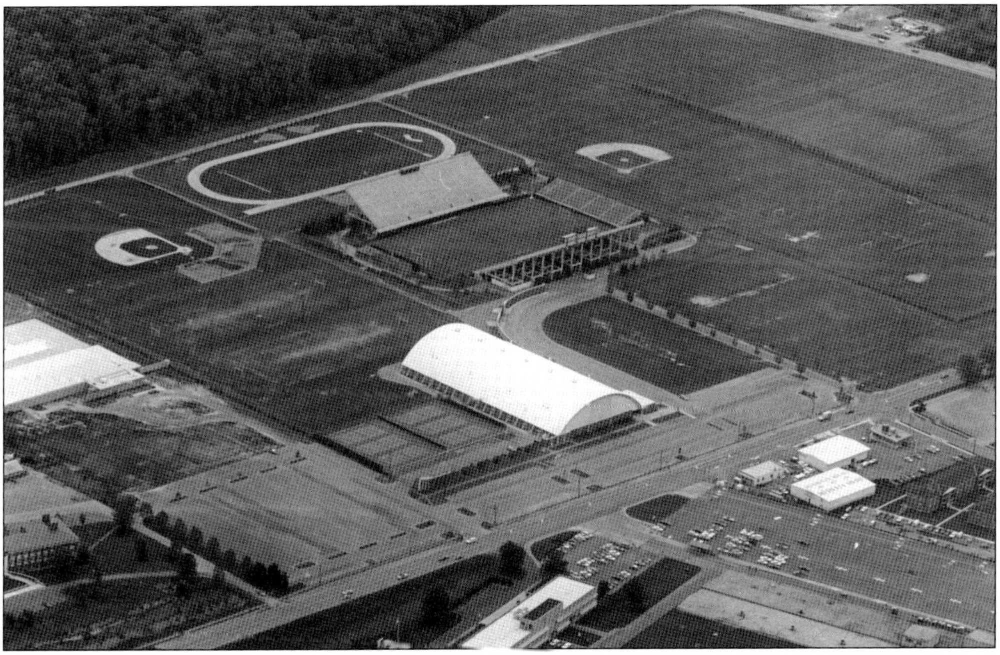

The University of Delaware's athletic facilities on South College Avenue are on land that had been part of the school's experimental farm. This 1971 aerial shot shows the football stadium and the soccer, baseball, and softball fields. The building with the arched roof is the 4,000-seat Delaware Field House, which was built in 1966 and was home to indoor sports and Blue Hen basketball until the Bob Carpenter Center opened in 1992. (Courtesy of Delaware Historical Society.)

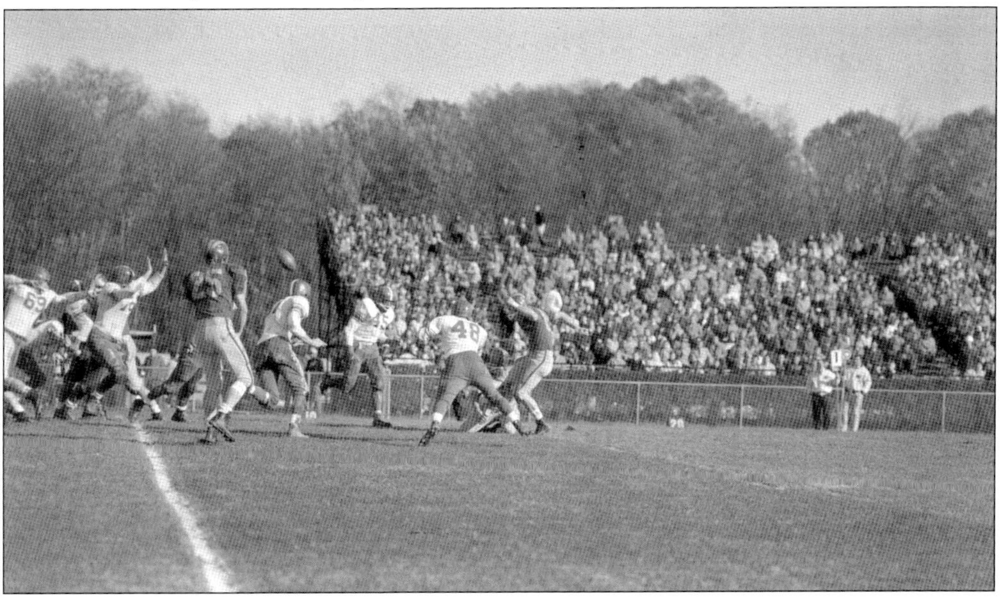

The University of Delaware Fightin' Blue Hens football program began in 1889. The team competed at Fraser Field and Wilmington Park before Delaware Stadium opened in 1952. This photograph shows an extra-point attempt by the Blue Hens during a 71-7 victory over Temple in 1957; the former visitor-side bleachers can be seen in the background. (Courtesy of Delaware Historical Society.)

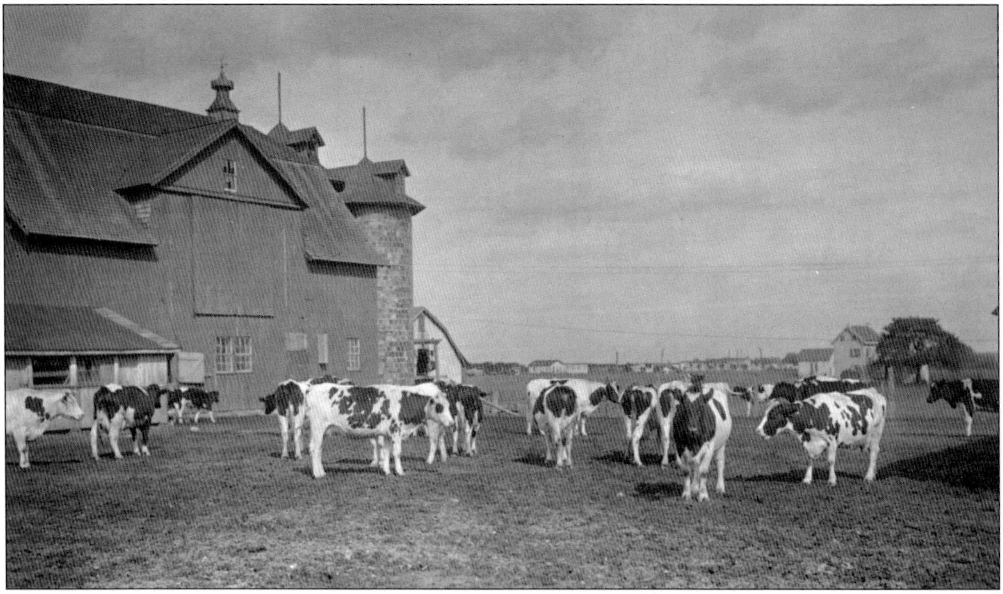

Seen here is a herd of Holstein cattle at the university's experimental farm in 1925. The farm began in 1907 on 212 acres as the Delaware Agricultural Experiment Station, to help farmers improve their agricultural yields. It is currently part of the school's College of Agriculture & Natural Resources on South College Avenue.

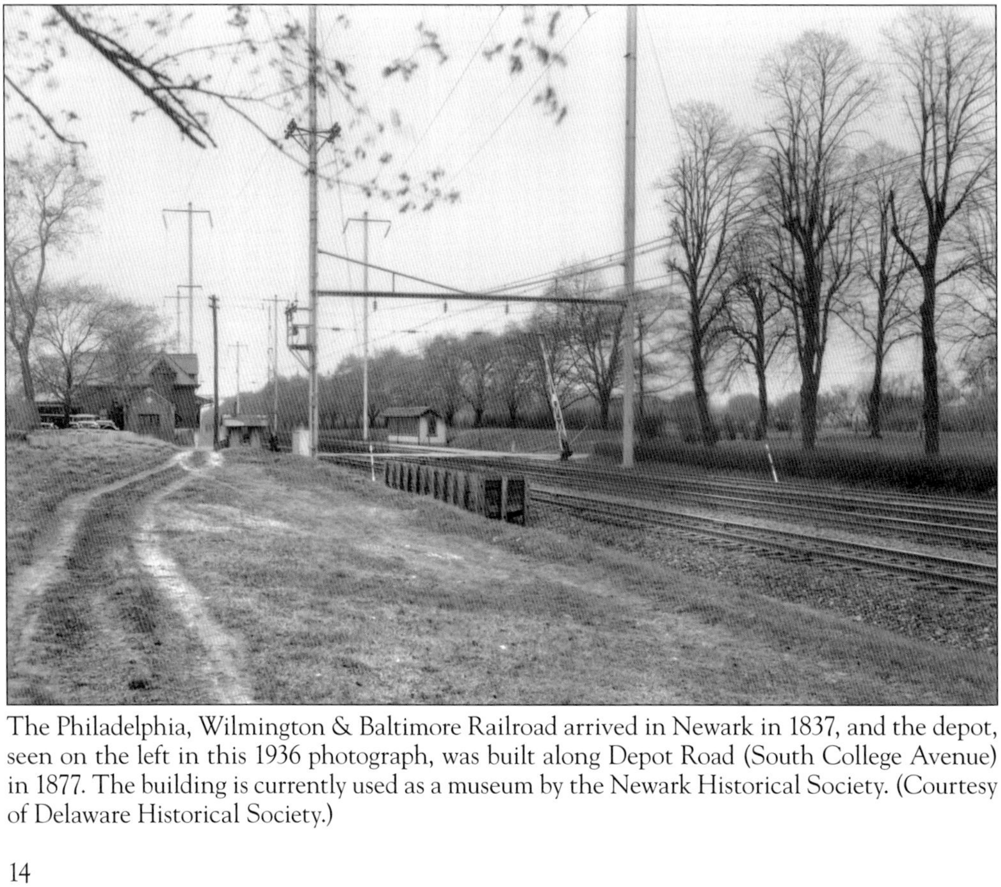

The Philadelphia, Wilmington & Baltimore Railroad arrived in Newark in 1837, and the depot, seen on the left in this 1936 photograph, was built along Depot Road (South College Avenue) in 1877. The building is currently used as a museum by the Newark Historical Society. (Courtesy of Delaware Historical Society.)

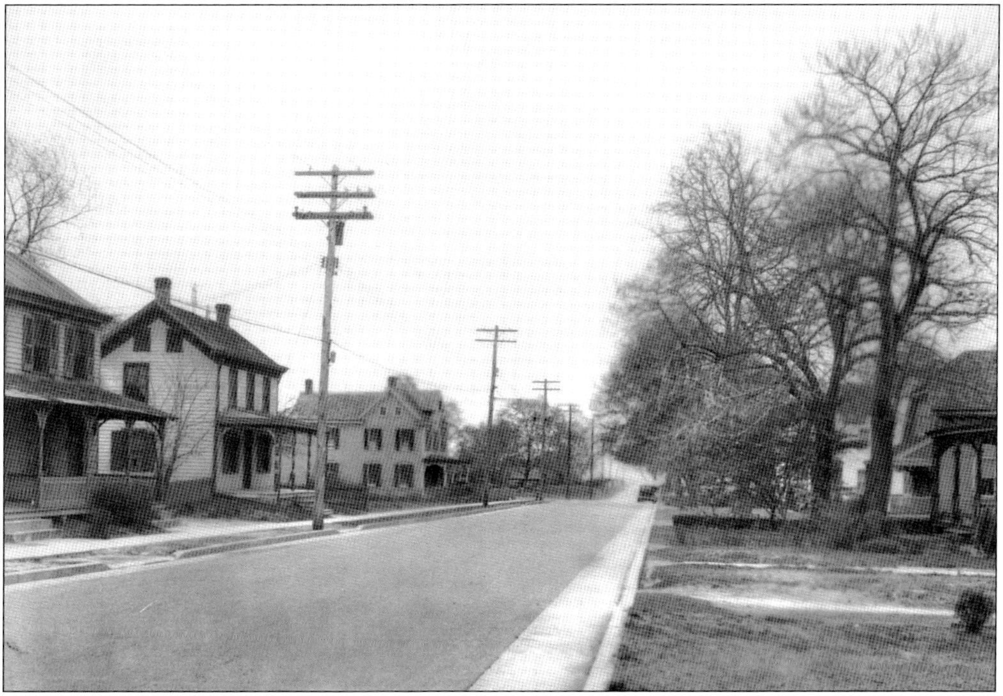

At the start of the 20th century, lots were sold from Main Street south along Depot Road (South College Avenue) to Pennsylvania Station. The Philadelphia, Wilmington & Baltimore Railroad line changed names over the years; currently, the rails are part of Amtrak's busy northeast corridor between Washington, DC, and Boston. This photograph, with a view looking south from Park Place, dates to 1936. (Courtesy of Delaware Historical Society.)

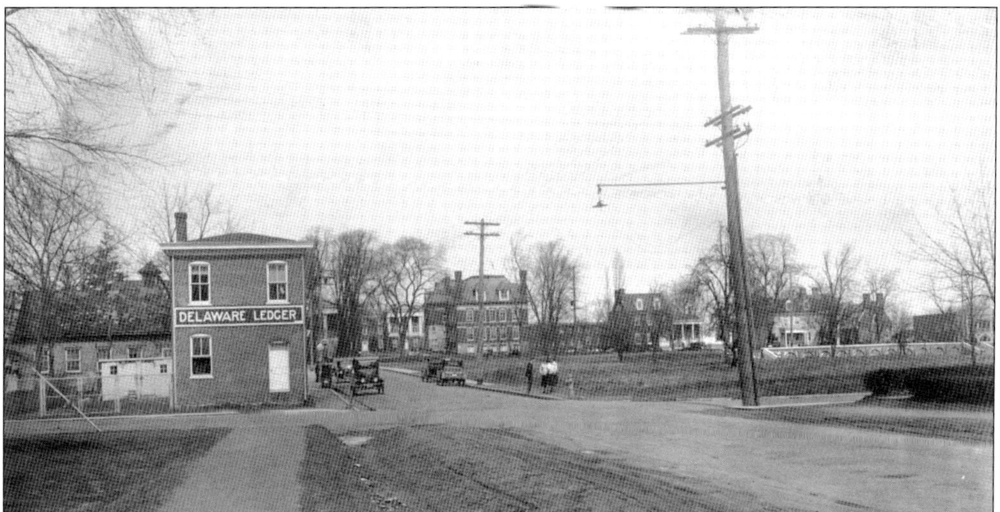

In this 1925 image of the intersection of Depot Road (South College Avenue) and Delaware Avenue, the building on the left houses the *Delaware Ledger,* which began in 1876 as the *Saturday Visitor* and was the first newspaper in Newark. The *Saturday Visitor,* started by J.H. Rowlinson, was a weekly paper that changed owners and names often until 1881, when it was purchased by Theodore Erling and named the *Delaware Ledger.*

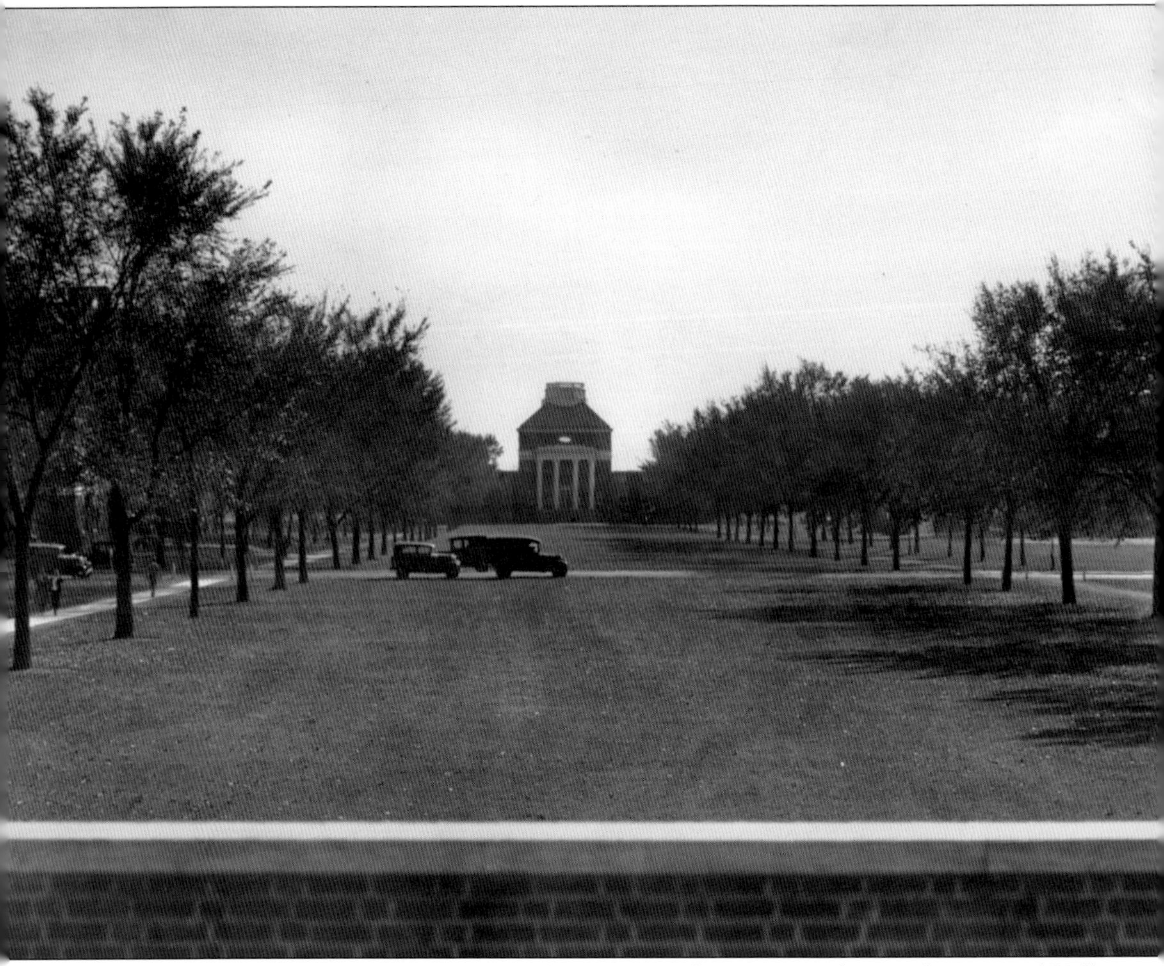

The historic Green at the University of Delaware is seen here in 1933 along with Memorial Hall in the distance and two-way automobile traffic on East Delaware Avenue. In 1915, Hugh Rodney Sharp, a Delaware College graduate and member of the board of trustees, got his brother-in-law Pierre S. du Pont to secretly buy the land between the all-male Delaware College on Main Street and the Delaware Women's College on South College Avenue. Sharp and Samuel Chiles Mitchell hired architects Frank Miles Day and Charles Z. Klauder and landscape designer Marian Cruger Coffin to provide a development plan for the new space. It took until the year 2002, with the expansion of Du Pont Hall, for their plan for the Green to be realized.

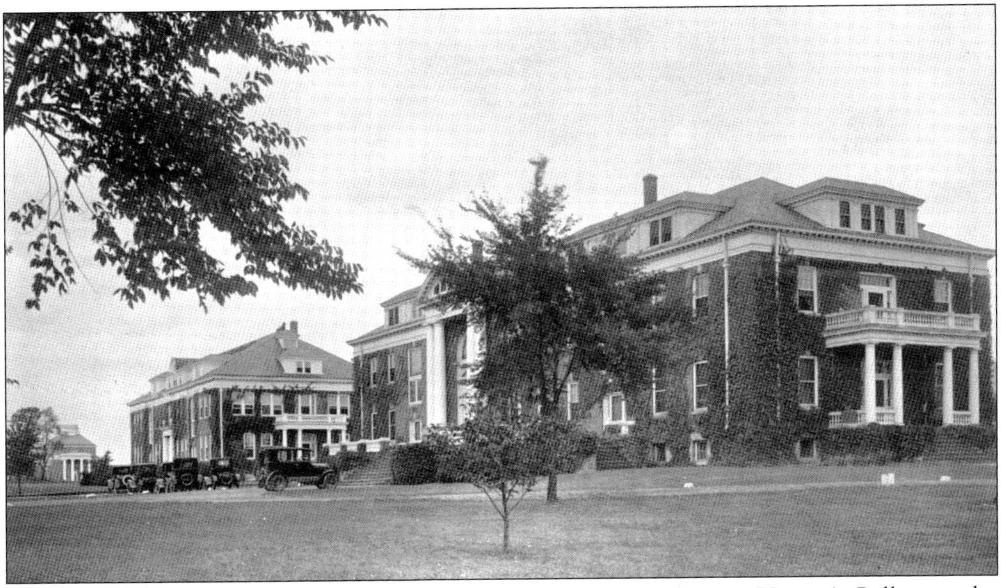

The University of Delaware's historic campus has the former Delaware Women's College at the corner of South College Avenue and Park Place. Seen here in 1925, it is represented by Residence Hall (now Warner Hall) in the foreground and the neighboring Science Hall (now Robinson Hall). Emalea Pusey Warner was instrumental in getting the school created in 1914, and Winifred Robinson was its first dean.

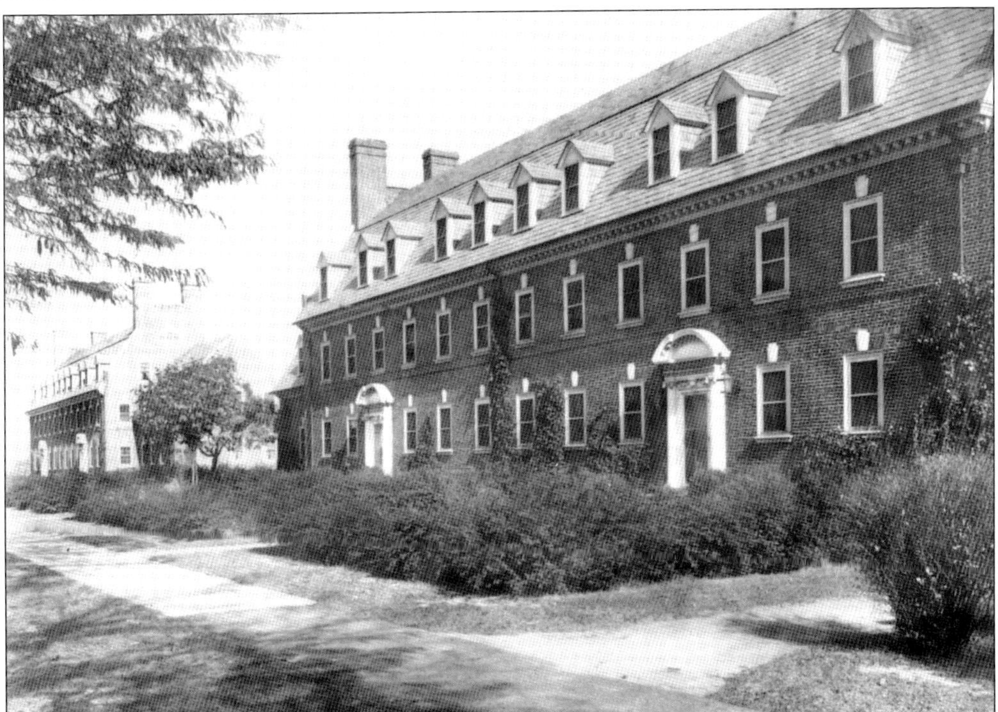

Sussex Hall, photographed in 1931, was built in 1918 as the second dormitory (after Residence Hall) on the Delaware Women's College campus. It continues to serves as a residence hall in what is now called the South Central Campus.

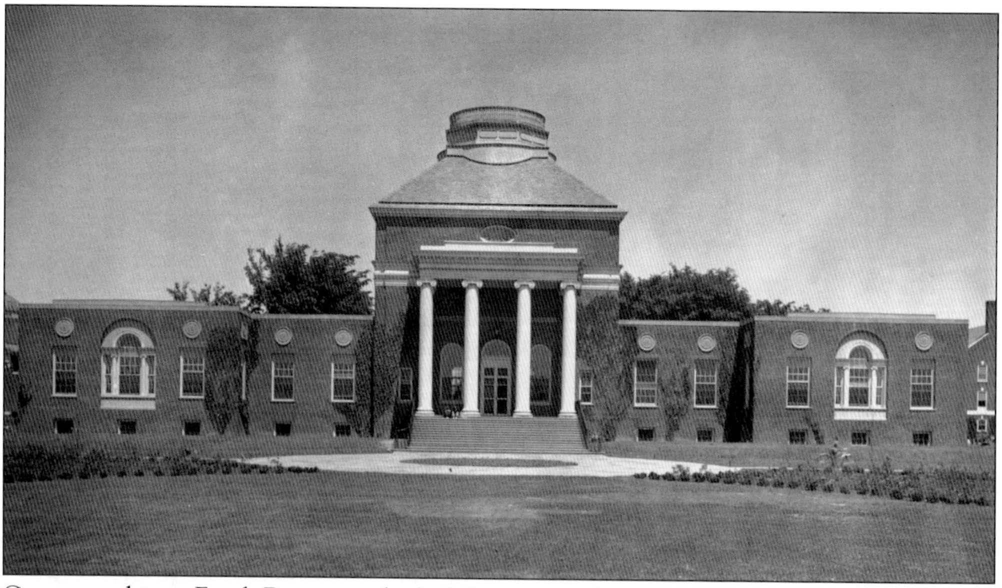

Campus architect Frank Day wanted a building centered on the Green that the students from Delaware College could share with the students from the Delaware Women's College. Memorial Hall, seen here in 1936, opened in 1925 and served as a library for both campuses. It continued as a library until Morris Library opened in 1963.

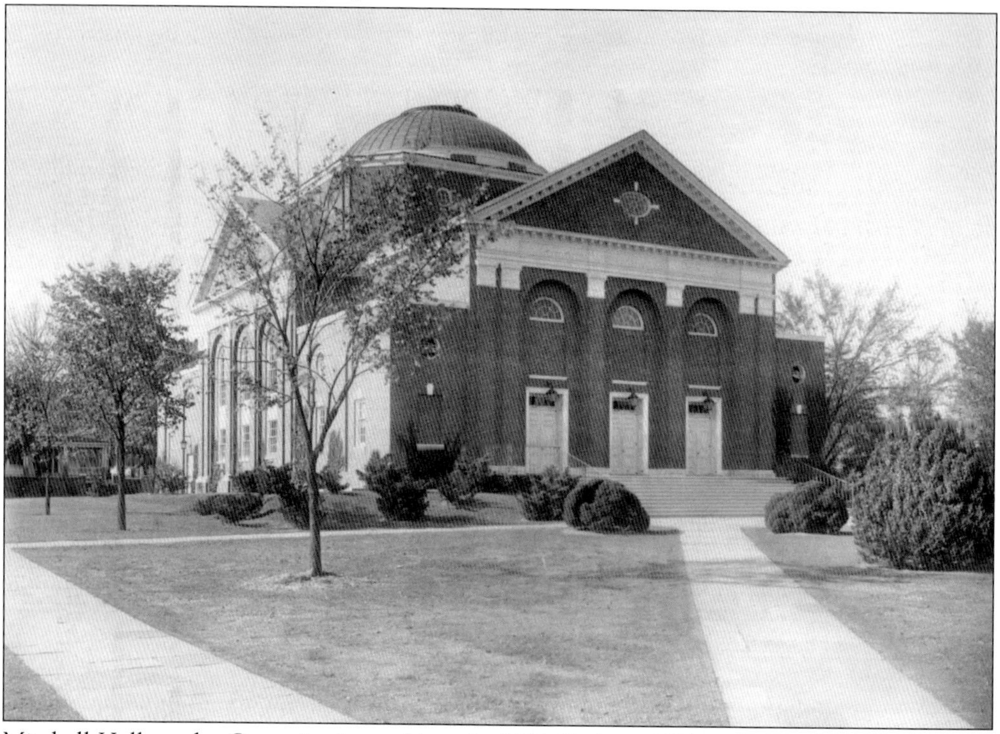

Mitchell Hall on the Green is pictured here in 1931. Built in 1929 and placed in the National Register of Historic Places in 1982, Mitchell Hall was named after former Delaware College president Samuel Chiles Mitchell. The university's first auditorium for the performing arts, it was a gift from Hugh Rodney Sharp.

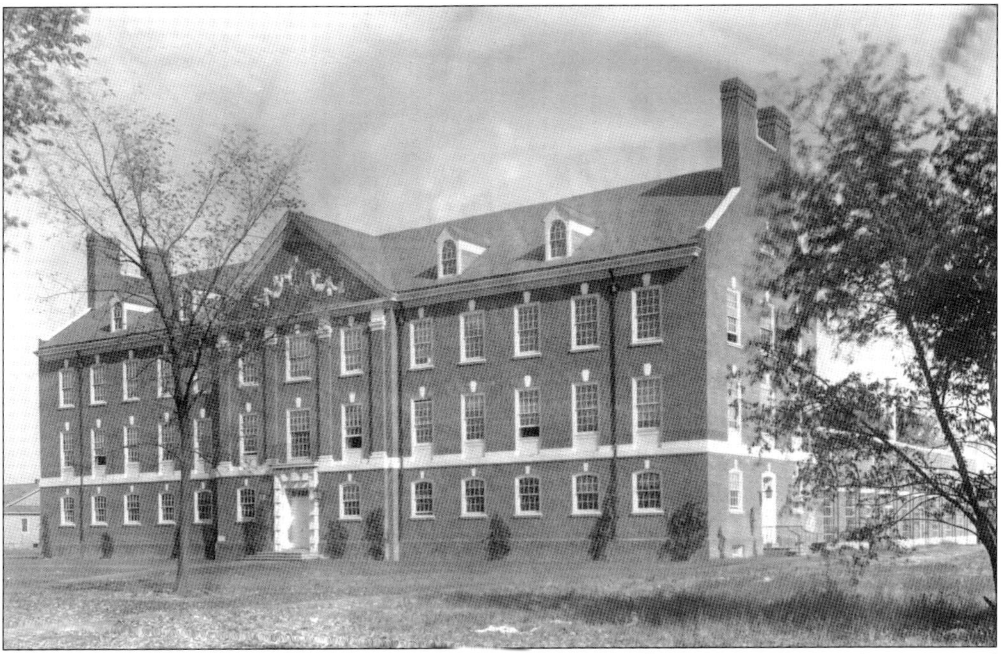

Wolf Hall was the first building on the Green and the first home to agricultural science and chemistry. Built in 1917 and shown here in 1931, it was named after Theodore R. Wolf, the first faculty member to earn a doctorate of philosophy and the longest-serving instructor at Delaware College.

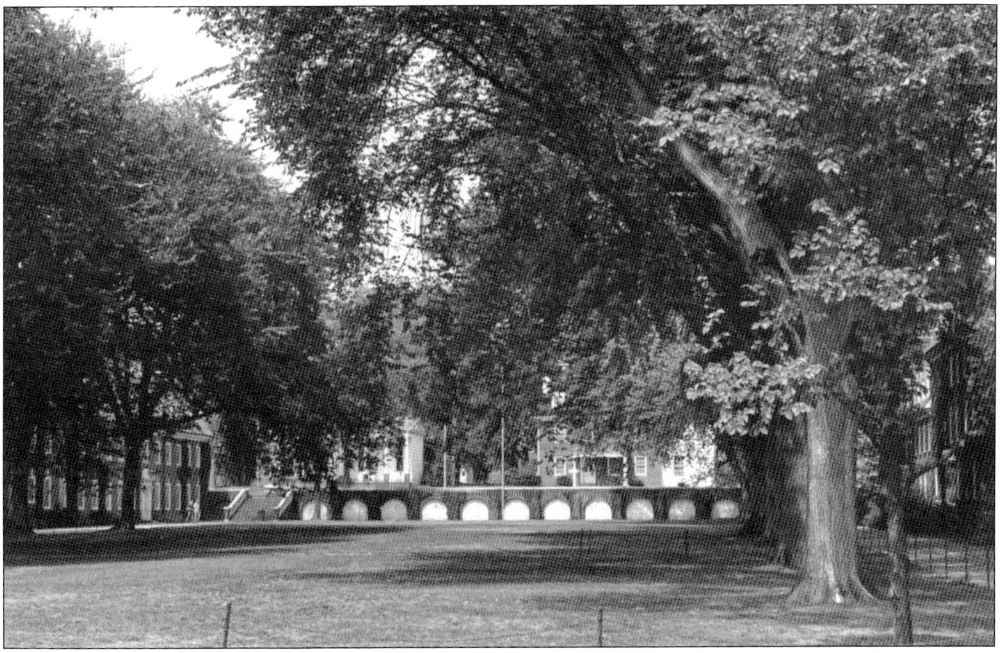

This 1968 view of the Green between Delaware Avenue and Main Street shows the opposing rows of American elms that had been planted by students in 1917. By 1972, some 163 elms existed, their leaves providing shade in spring and summer and great color in autumn. Unfortunately, Dutch elm disease has left few survivors.

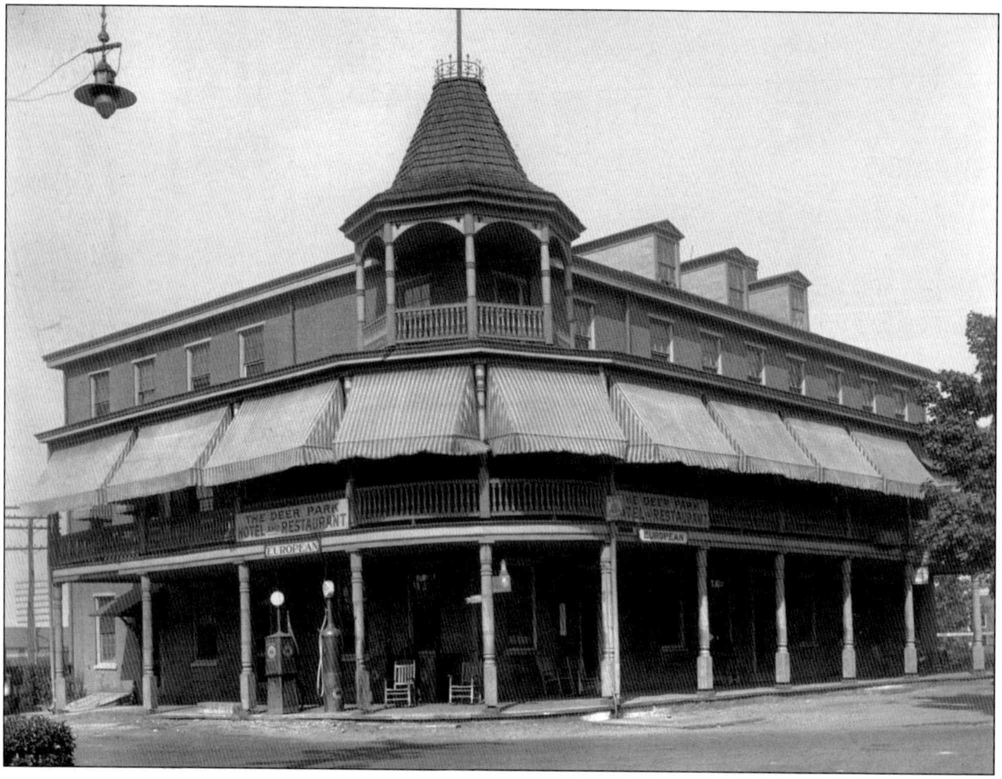

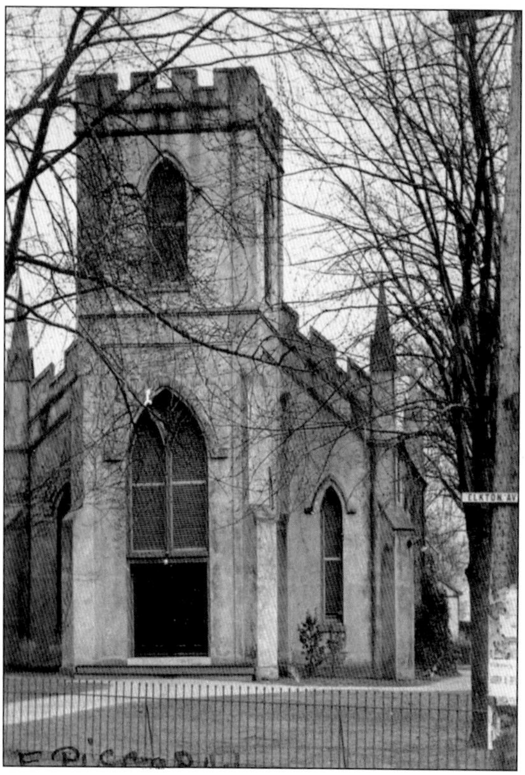

The Deer Park Tavern stands at the junction of East, West, and South Main Streets and New London Road, intersecting routes that were once Native American trails and trade routes. Newark was chartered as a market town by King George II in 1758. The Deer Park Tavern, built in 1851, is a familiar landmark on Newark's west side.

The St. Thomas Episcopal Church at South Main Street and Delaware Avenue is captured here in 1906. Built in 1843 and used as a church for 114 years, it was converted and functioned as the Newark Free Library from 1957 to 1974. It is currently part of the University of Delaware as Bayard Sharp Hall.

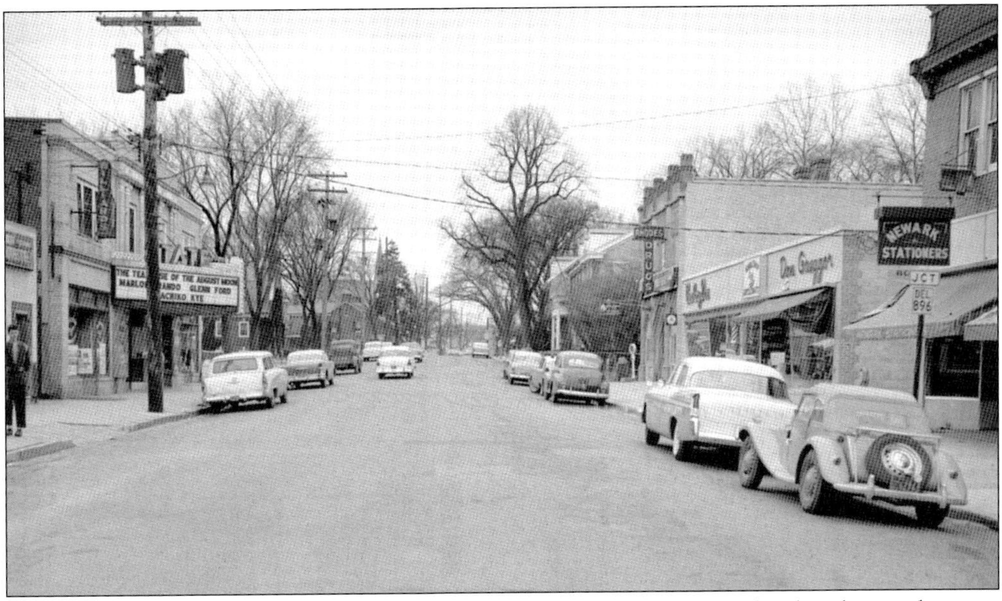

Main Street has changed dramatically over the past 40 years. Two former landmarks seen here are the State Theatre (left) and, across the street, Rhodes Drug Store. The State Theatre operated from 1929 to 1989, and the building was torn down for retail and restaurant space. Dr. George Rhodes had a pharmacy at 168 East Main Street before moving to the Gothic-facade building, complete with gargoyles, at 35 East Main in 1917.

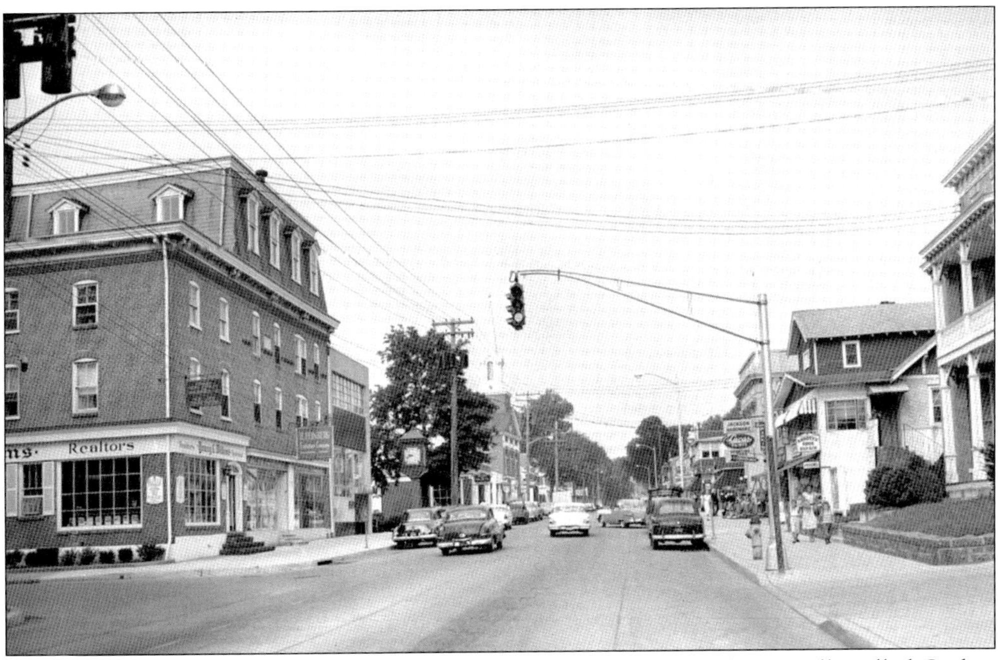

The Newark Opera House (left), built by David Caskey in 1885 and originally called Caskey Hall, is shown here in 1958, on the southwest corner of Main and Academy Streets. It hosted plays, lectures, musical events, and movies. Caskey lived across the street in the house with the double-deck porch.

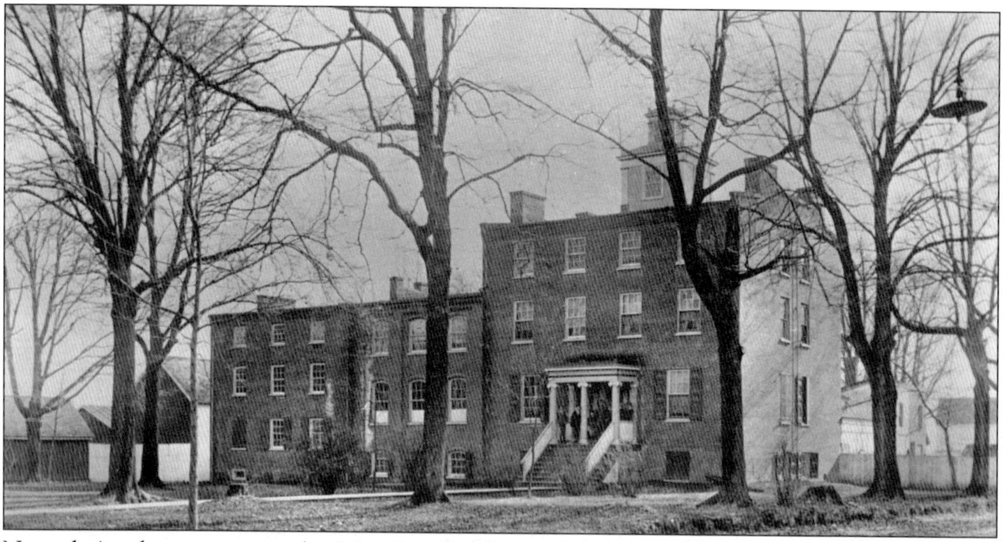

Newark Academy was started at New London, Pennsylvania, in 1741 by Rev. Dr. Francis Alison. The school moved to Newark in 1767, merged with Newark College in 1834, separated from the college in 1869, and operated independently as a boys' academy until 1898. The building at Main and Academy Streets, which has also served as Newark High School and the Newark Free Library, is currently owned by the University of Delaware.

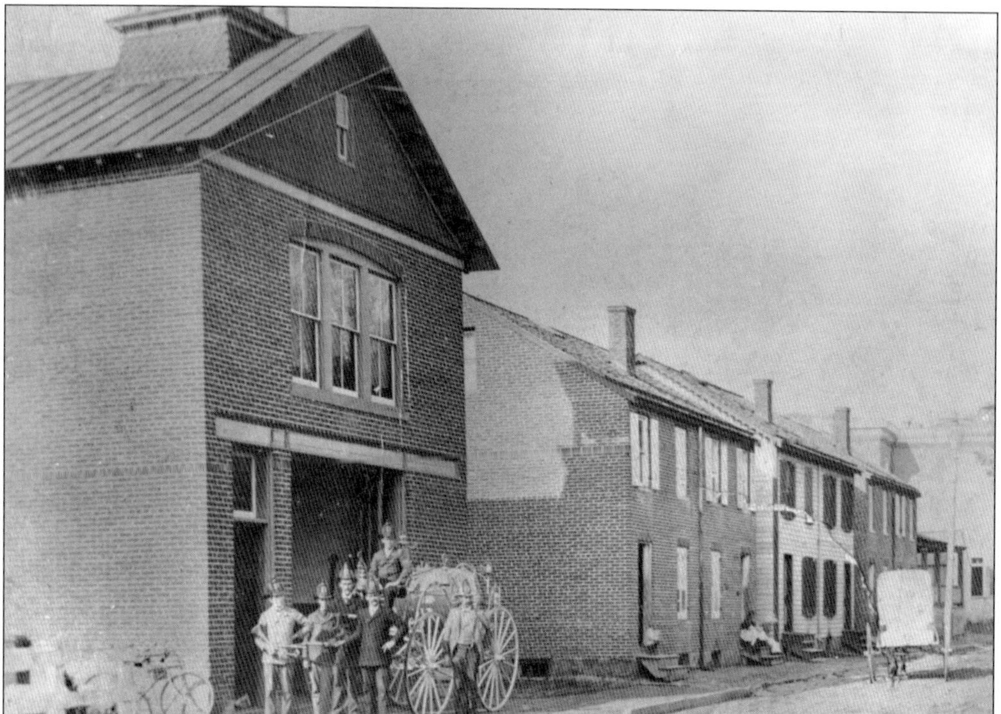

The original firehouse for the Aetna Hose, Hook & Ladder Company on Academy Street, photographed in 1893, still stands today. The volunteer company organized in 1888 following a devastating fire at the Dean Woolen Mills on Christmas Day 1886. (Courtesy of the Newark Historical Society.)

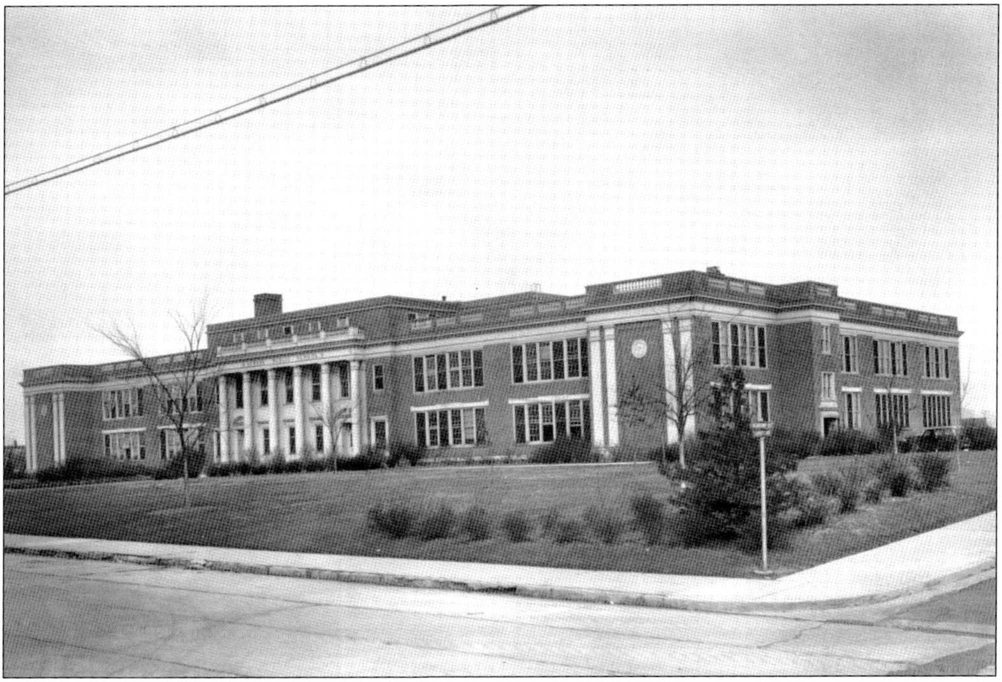

This structure was built in 1924 as Newark High School, on Academy Street (then called High Street). Its front and back are pictured in 1936, after the addition of the south wing. Pierre Samuel du Pont had contributed $125,000 toward its original construction costs of $247, 809. Du Pont had led the way in reforming public education in Delaware during the 1920s through his Delaware School Auxiliary Association. In 1957, the building was converted into Central Middle School upon the opening of the current Newark High School on East Delaware Avenue. Central Middle School existed until 1981, and the University of Delaware acquired the building two years later, renovated it, and named it Pearson Hall, a multipurpose facility.

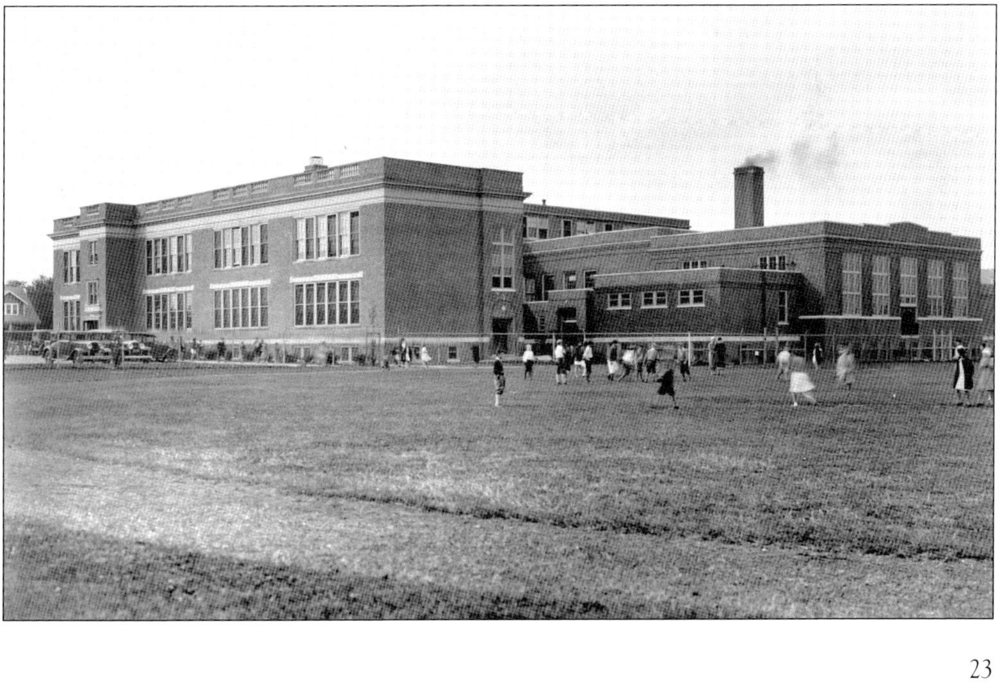

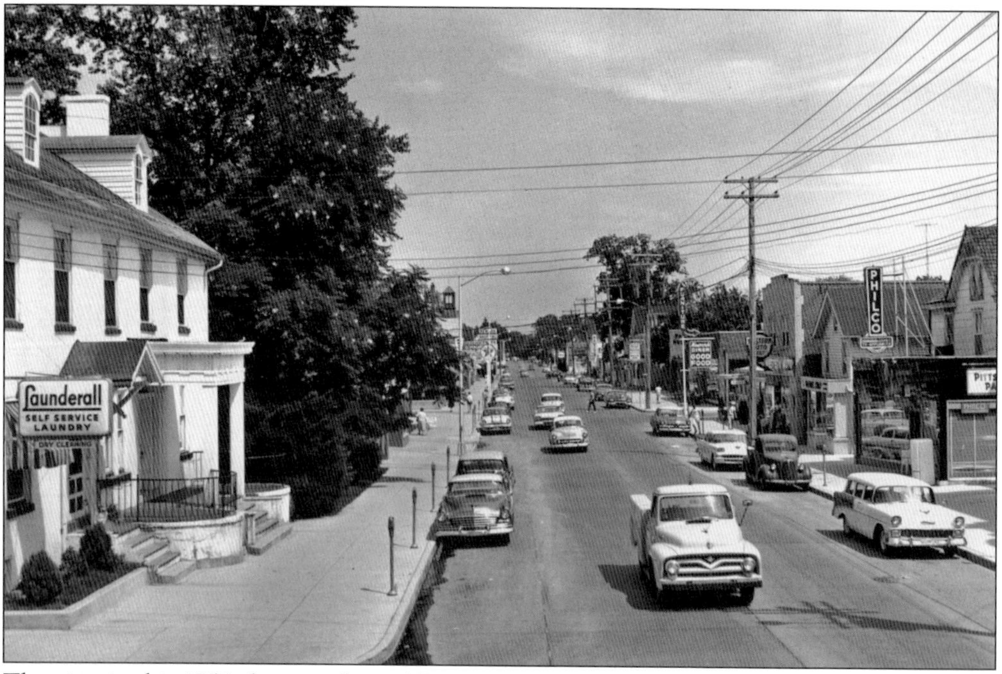

The view in this 1958 photograph is of East Main Street, looking east from Center Street. The city of Newark, incorporated in 1887, was first chartered in 1758 by King George II of the United Kingdom as a market town because of its numerous overland routes from southeastern Pennsylvania and eastern Maryland and south to Dover.

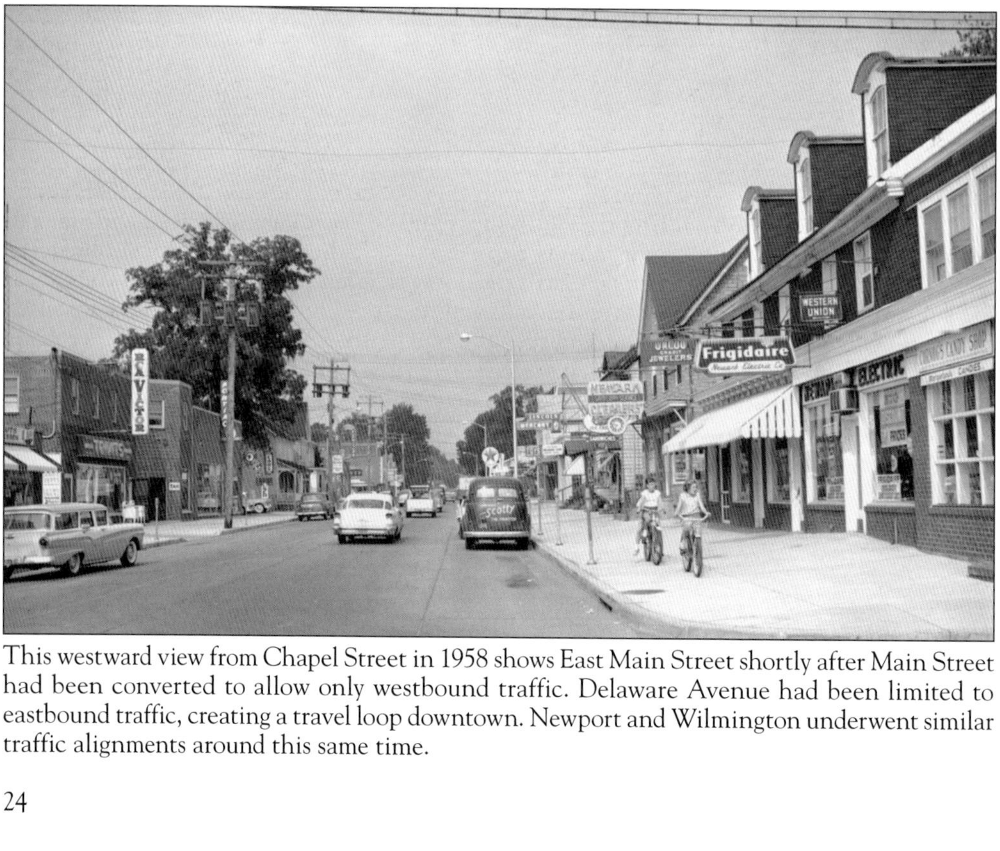

This westward view from Chapel Street in 1958 shows East Main Street shortly after Main Street had been converted to allow only westbound traffic. Delaware Avenue had been limited to eastbound traffic, creating a travel loop downtown. Newport and Wilmington underwent similar traffic alignments around this same time.

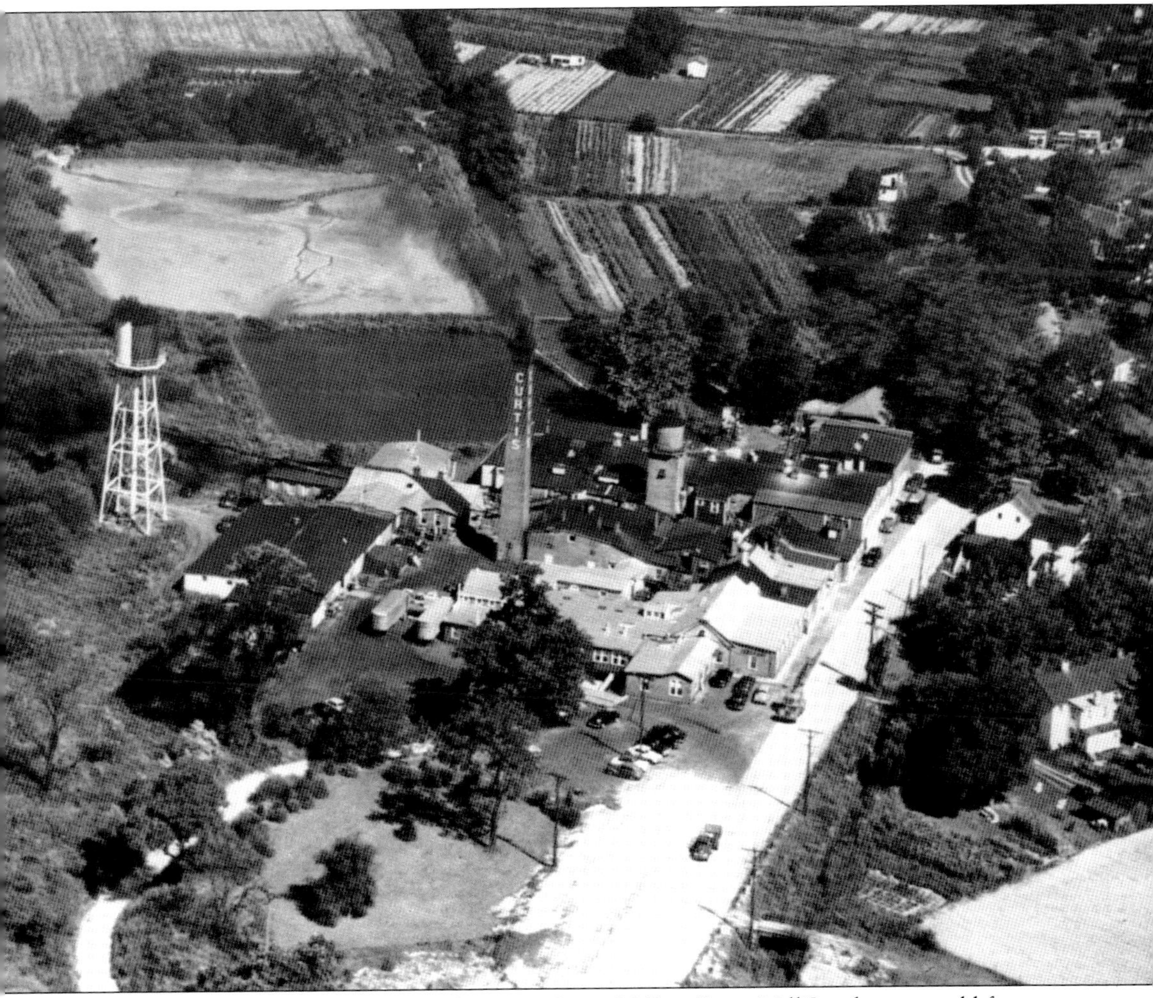

Founded by Thomas Meeteer in 1789, the Curtis Paper Mill on Paper Mill Road was a world-famous operation that produced high-grade, quality paper until 1997. In a series of several subsequent owners, brothers George and Solomon Curtis took over the mill in 1848. Alfred A. Curtis was the last member the family to manage the mill, and he retired in 1926. Curtis paper was used for books, annual reports, advertising, and even the treaties that ended World War II. For many years, paper for UNICEF Christmas cards came from Curtis. The Crown Vantage Corporation/Curtis Paper Division was shut down in 1997, and despite efforts to preserve the mill, the facility no longer stands. The City of Newark plans to convert the property into parkland.

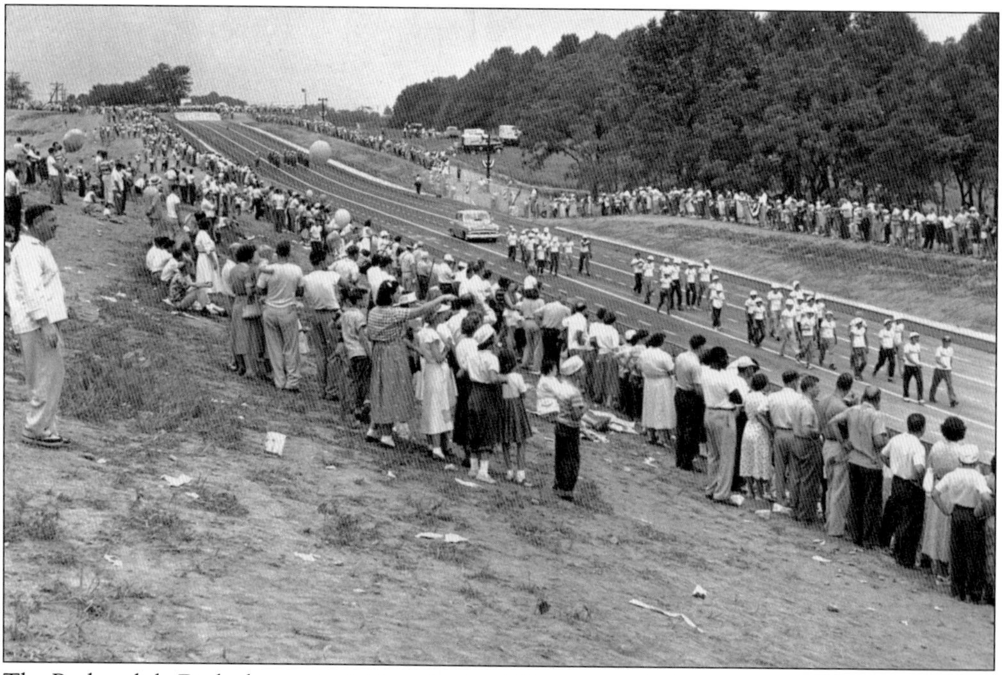

The Pushmobile Derby began in 1929 under the Wilmington Parks and Recreation Department. Originally, it was a race between boys-only teams over a flat and hilly course; one boy pushed the car while the other steered, hence the term *pushmobile*. In 1954, the derby relocated to a track in Milford Crossroads built on the property of S. Hallack du Pont, a longtime president of the event. That course closed in 1986.

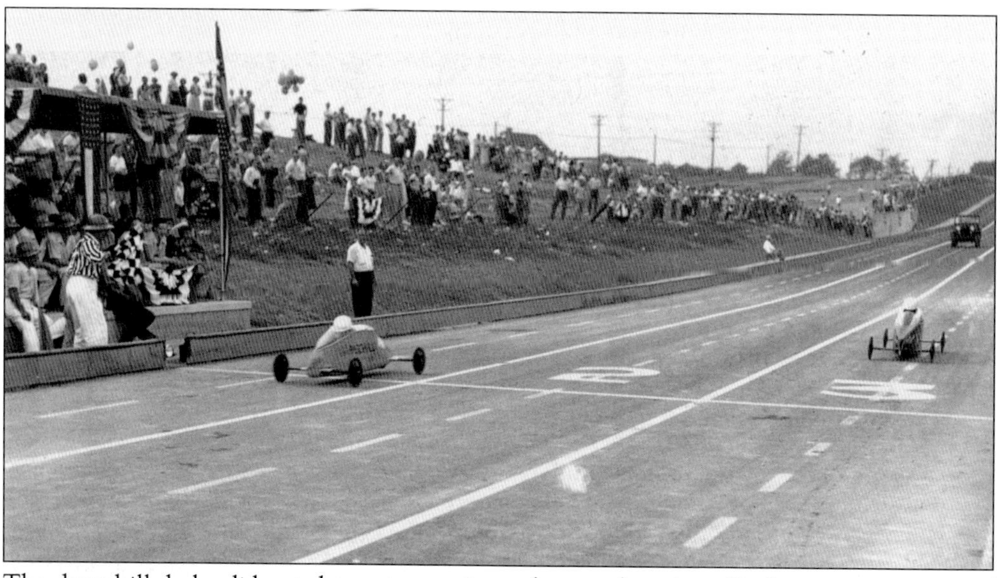

The downhill derby did not determine a winner by speed or time. Rather, it was a series of elimination races. Two cars at a time lined up at a starting ramp until one car per age group was left undefeated. Pushmobiles could reach 40 miles per hour by the time they reached the finish line, and a race took an average of 30 seconds to complete.

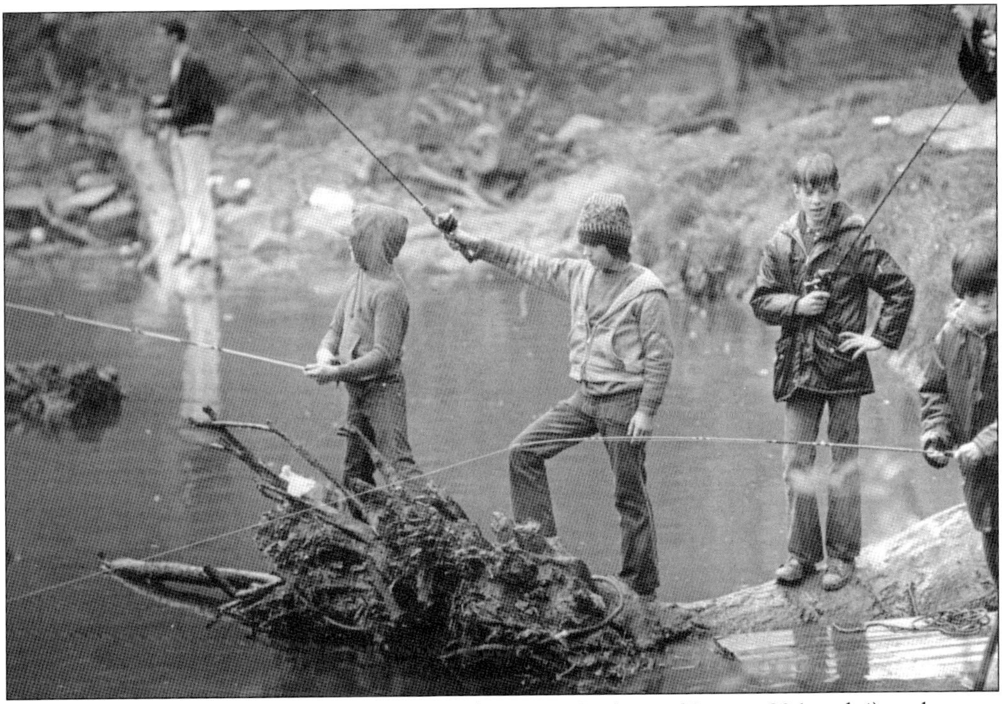

The Christina continues south under the Christiana Parkway (Routes 896 and 4) and enters the heavily wooded Rittenhouse Park, one of the few spots for recreation along the waterway. Rittenhouse Park at 228 West Chestnut Hill Road started with the $10 sale of 5.067 acres by Hugh and Alice Gallagher to the City of Newark in 1953. In 1969, an additional 40 acres was deeded from Arthur and Lidie Rittenhouse. The park is an attractive natural area with almost two miles of hiking trails, picnic facilities, and areas for fishing and canoeing. (Both, courtesy of the City of Newark Parks and Recreation Department.)

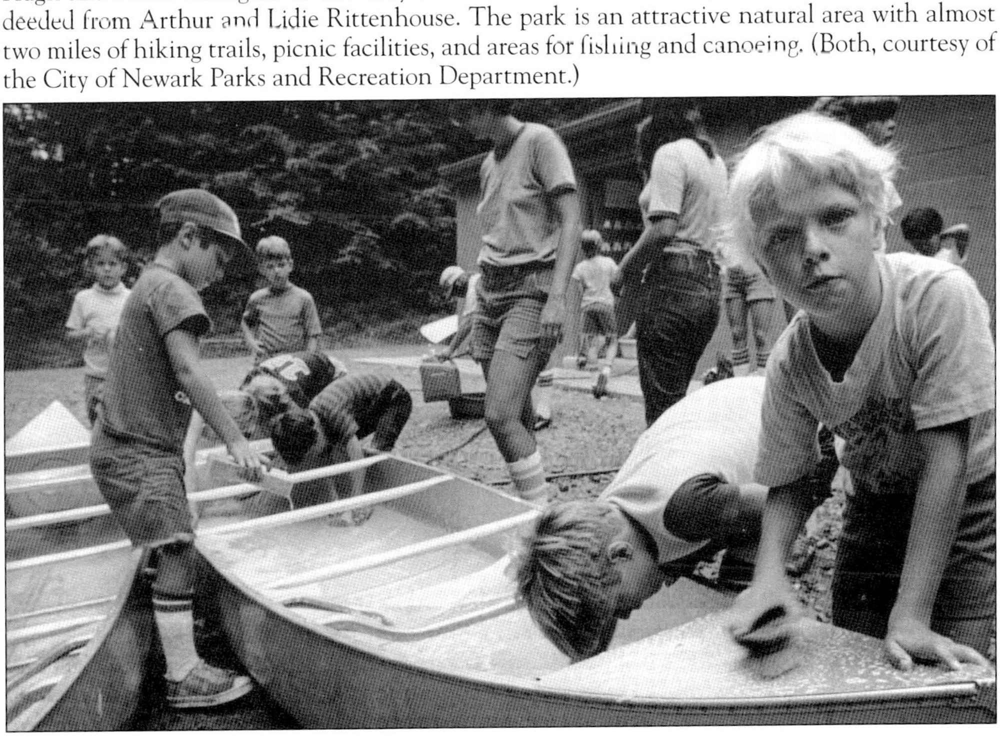

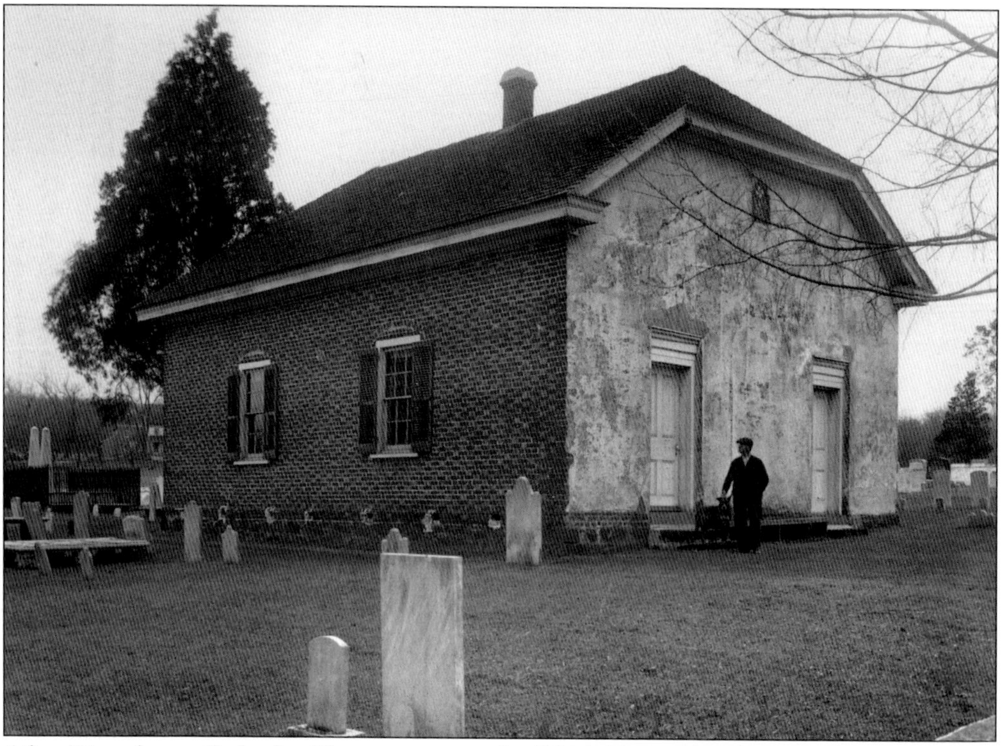

After Rittenhouse Park, the Christina passes the Welsh Tract Church on Welsh Tract Road. Photographed in 1936, the church was built in 1746 to replace an earlier log structure. Settlers from Southern Wales had been drawn to the region because of nearby iron mines on Iron Hill.

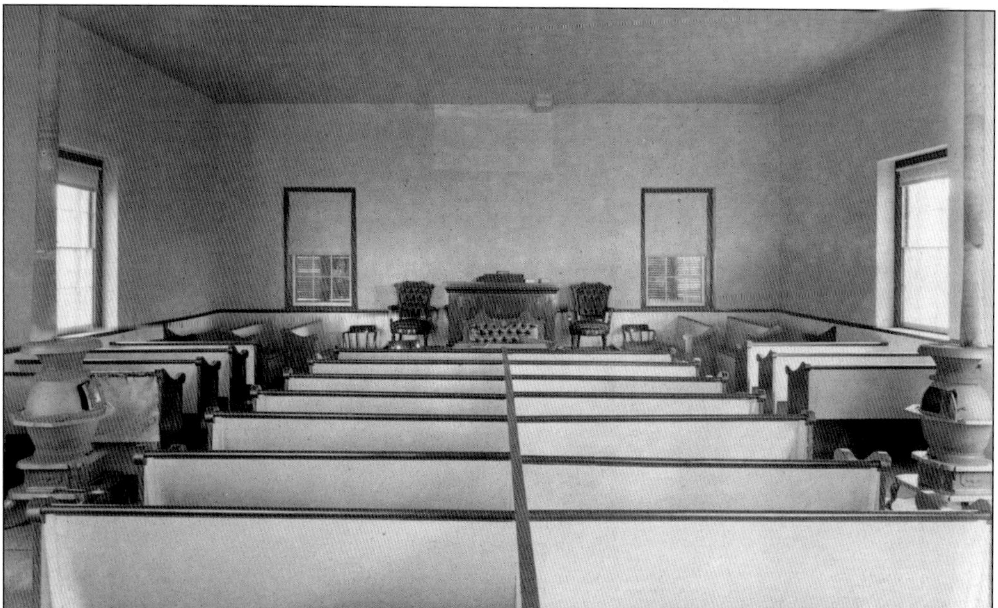

The church's interior is seen here. In 1701, attempting to strengthen his claim over the region against Lord Baltimore and the Marylanders, William Penn granted 30,000 acres, called the Welsh Tract, to Welsh settlers. They named the area Pencader, meaning "highest place."

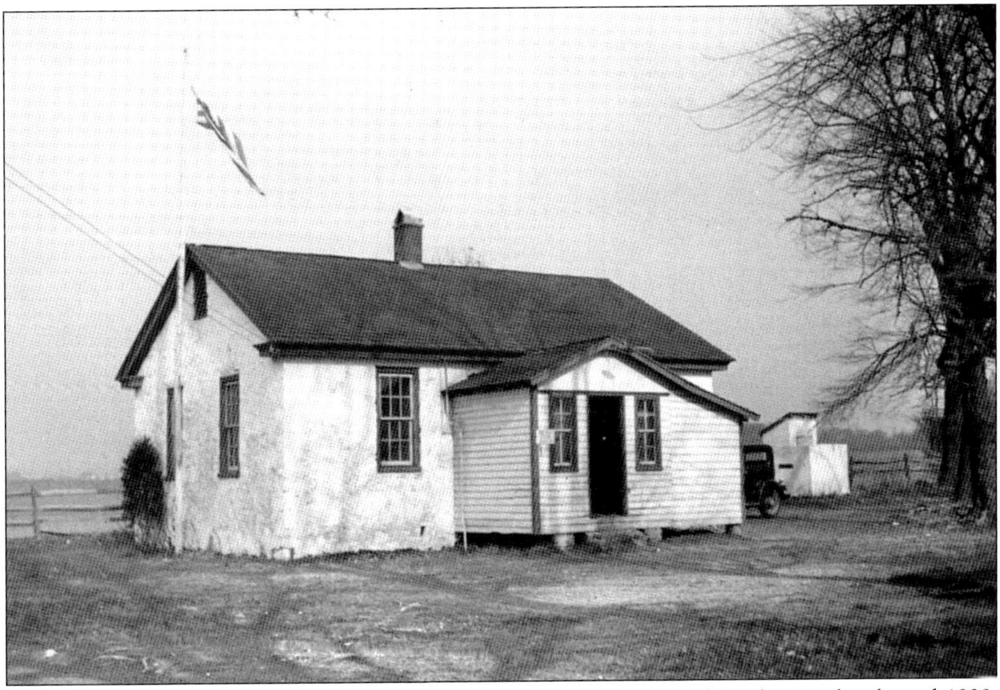

Welsh Tract School No. 54, seen here in 1932, was built in 1851 and used as a school until 1939, when it became a private residence. The building was demolished in 1981 when the intersection at Old Chestnut Hill Road and South College Avenue was enlarged.

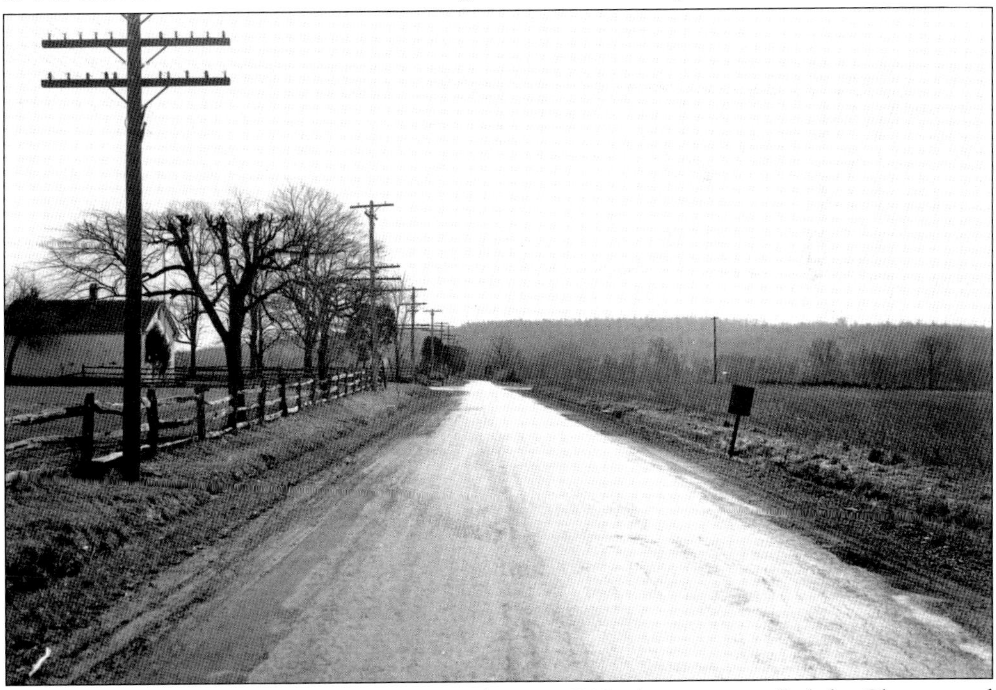

South College Avenue, or Route 896, is seen here in 1938 when it was called the Glasgow and Newark Road. The view is looking south toward Iron Hill near Welsh Tract Road. At 331 feet above sea level, Iron Hill is the highest hill—but not the highest point—in Delaware.

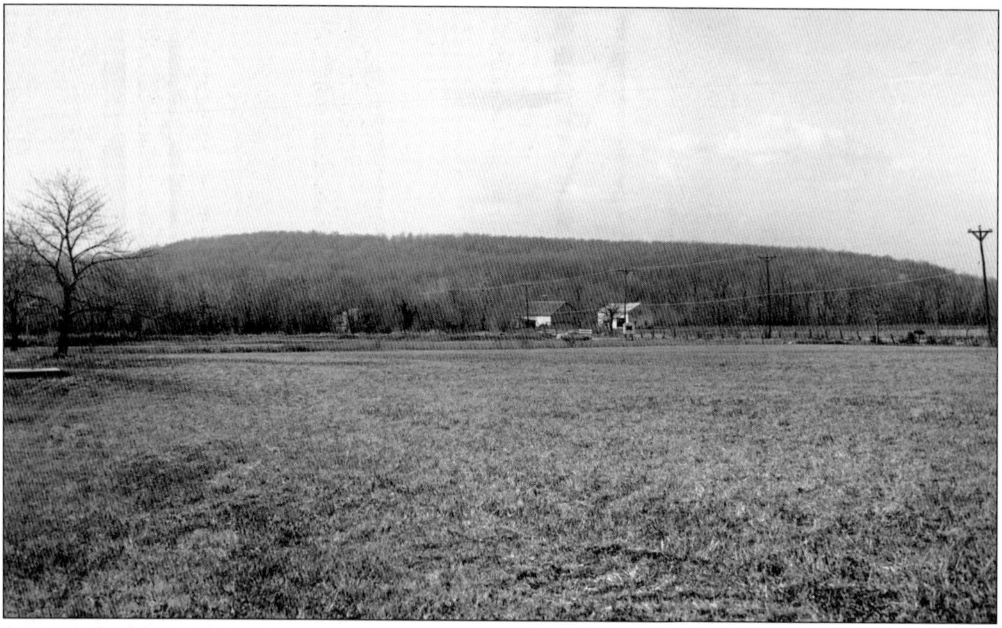

Iron ore had been discovered on Iron Hill by 1661. The Welsh were among many to mine the hill, the last being J.P. Whitaker, owner of Principio Furnace, which ended operations in 1884. Numerous arrowheads found in the vicinity indicate the hill was well used by Minquas and Lenni Lenape tribes. American generals Washington, Greene, and Lafayette stood atop the hill to watch British troop movements on August 26, 1777.

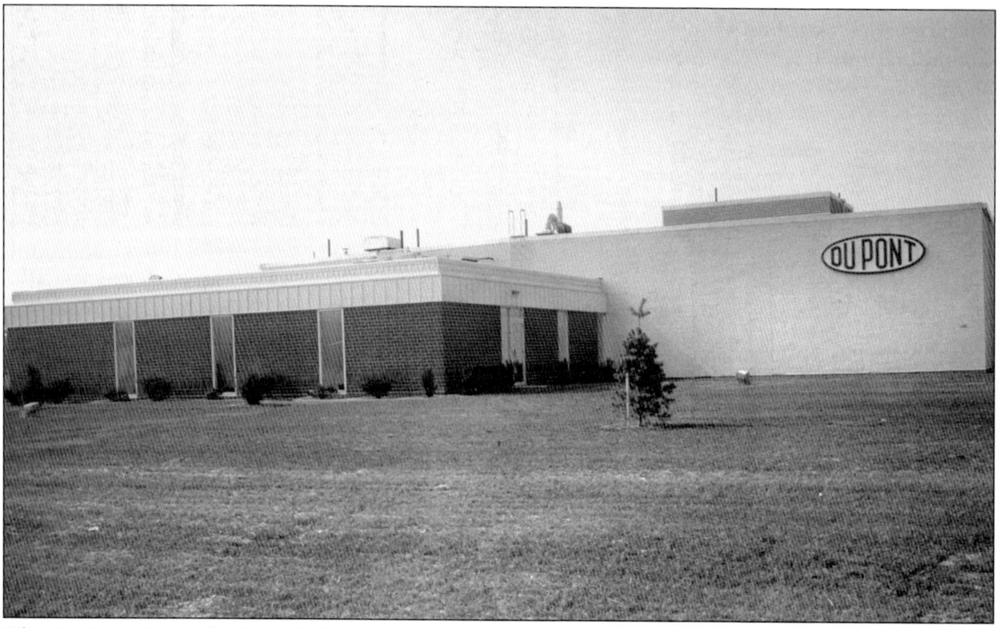

The DuPont Pencader Vespel Division is one of the businesses at the Diamond State Industrial Park on Bellevue Road off Old Cooch's Bridge Road. The industrial park is near the intersection of South College Avenue (Route 896) and Interstate 95. This portion of Old Cooch's Bridge Road was converted into a dead end when the interstate was built; prior to that, it had connected to Old Baltimore Pike.

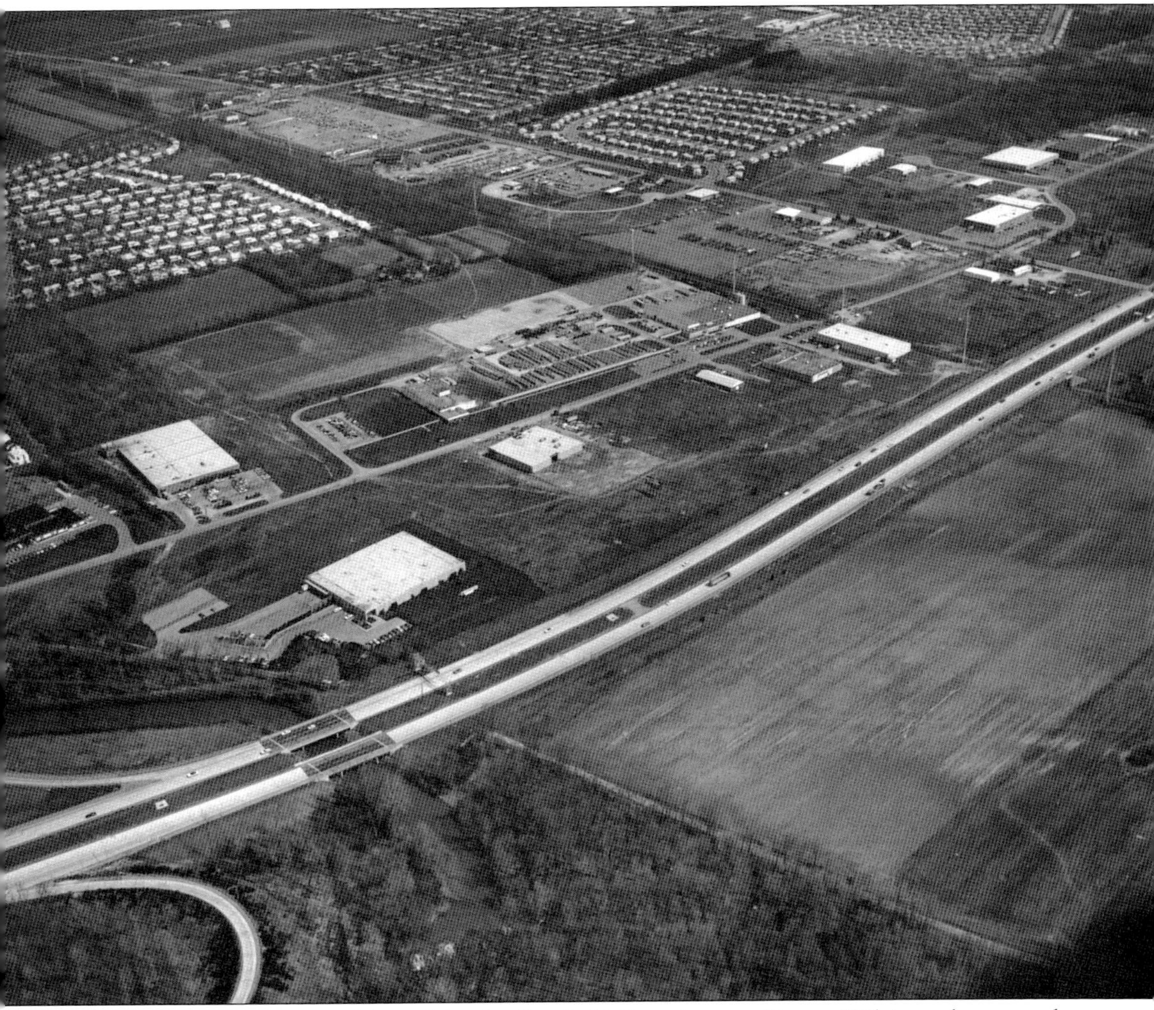

This is a 1963 aerial view of Newark by the South College Avenue (Route 896) interchange and what was then called the Maryland Northeastern Expressway–Delaware Turnpike. It was actually two separate highways that met at the Maryland/Delaware border, and they would eventually be incorporated into Interstate 95. Pres. Dwight D. Eisenhower had championed a modern highway system, and his administration passed the Federal-Aid Highway Act of 1956 on June 26, setting aside $25 billion for construction costs. It was the largest public works project in US history. In Delaware, Interstate 95 was completed in 1968, and Interstate 495 was done 10 years later. The Christina River can be seen flowing by the Diamond State Industrial Park and beneath the north- and southbound lanes of the highway. The two sections of Old Cooch's Bridge Road are visible just above the river. (Courtesy of Delaware Historical Society.)

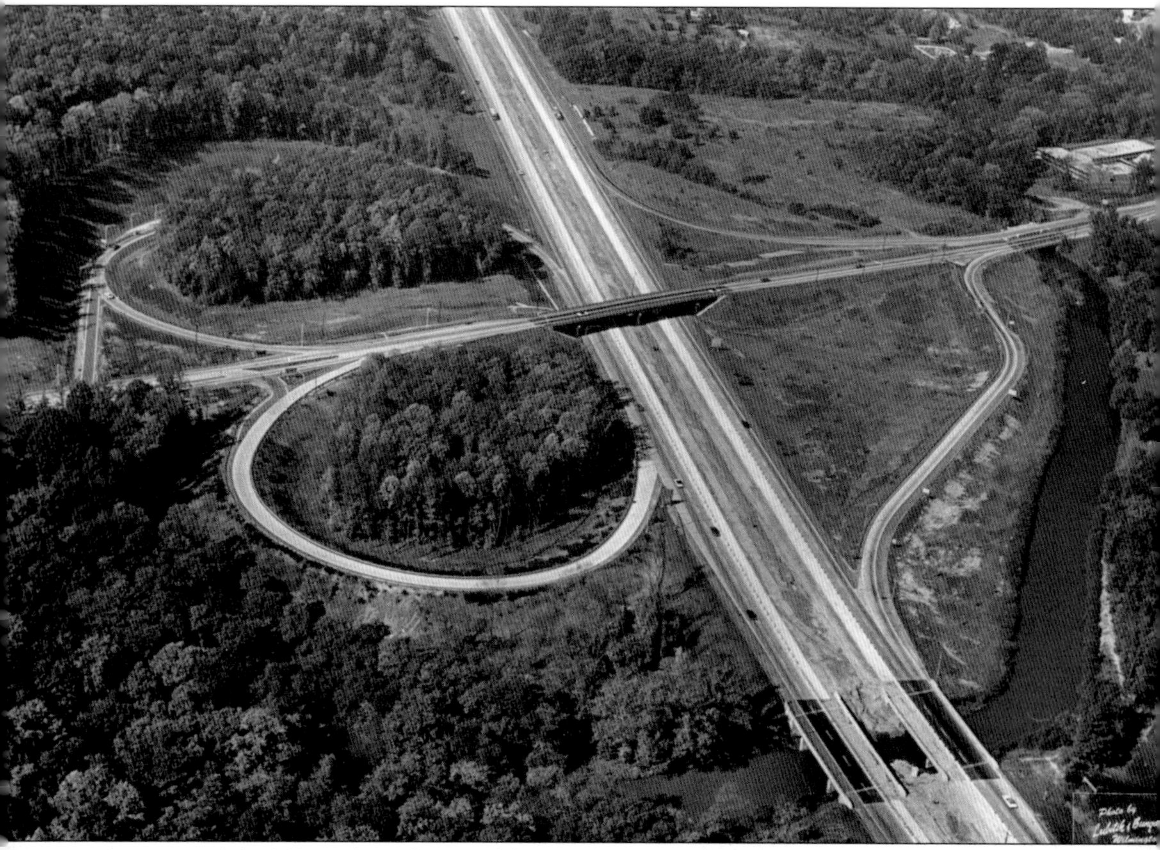

As seen in this 1963 southward view of the South College Avenue (Route 896) interchange with Interstate 95, the Christina River flows under South College Avenue (right) and then beneath the interstate (bottom) on its way to Cooch's Bridge. Route 896 has been a major north-south corridor through Delaware for more than 200 years. As such, there are a number of historic farms and houses along the way. In 1938, the road was straightened and paved to provide a better transportation route between Newark and Glasgow. By 1993, this stretch of road had been expanded to four lanes and realigned 900 feet east of its former intersection with Route 40, now bypassing Glasgow. (Courtesy of Delaware Historical Society.)

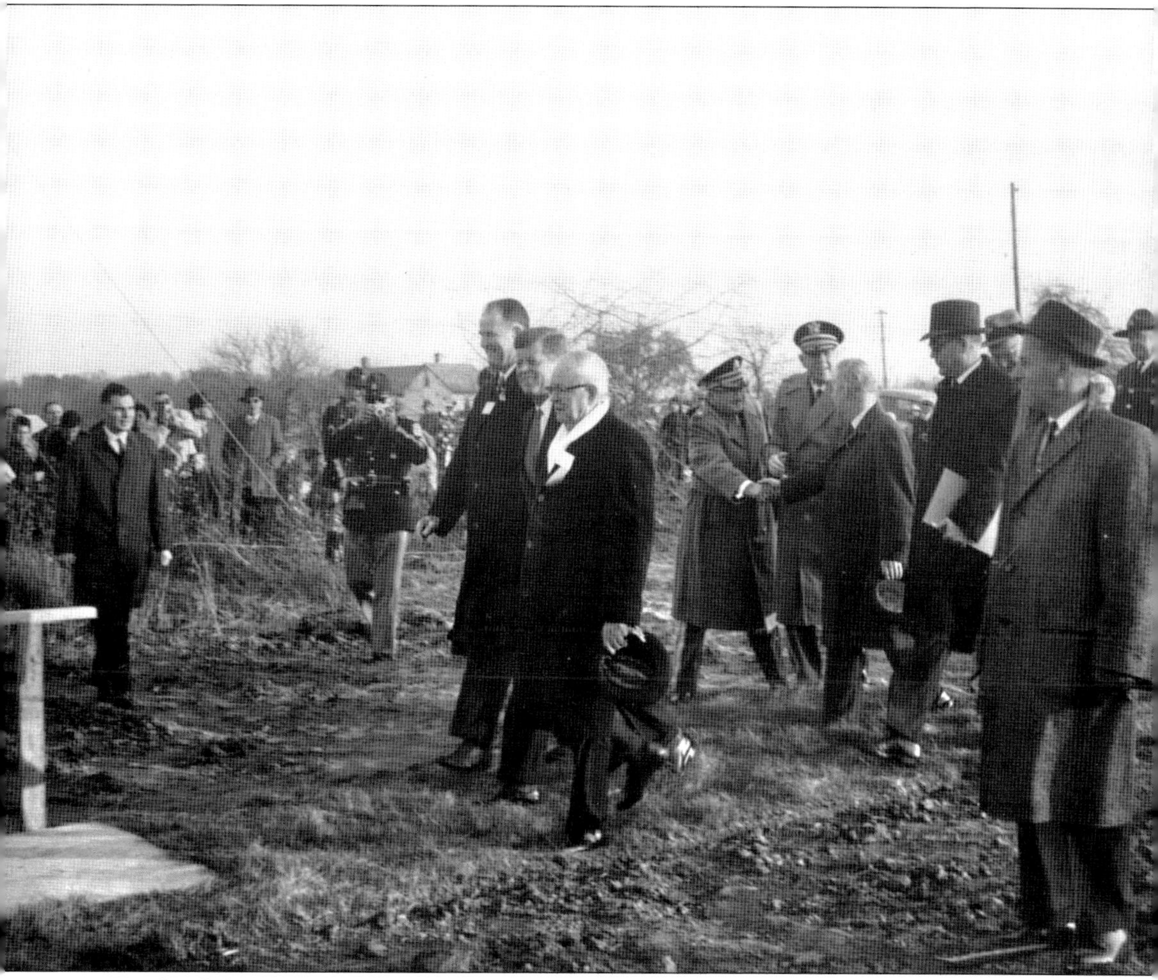

Just south of the Route 896 and Interstate 95 interchange, at the Delaware and Maryland border, Pres. John F. Kennedy (forward center), Delaware governor Elbert Carvel (forward left), and Maryland governor J. Millard Tawes (forward right) attend a ribbon-cutting ceremony on November 14, 1963, to officially open the first 59 miles of what was then called the Maryland Northeastern Expressway–Delaware Turnpike. President Kennedy spoke at 3:15 p.m., saying, "It is a pleasure for me to join the citizens of Delaware and Maryland in opening this new highway. This highway has been built by the dedicated effort of the citizens of these two states, and it joins a great interstate highway which represents a cooperative effort between the United States Government and the people of the various states, through which this long ribbon will pass." The president was assassinated a week later, and the highway was renamed for him soon after.

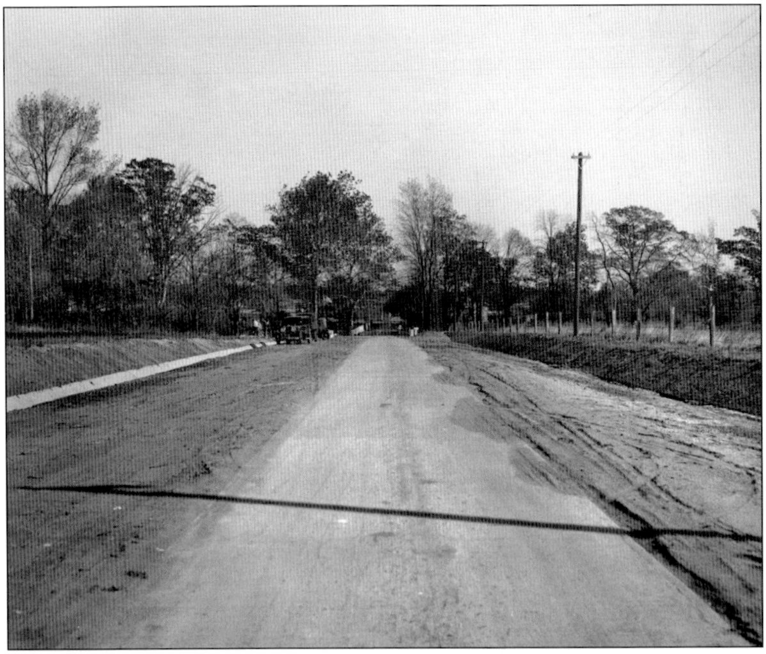

The Christina River flows under Old Baltimore Pike, shown here in 1931, at Cooch's Bridge. The pike is one of the oldest routes in Delaware, initially carved out by Native Americans for travel between the Delaware River and Chesapeake Bay. The corridor has also been known as the Great Road from Head of Elk to Christiana Bridge, and the Christiana-Elkton Turnpike.

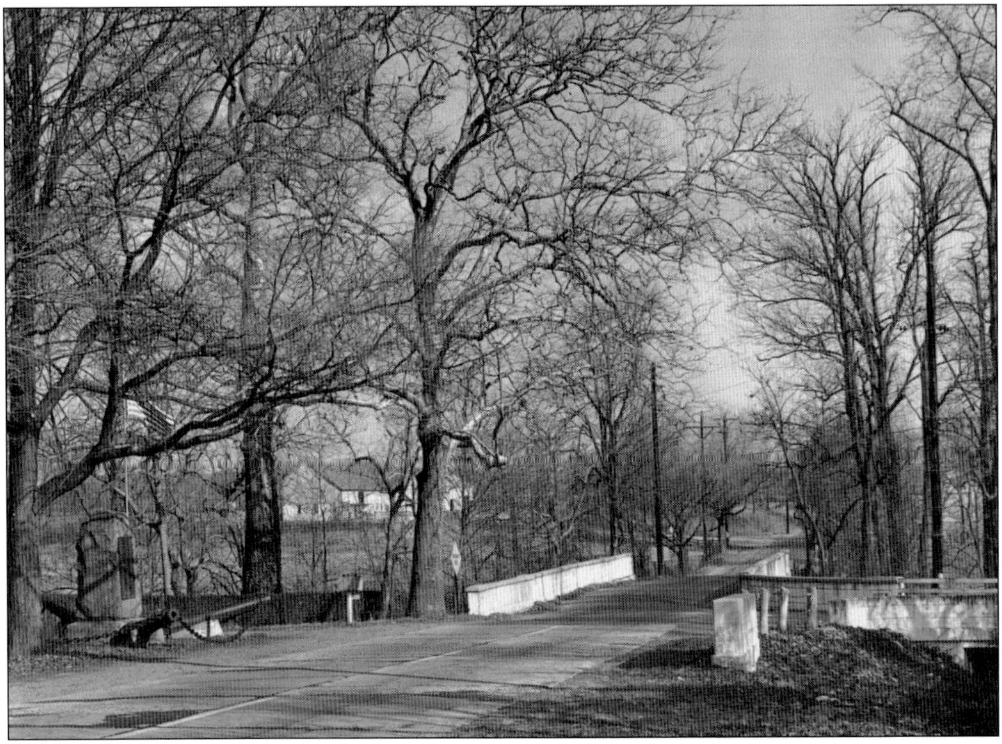

The Christina River played a part in the American Revolution on September 3, 1777, at the Battle of Cooch's Bridge. The British marched overland from the Head of Elk (Elkton) toward Philadelphia. About 500 Americans under William Maxwell skirmished with the redcoats around this location to slow their advance, giving General Washington time to fortify his position along the Brandywine River at Chadd's Ford.

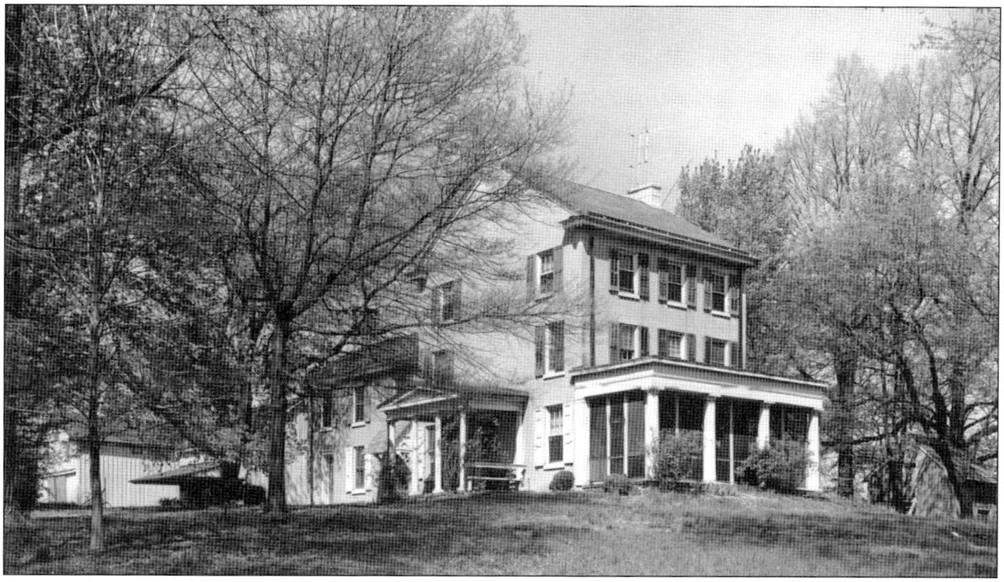

Pictured in 1925, the Cooch House along Old Baltimore Pike faces the Christina River and was built in 1760. Members of the Cooch family resided in the home for over 200 years. British commander Lord Cornwallis used it for his headquarters after the Battle of Cooch's Bridge, and though he and his men left the home intact, they burned down the family mill.

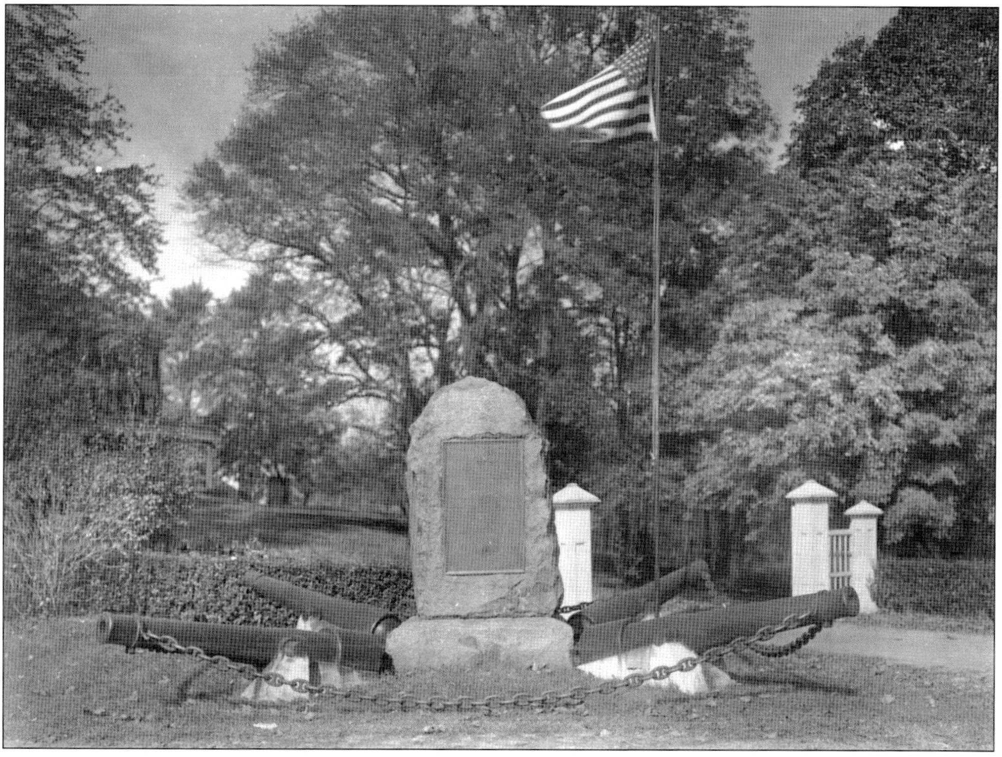

Pictured in 1933, this granite monument was erected in 1901 to commemorate the September 3, 1777, Battle of Cooch's Bridge. It continues to stand along Old Baltimore Pike near the bridge. Legend has it that the American flag was first unfurled during this conflict.

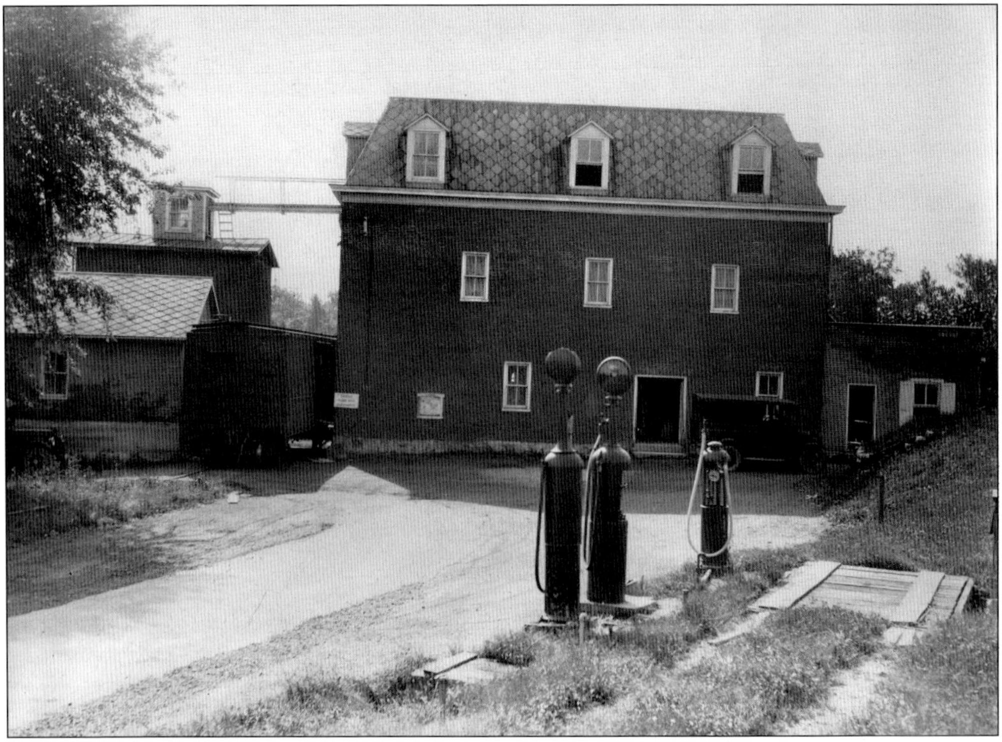

Dayett Mills is located near the intersection of Old Baltimore Pike and Route 72, not far from Cooch's Bridge. Built in 1838 by William Cooch Jr. as a gristmill, it remained in the family until it was sold to John Dayett in 1884. The mill operated until the 1980s, when it was sold to the State of Delaware's Division of Historical and Cultural Affairs. (Courtesy of Delaware Historical Society.)

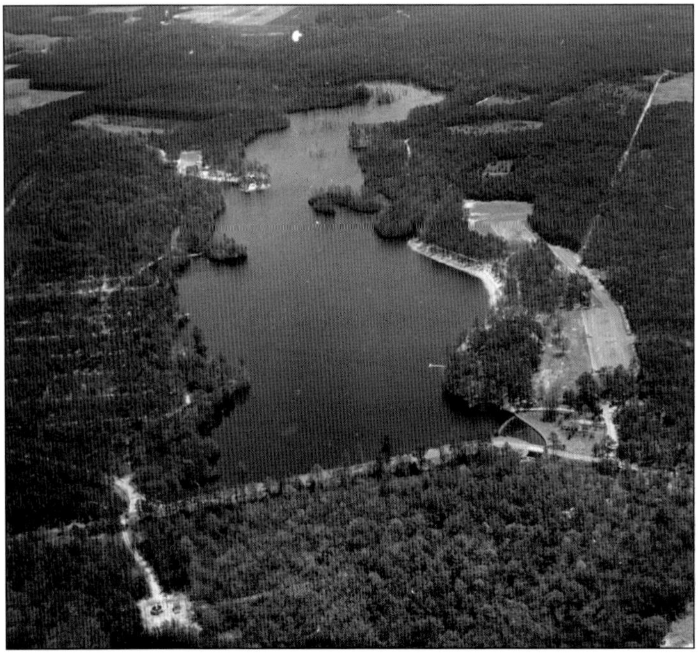

The Christina River is affected by tides to Smalley's Pond, about 15.8 miles from its confluence with the Delaware River and a mile west of Christiana, the next town on its easterly route. The pond was created by a dam dating back to a 1737 gristmill and sawmill complex called Christiana Mills. This aerial photograph is from 1971. (Courtesy of Delaware Historical Society.)

Two

Christiana Before the Mall

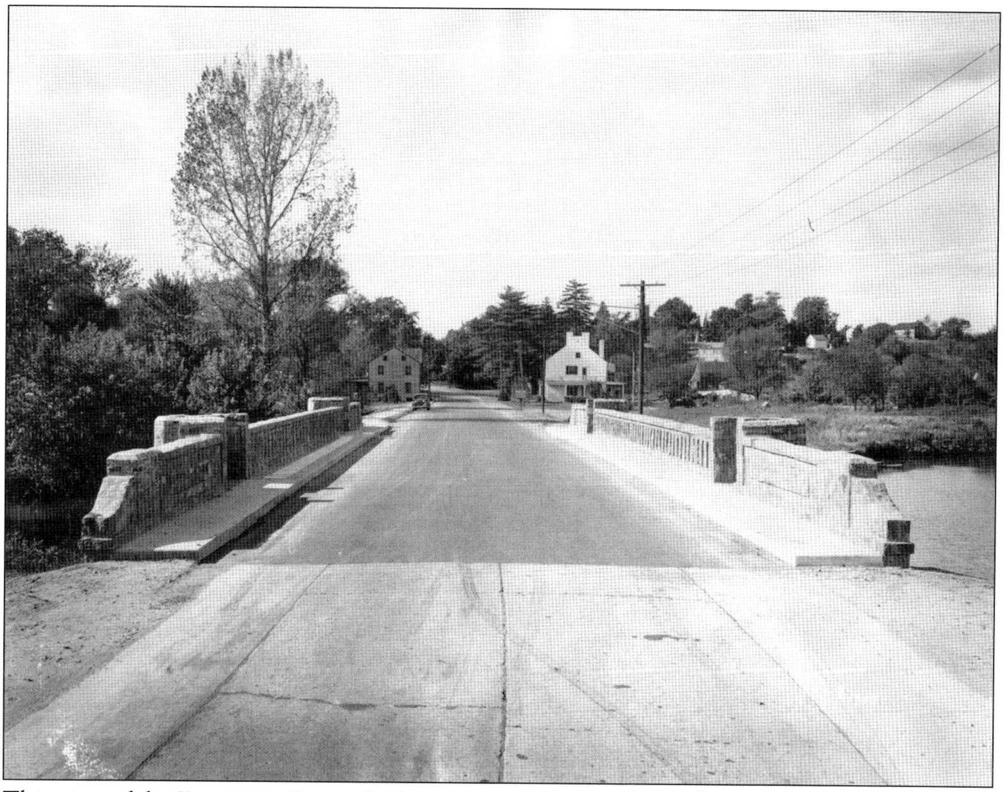

This view of the East Main Street Bridge over the Christina River dates to 1938. Christiana had been originally referred to as Christiana Bridge because the Christina River was only navigable to "Christiana's Bridge." In Colonial times, the village was a major hub for trading, and it played a vital role in the American Revolution. Today, Christiana has become synonymous with a large shopping mall and hospital, but in 1974 it was designated a National Historic District because of its numerous surviving 18th-century buildings.

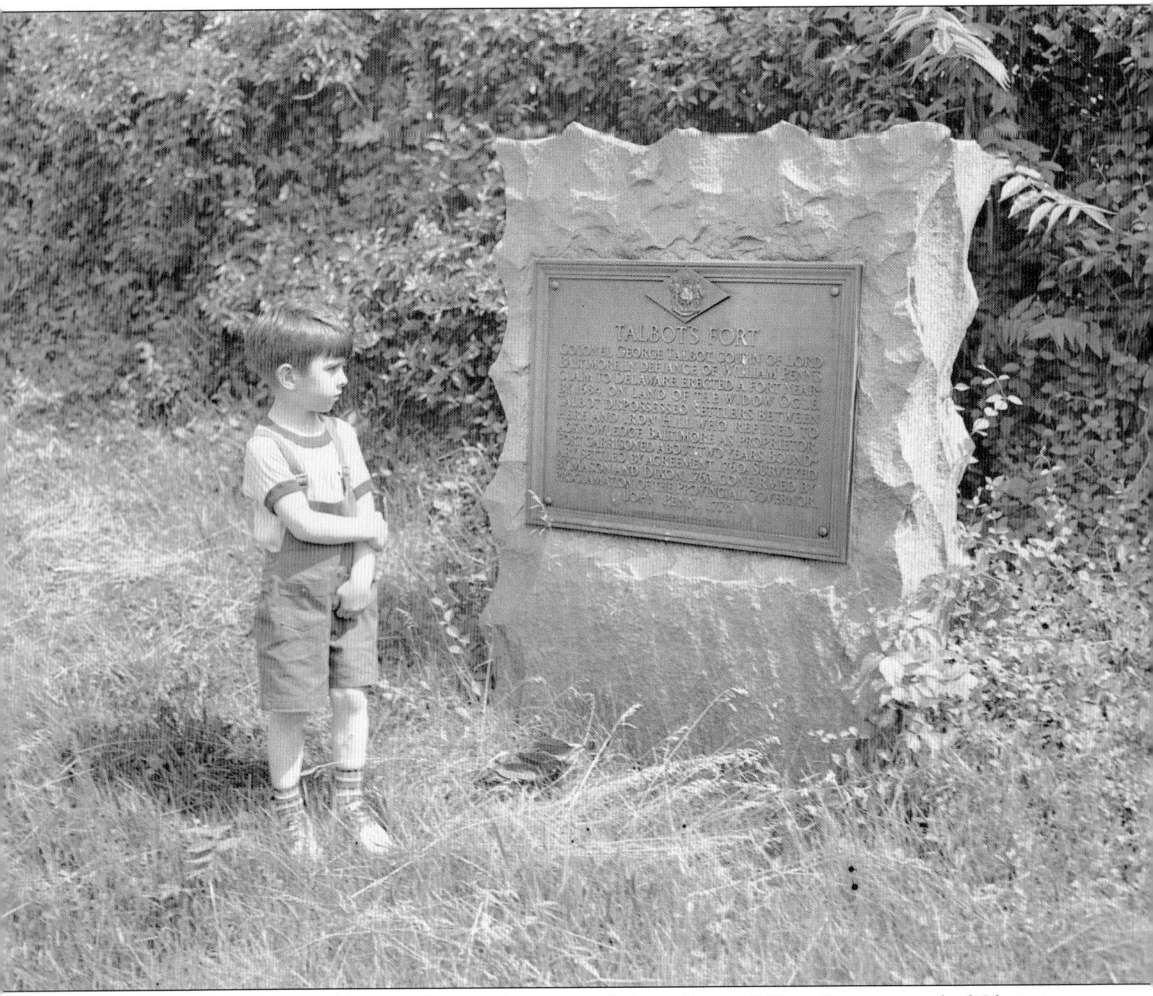

In 1940, an unidentified boy reads a marker erected along Route 273 at the west end of Christiana that reads: "Colonel George Talbot, cousin of Lord Baltimore, in defiance of William Penn's claim to Delaware, erected a fort nearby in 1684, on land of the Widow Ogle. Talbot dispossessed settlers between here and Iron Hill who refused to acknowledge Baltimore as proprietor." The fort was garrisoned about two years, until the boundary was settled by agreement in 1760 and surveyed by Charles Mason and Jeremiah Dixon in 1763. Talbot was an Irishman who became surveyor general of Maryland. He had been granted 32,000 acres, known as the Susquehanna Manor, to help settle English and Irish immigrants in Maryland. Talbot not only had a dispute with the Penn family, but he was also found guilty of the murder of Christopher Rousby in 1684 but was later pardoned by King James II. The 1933 Fort Talbot marker can still be seen near Route 273 by the entrance to the shops at Christiana Town Center.

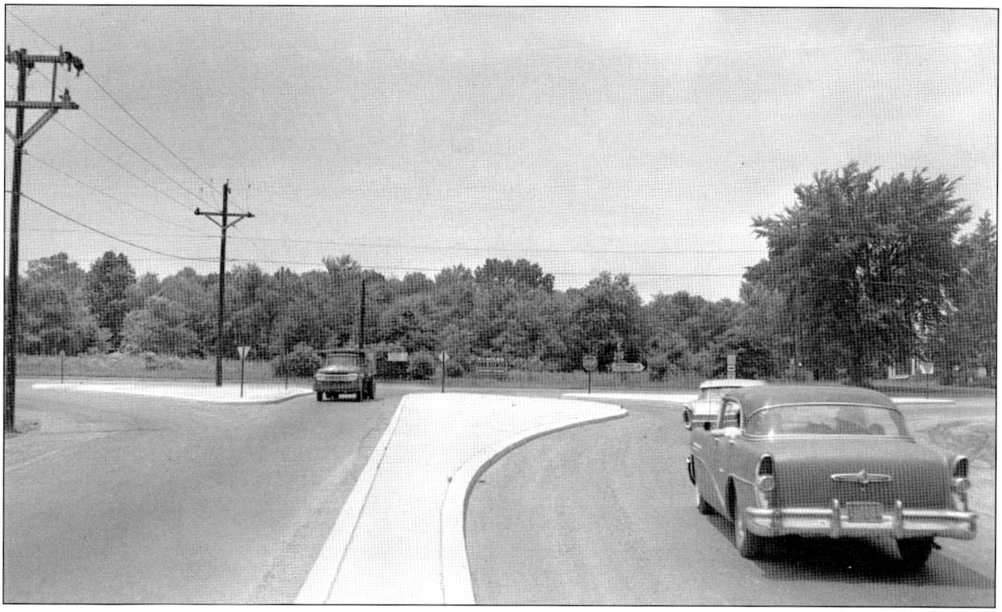

As seen in this 1961 photograph of Route 7 at the east end of Christiana, northbound traffic veered right and then entered East Main Street. Route 7 then turned onto North Old Baltimore Pike and temporarily linked with Route 4 before breaking off in Stanton onto Limestone Road.

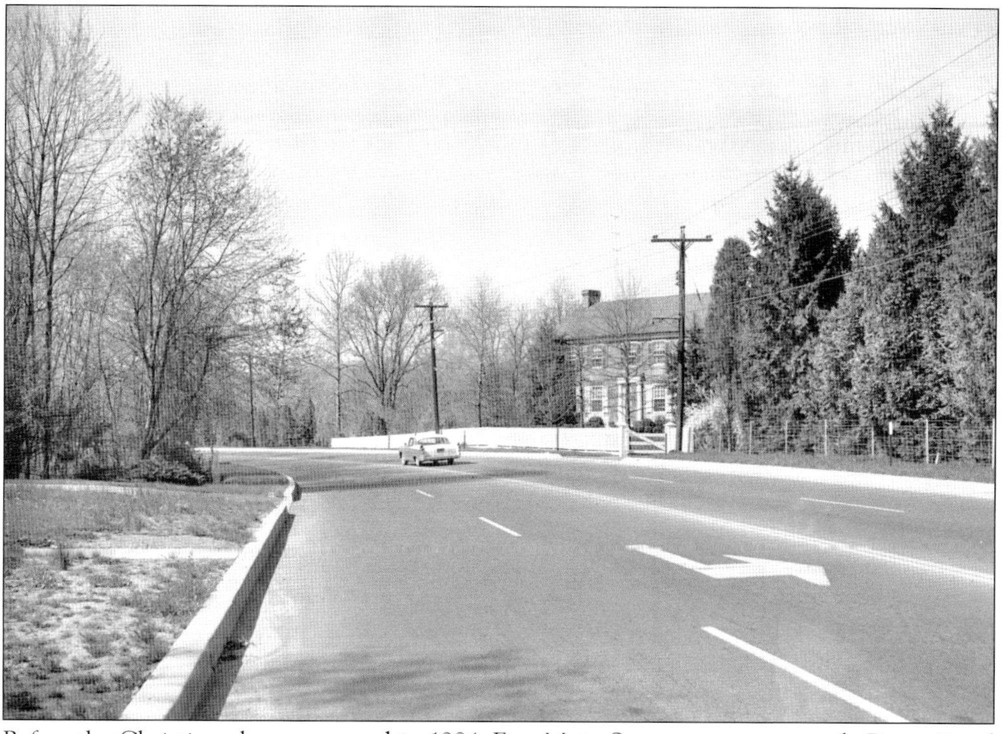

Before the Christiana bypass opened in 1984, East Main Street was concurrently Route 7 and Route 273 (with Route 273 encompassing the full length of Main Street). By the 1970s, the large volume of automobile traffic just passing through town was getting backed up at the village's one light at Old Baltimore Pike, prompting the need for a bypass.

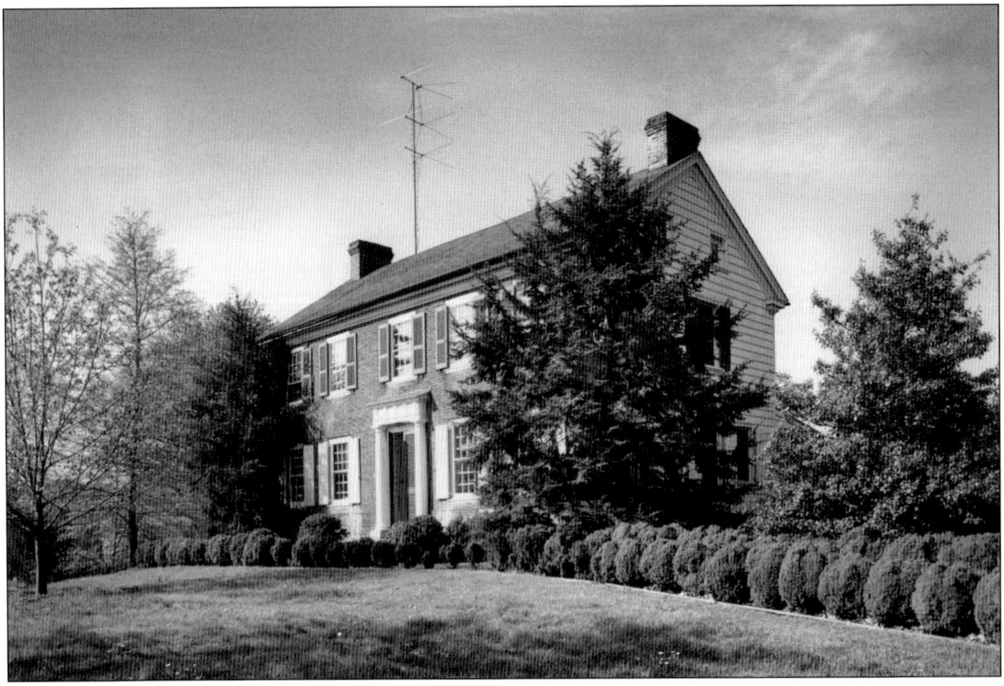

The Josiah Lewden House at 107 East Main Street is a Georgian mansion built in 1770 by Quaker merchant Josiah Lewden. The Lewden family was prominent in the history of Christiana, operating stores and living in the village during the 18th and 19th centuries. The family originally lived in Newport on a parcel of land called Lewden's Island. In his will, John Lewden I left land (known as "the meadowland") in Christiana to one of his sons, John Lewden II, and the family relocated. The photograph below shows the house in 1958.

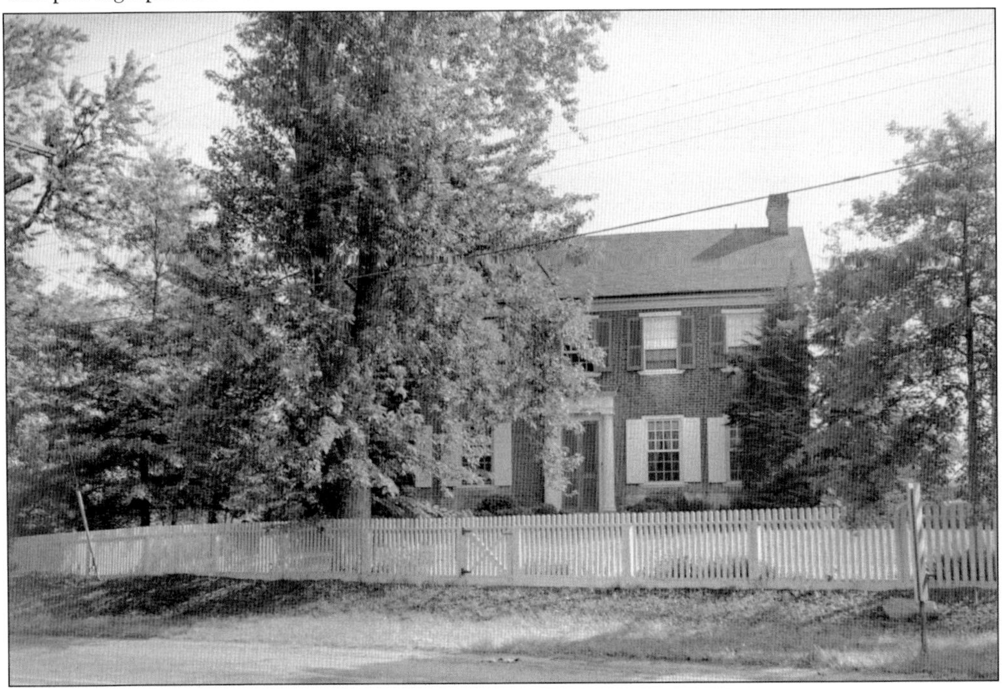

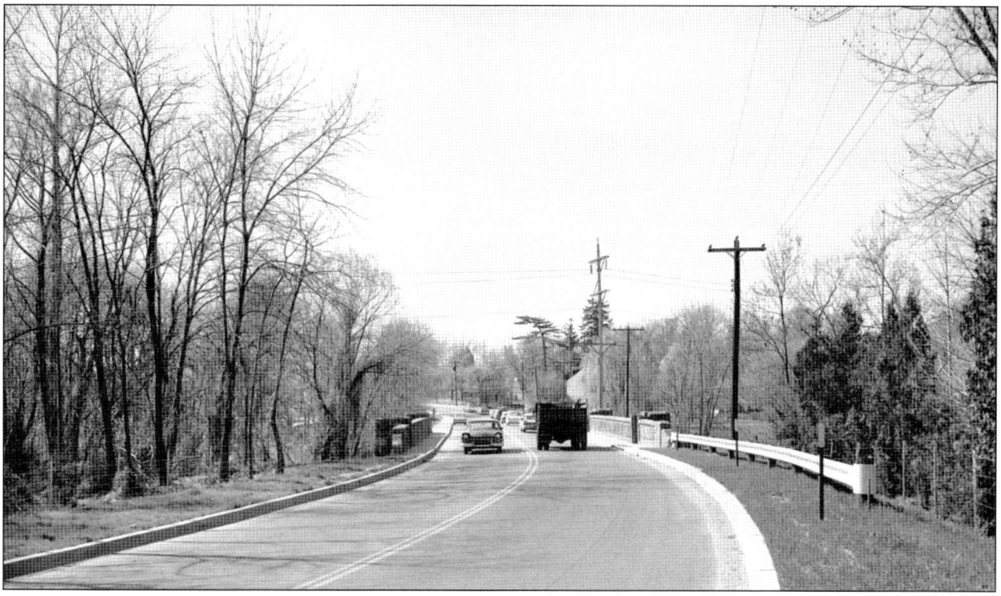

Ye Old King's Road, or King's Highway, was a Colonial route built sporadically between 1673 and 1735. The 1,300 miles of dirt paths and ferry crossings linked Boston, Massachusetts, and Charles Town (Charleston), South Carolina, and passed through Christiana.

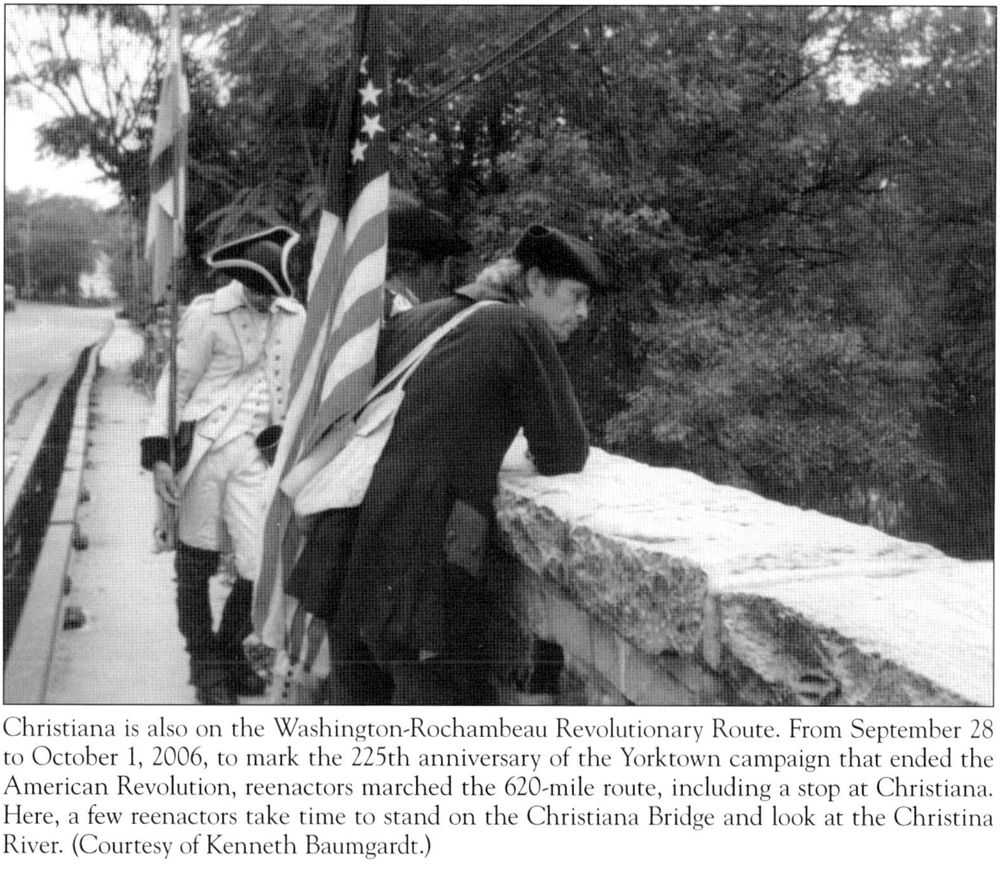

Christiana is also on the Washington-Rochambeau Revolutionary Route. From September 28 to October 1, 2006, to mark the 225th anniversary of the Yorktown campaign that ended the American Revolution, reenactors marched the 620-mile route, including a stop at Christiana. Here, a few reenactors take time to stand on the Christiana Bridge and look at the Christina River. (Courtesy of Kenneth Baumgardt.)

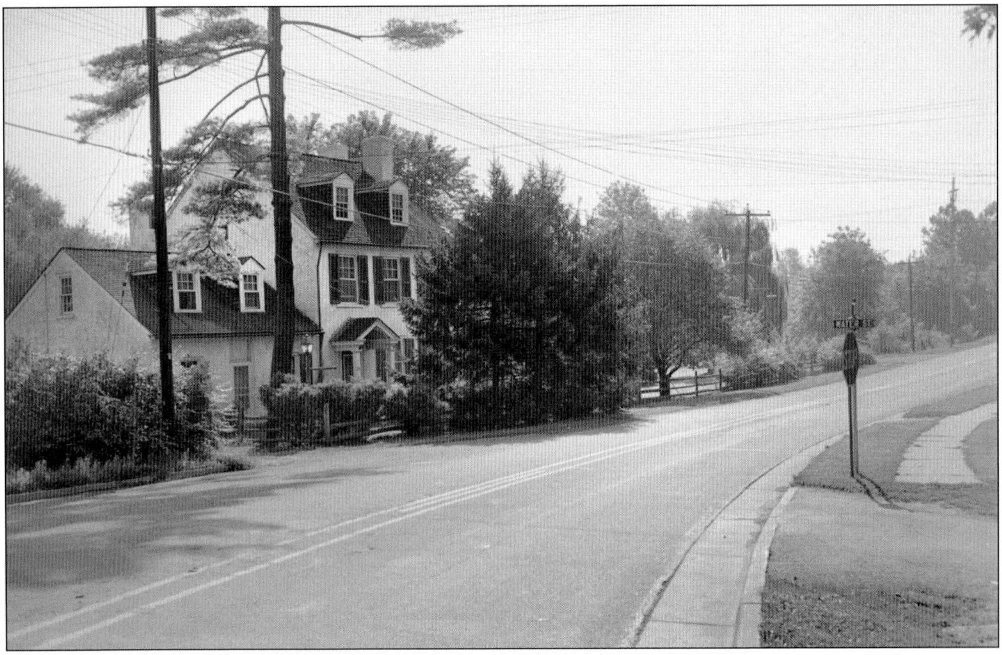

The John Read House at 29 East Main Street was also known as the Brinkle-Maxwell House. It was built by John Read, the father of George Read (who signed the Declaration of Independence and the Constitution). After John Read's death in 1756, the house passed to his son Thomas Read, the first commodore of the Continental navy.

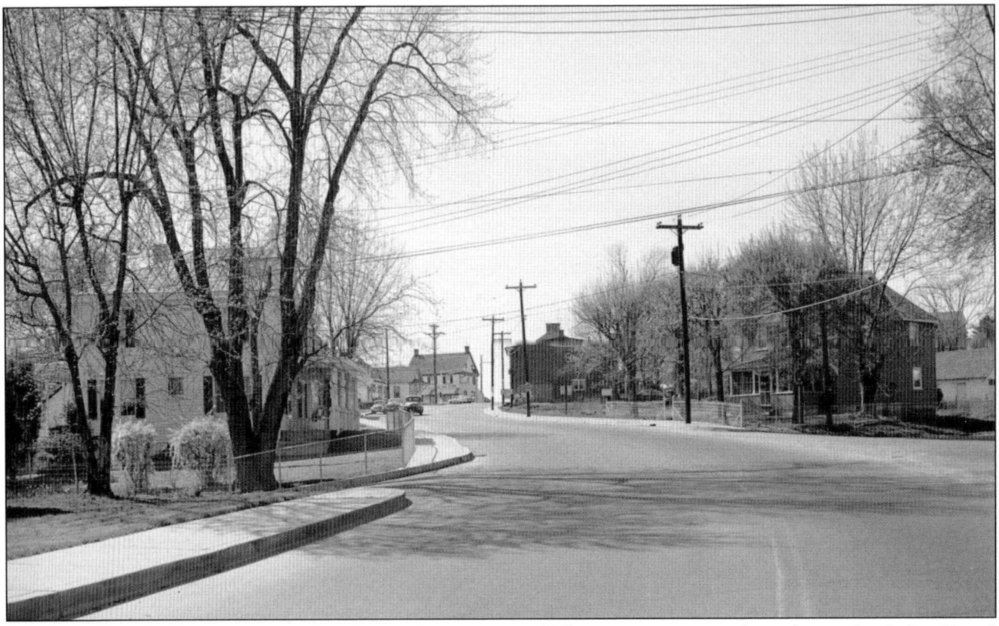

This photograph of Christiana's Main Street toward downtown was taken from the John Read House in 1960. Author Lorenzo Dow Blackson, one of the earliest African American novelists in American history, was born and raised in Christiana. His most famous work, *The Rise and Progress of the Kingdoms of Light and Darkness*, also known as *The Reign of Kings Alpha and Abadon*, was published 1867.

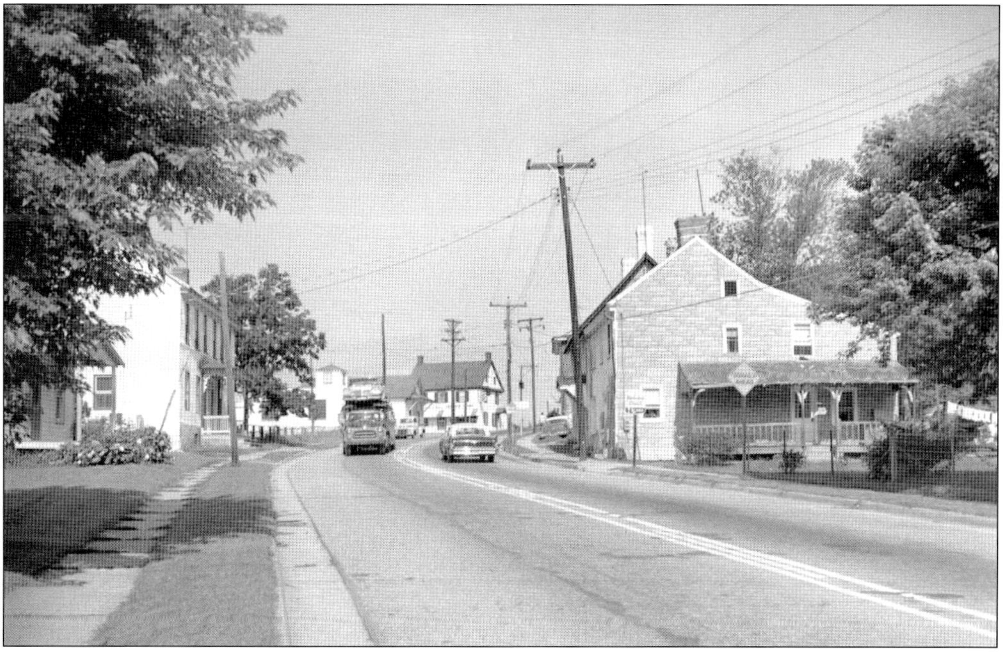

Christiana was born of simple geography, springing from the intersection of both overland and river transportation routes. In Colonial times, it was a central location for trade in the Mid-Atlantic region. It was also a hotbed for smugglers trying to avoid paying import and export duties, trade tariffs, and taxes, especially during the Revolutionary period.

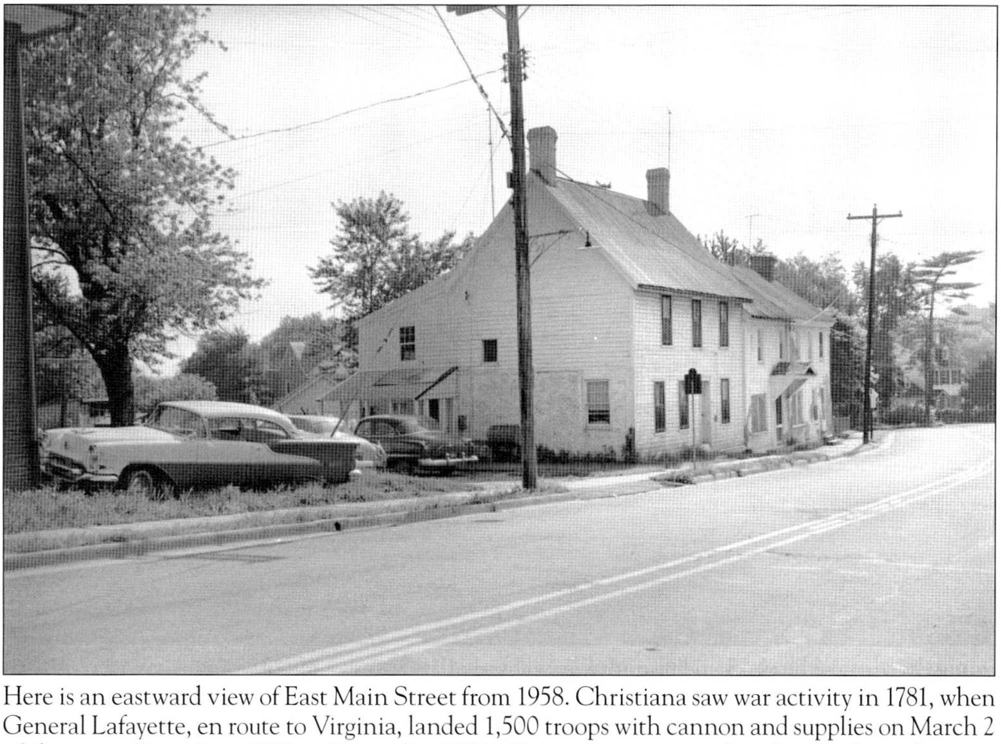

Here is an eastward view of East Main Street from 1958. Christiana saw war activity in 1781, when General Lafayette, en route to Virginia, landed 1,500 troops with cannon and supplies on March 2 of that year. From June 1781 to December 1782, Christiana saw record trade pass through town.

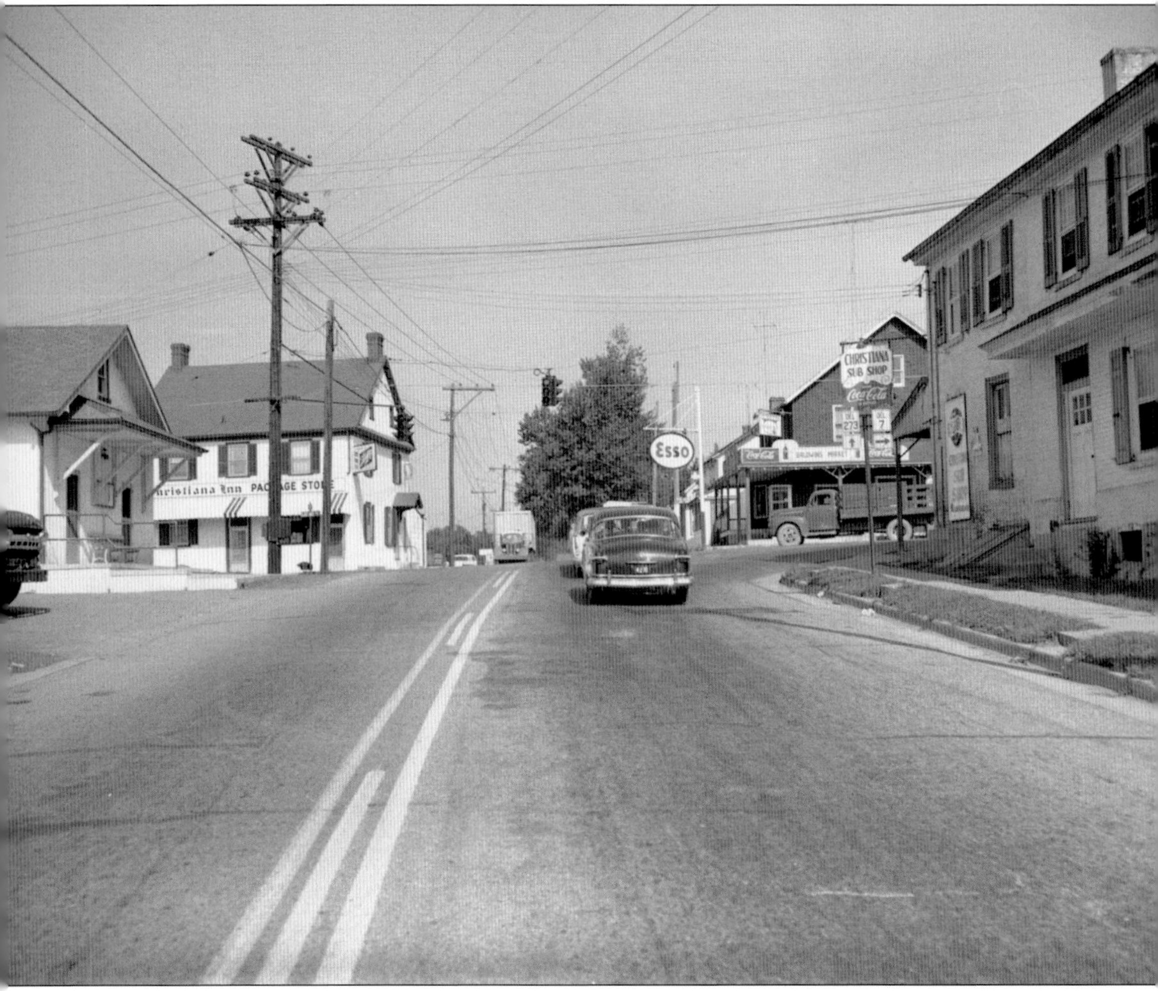

Old-timers refer to the intersection of Main Street and Old Baltimore Pike as "the Corner." It features the village's only traffic light, the Christiana Firehouse (left foreground), Christiana Inn (left background), Baldwin's Market (right background), and the historic Shannon Hotel (right foreground). Functioning as a sub shop in 1958, the Shannon Hotel was built before 1759 as the store of Thomas Montgomery. Around 1800, it was converted into an inn under the ownership of William Shannon. General Washington remarks about the Shannon Hotel and its fine accommodations in letters. Other famous hotel guests included the Marquis de Lafayette, the surveyors Charles Mason and Jeremiah Dixon, and possibly Meriwether Lewis and William Clark.

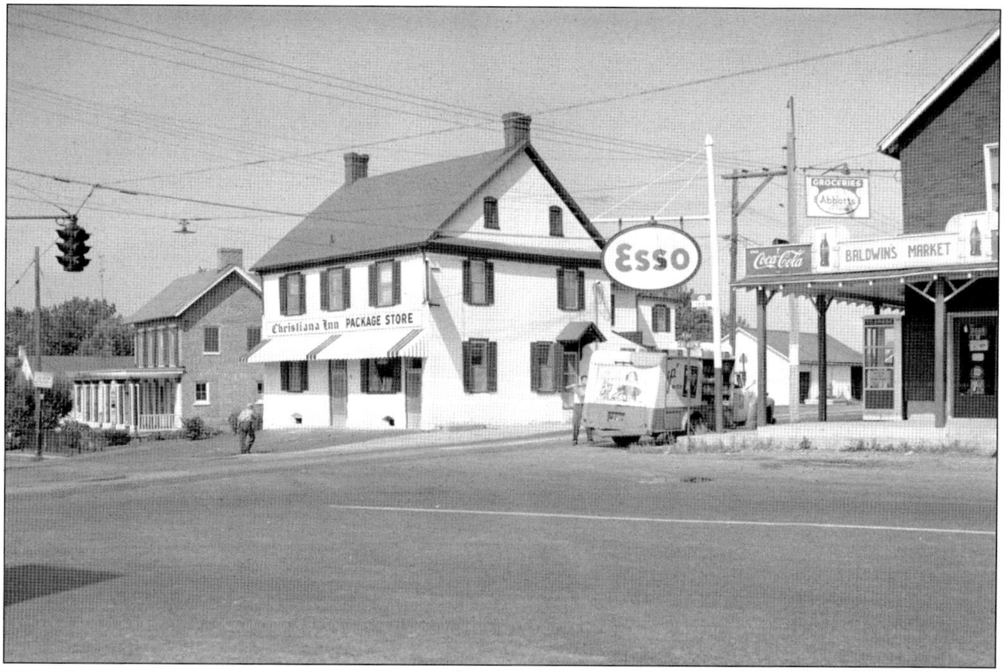

The Christiana Inn was a package store, with white paint over its brick facade, at the time of the 1958 view above. Originally built around 1770 at the corner of South Old Baltimore Pike and West Main Street, the inn was a popular stop along the Olde King's Road and remained a lodging house into the 19th century. The photograph below shows the Christiana Inn as it looked in 1938, operating as a grocery store and gas station.

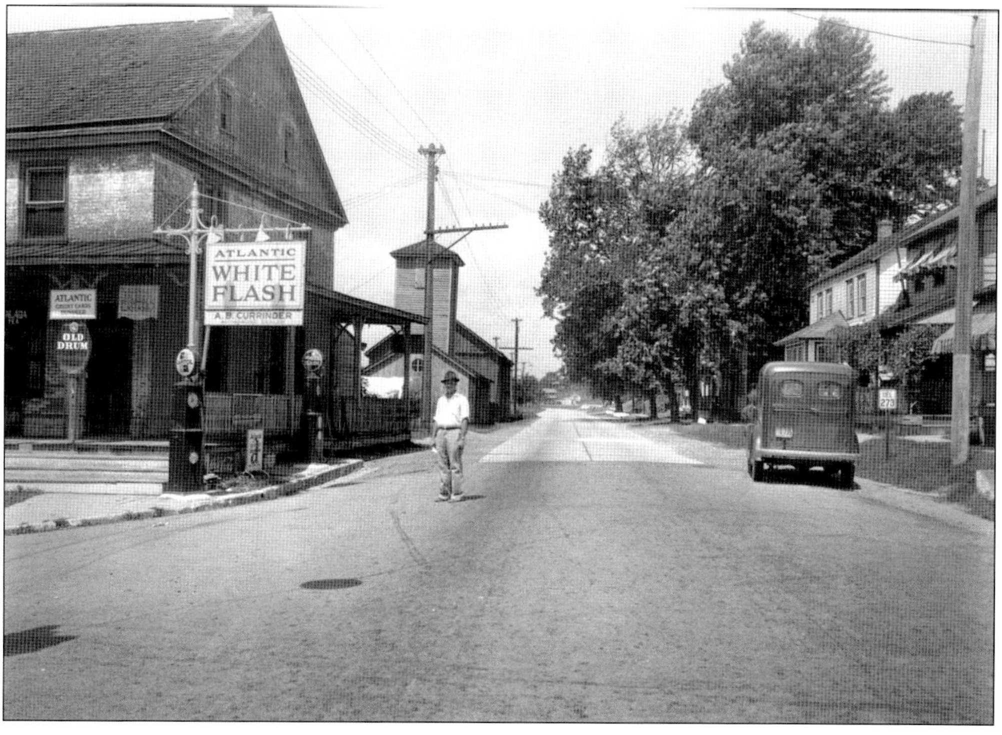

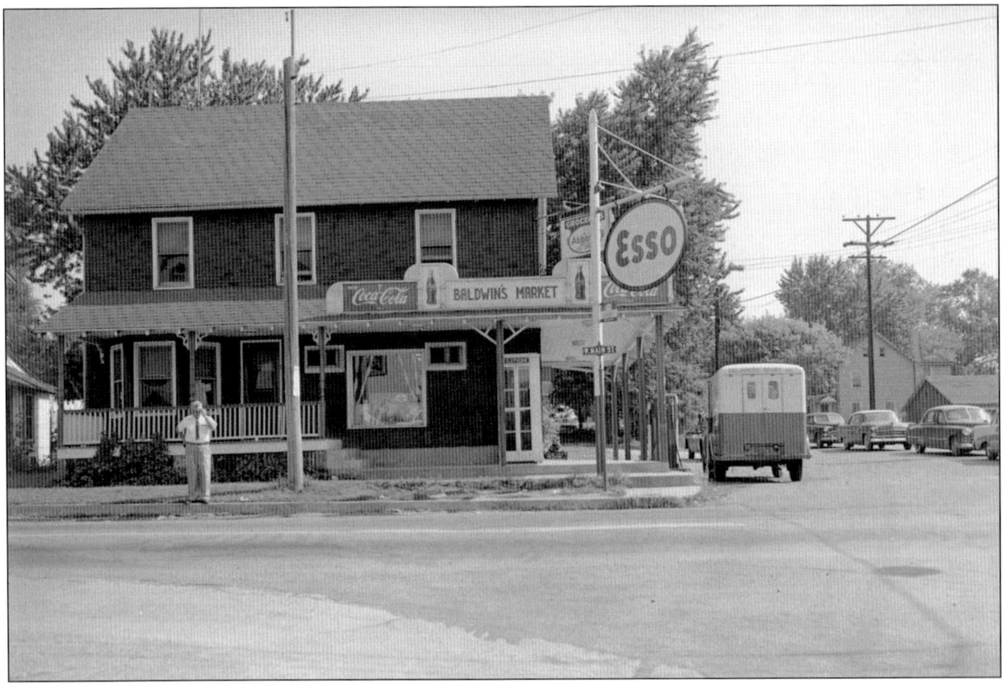

Baldwin's Market, located across from the Christiana Inn, had a wraparound porch on the south and east sides and served as a gas station as well. Proprietor Edward Baldwin, known affectionately as "Baldie," opened the store in 1946 and operated it with his wife, Eleanor, until it closed in 1977—unable to compete with the stores at University Plaza, which opened in 1974. The land is currently a vacant lot.

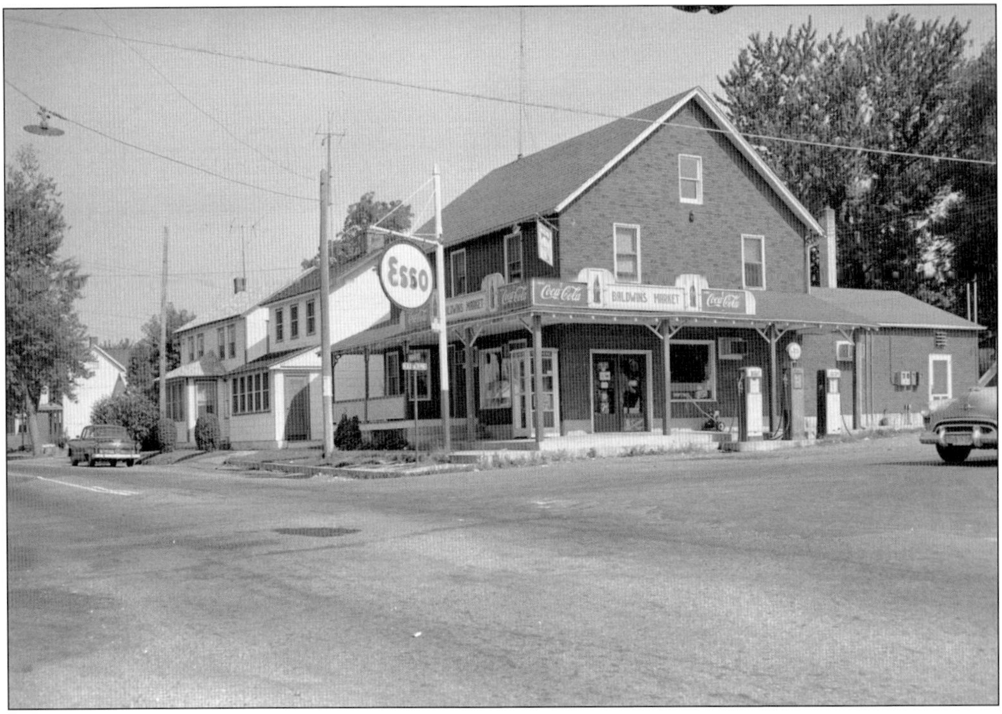

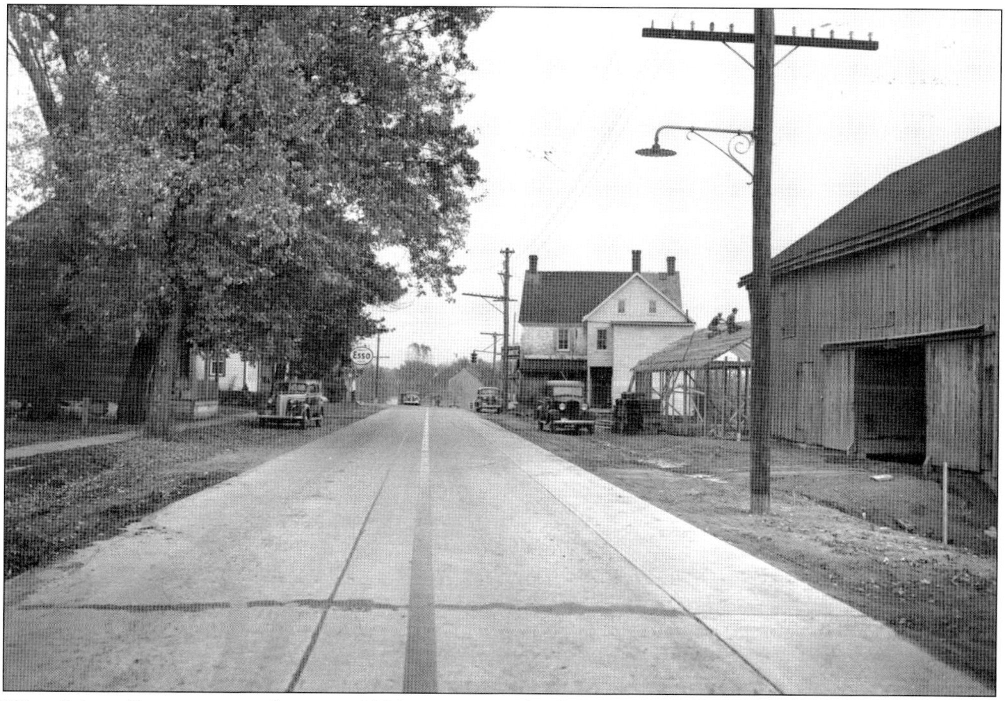

West Main Street is seen here in 1938, in a view looking east on what was then part of Route 273 toward the center of the village. Christiana began in 1684 when John Ogle divided his 75-acre property and sold lots to people for houses and businesses. Ogle had gotten the land from William Penn.

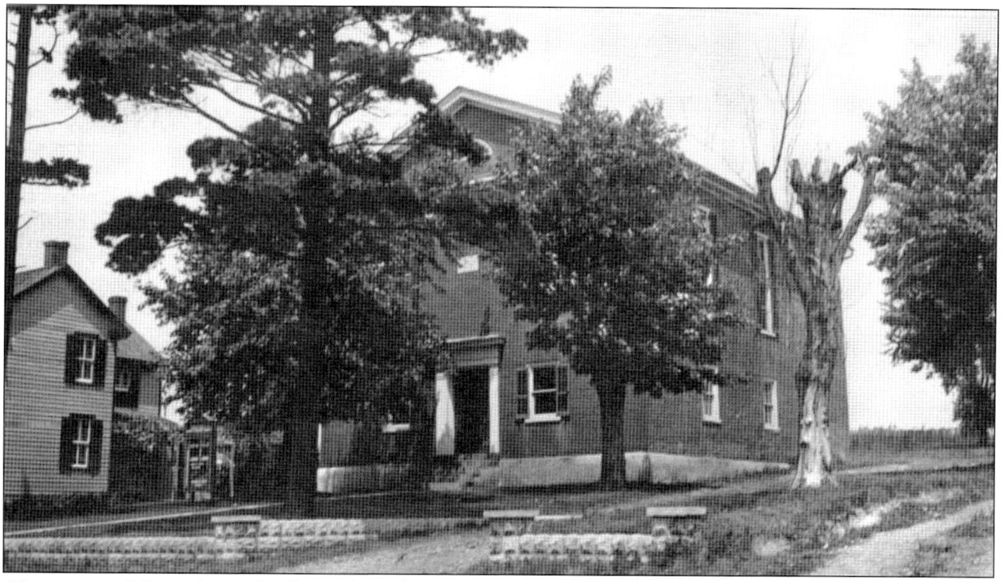

Christiana United Methodist Church on West Main Street was built on land bought from Abraham and Mary Cannon and dedicated by Bishop Levi Scott on January 28, 1858. The origin of the congregation can be traced to the earliest days of Methodism in America. In March 1771, Joseph Pilmore, one of the first Methodist missionaries from England, preached outdoors at Christiana.

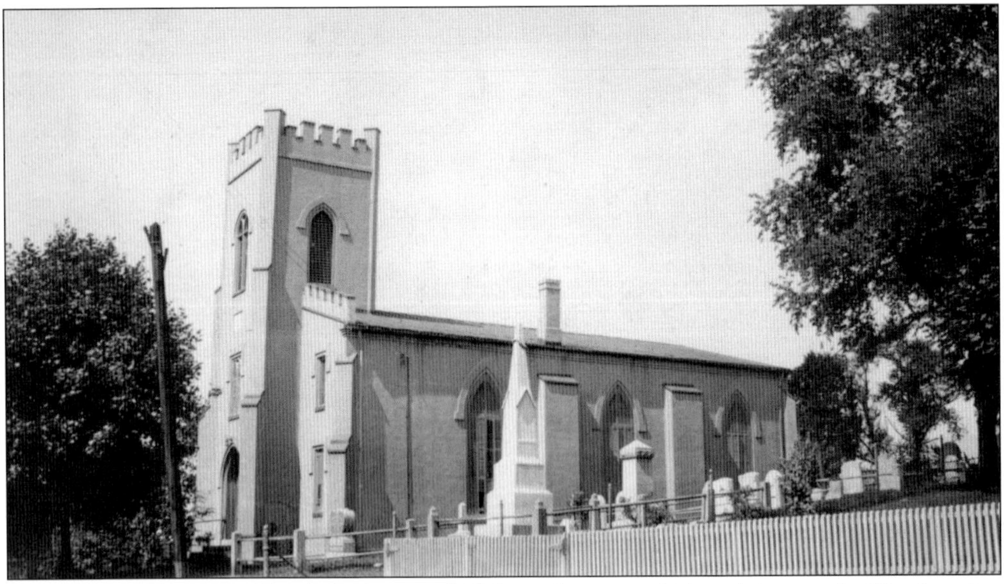

Christiana Presbyterian Church, built around 1732, was known in Colonial times as the "Presbyterian Church at Christiana Bridge." The congregation was organized in the 1730s, and the original church was replaced by the current structure in 1857. The structure is listed in the National Register of Historic Places.

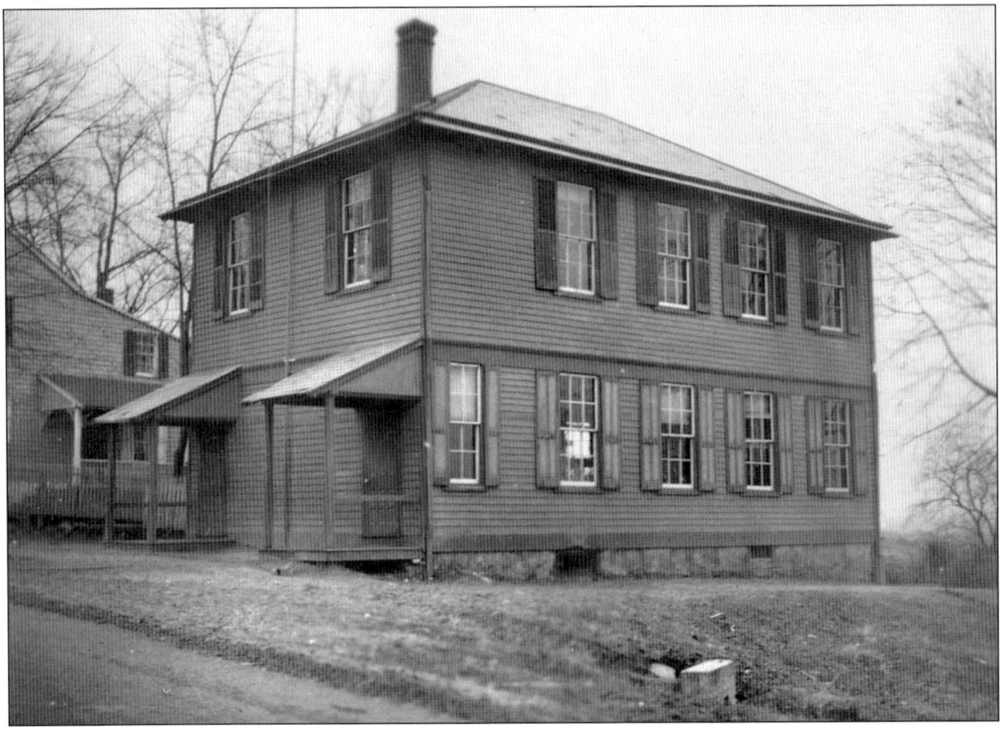

Public School No. 44 for white children, pictured in 1926, was across from the Presbyterian church on Old Baltimore Pike. Education was segregated by race, and the first school for white children in Christiana opened in 1829. The school in the photograph came later and was seriously inadequate for its purpose. A new facility—Albert H. Jones Elementary School—opened in 1935.

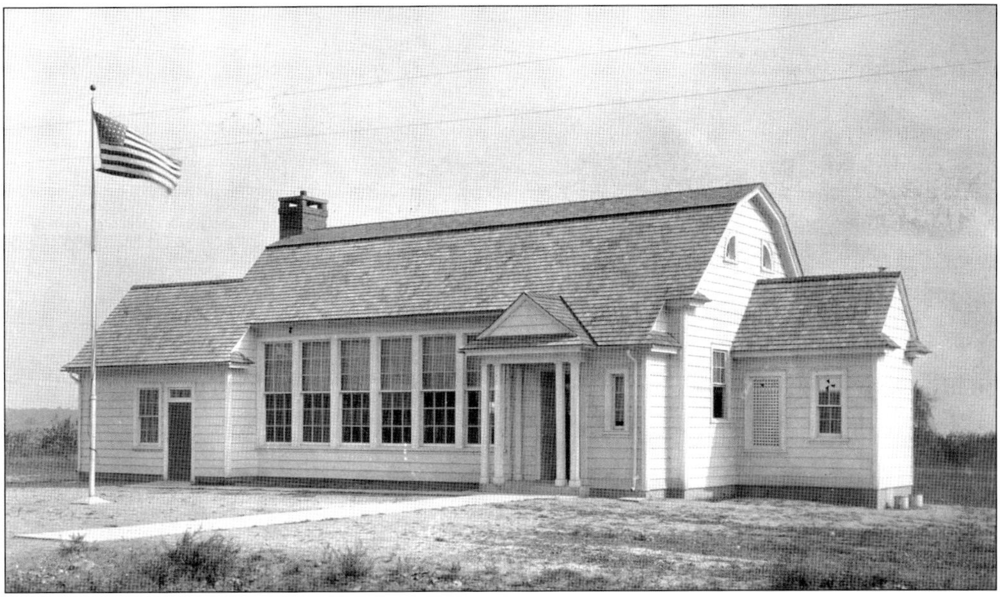

This building is Christiana Colored School No. 111-C. Pierre S. du Pont (1870–1954), unhappy with the condition of public education in Delaware, organized the Delaware School Auxiliary Association to oversee the construction of new schools for both races. He also personally donated more than $6 million, most of which was spent for African American schools. He dedicated the Christiana Colored School on September 6, 1920. It closed because of dwindling attendance in 1952, but the building remains.

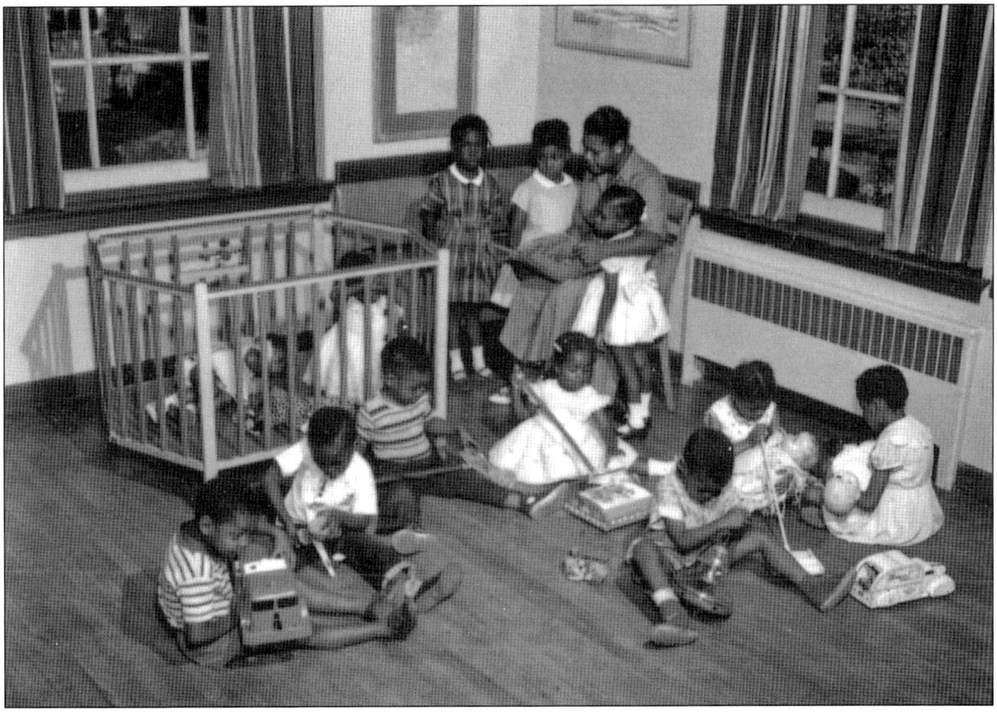

This photograph from 1959 shows the school when it was used as a day care and community center. The building still stands on North Old Baltimore Pike. (Courtesy of Delaware Historical Society.)

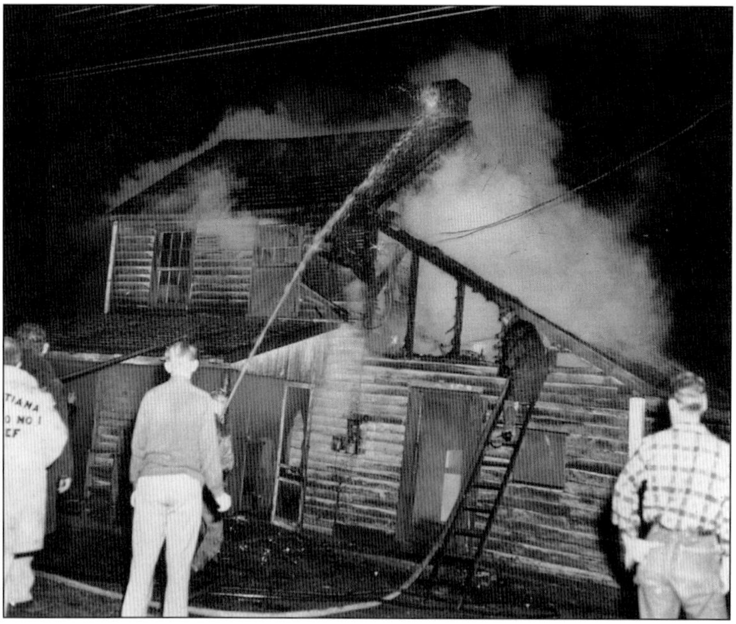

Fighting this house fire are members of the Christiana Fire Company, which was officially chartered and incorporated on January 4, 1922. In 1927, the fire company purchased the lot on which a portion of the current Station 12 now stands. To meet the growing fire-protection and life-support needs of the region, Fire Company 6 opened on Porter Road in 1972, and Station 3, on Salem Church Road in 1994.

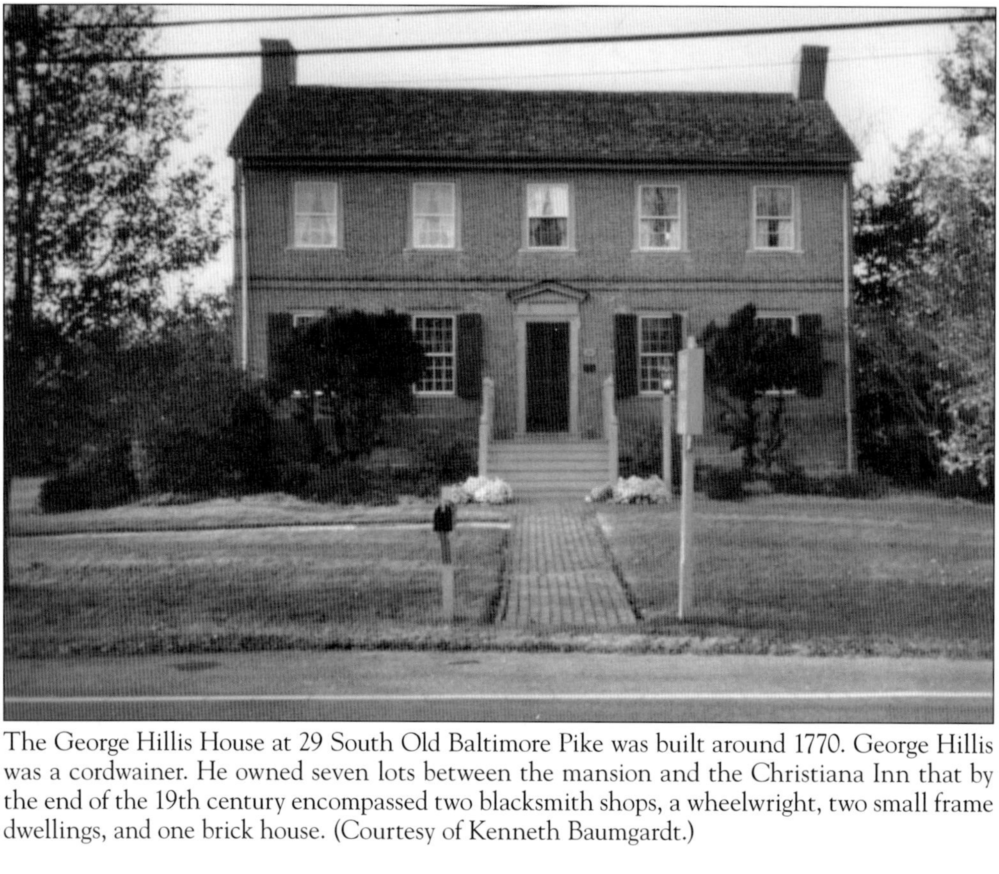

The George Hillis House at 29 South Old Baltimore Pike was built around 1770. George Hillis was a cordwainer. He owned seven lots between the mansion and the Christiana Inn that by the end of the 19th century encompassed two blacksmith shops, a wheelwright, two small frame dwellings, and one brick house. (Courtesy of Kenneth Baumgardt.)

Three

Newport Ayre

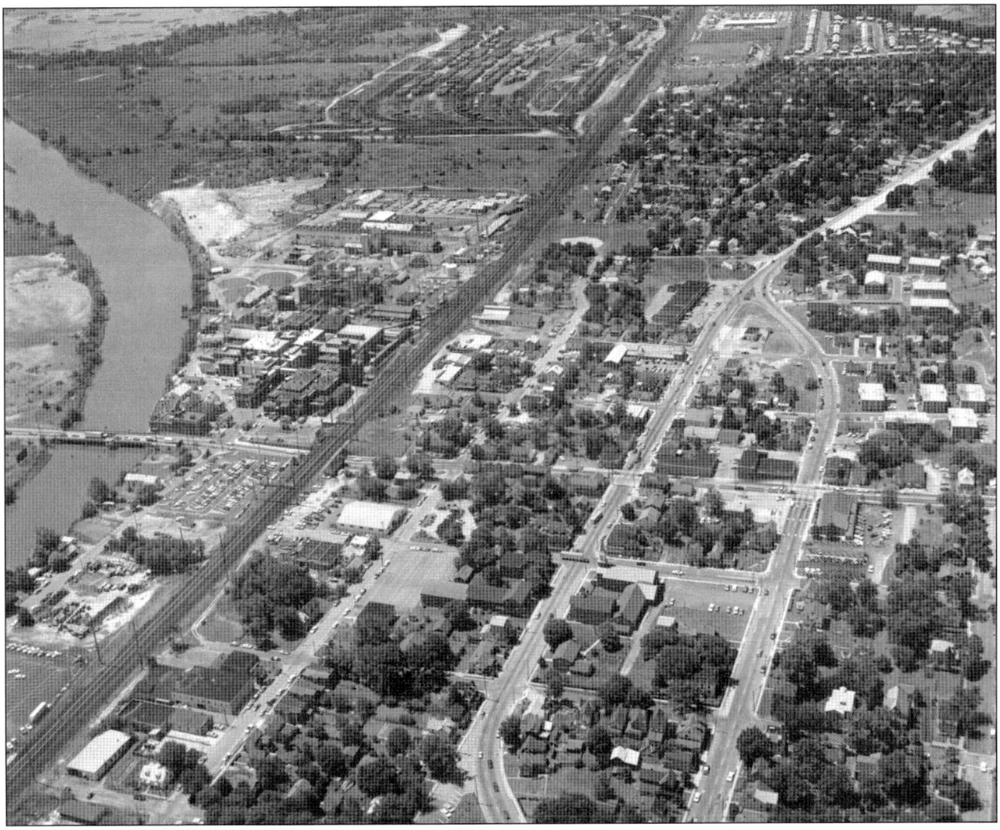

The James Street Bridge over the Christina River is visible in this 1968 aerial view of Newport. In 1731, John Justis purchased 100 acres of land to build a town for business purposes. He called it Newport Ayre. In 1735, Samuel Marshall purchased 18 acres from Justis and laid out lots for sale. His original town plan includes many of the street names still in use today. Newport thrived as a shipping center for flour and grain because of the Christina River and its location along the Olde Kings Road, but the town's importance faded with the rise of railroads.

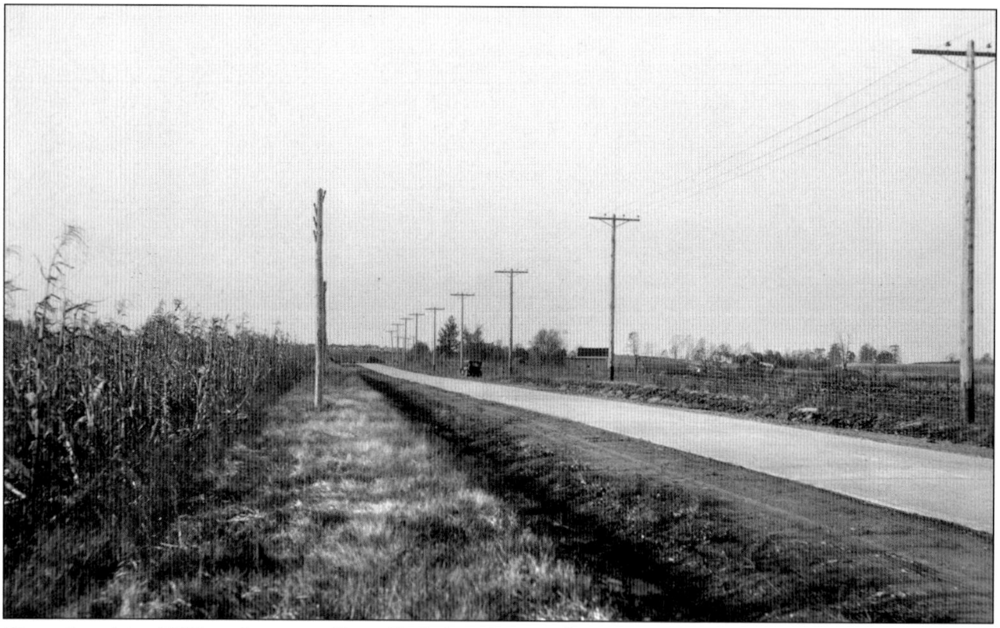

Completed in 1818 and originally called the Gap and Newport Turnpike, Delaware's first toll road connected Newport, Delaware, and Gap, Pennsylvania. Early on, private companies built roads and charged a toll. Tollgates were originally a long pole, or pike, that crossed the road and blocked the traveler from proceeding. When the toll was paid, the pike was turned upwards; hence the term *turnpike*.

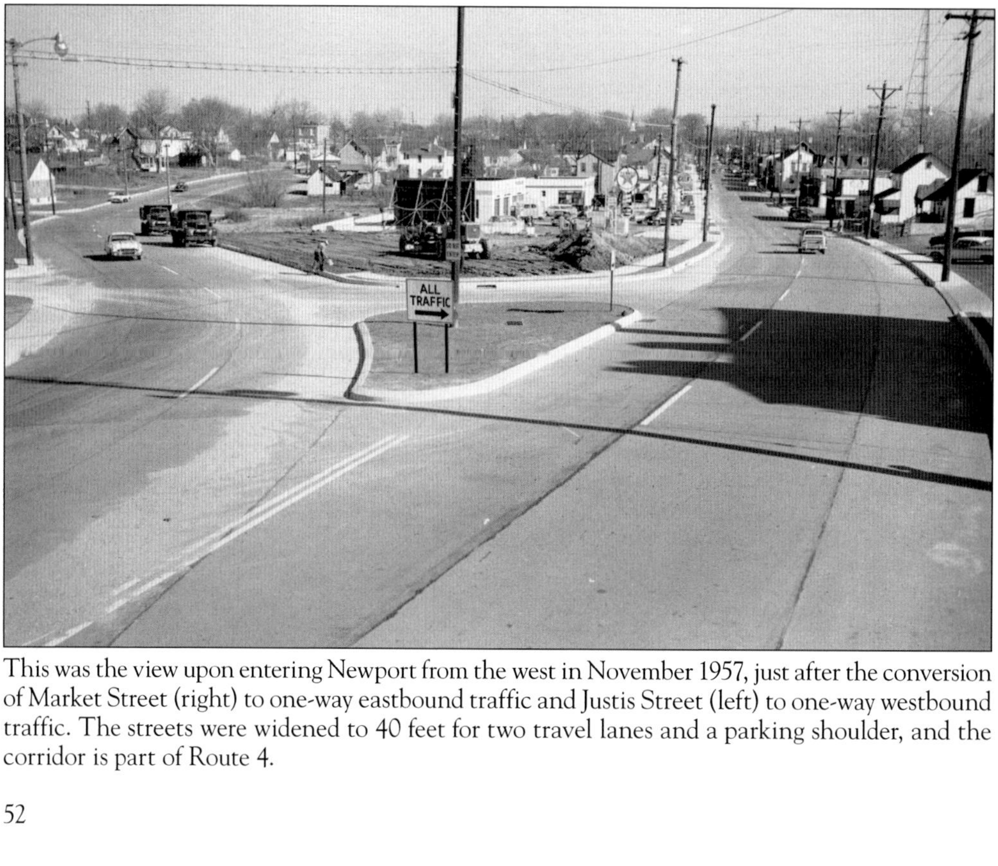

This was the view upon entering Newport from the west in November 1957, just after the conversion of Market Street (right) to one-way eastbound traffic and Justis Street (left) to one-way westbound traffic. The streets were widened to 40 feet for two travel lanes and a parking shoulder, and the corridor is part of Route 4.

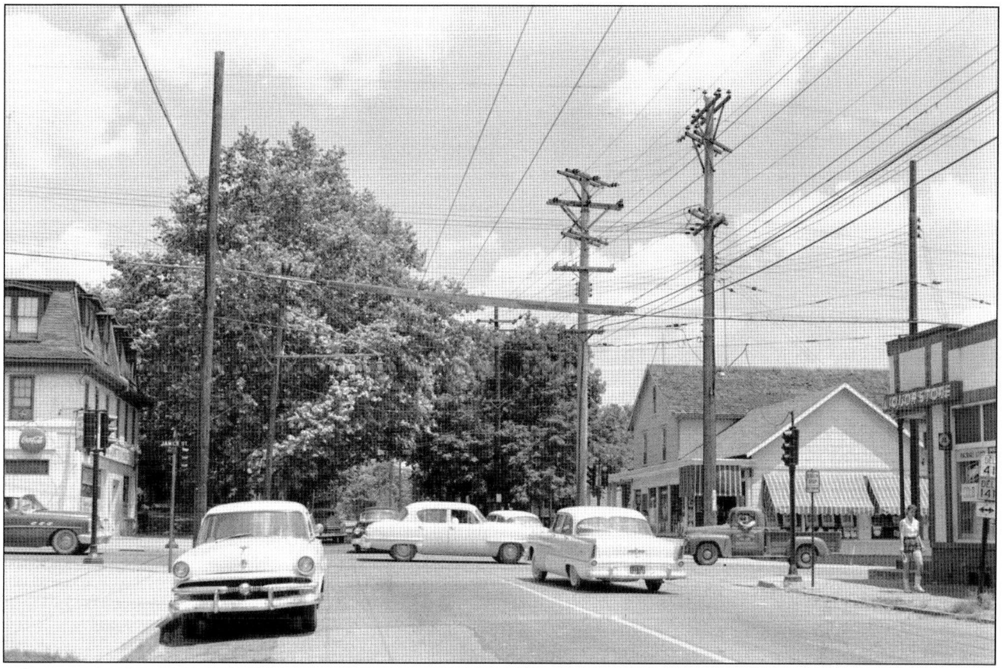

This 1956 photograph depicts West Market Street with two-way traffic and trees. The crossroad, James Street, had for a time been part of Routes 41 and 141 and connected to Basin Road (south) and the Newport Gap Pike (north). When Delaware assigned state route numbers by 1936, Routes 41 and 141 ran concurrently from US 13 up Frenchtown Road (Route 273) in New Castle, turning onto Basin Road, and then running along James Street before separating north of Newport.

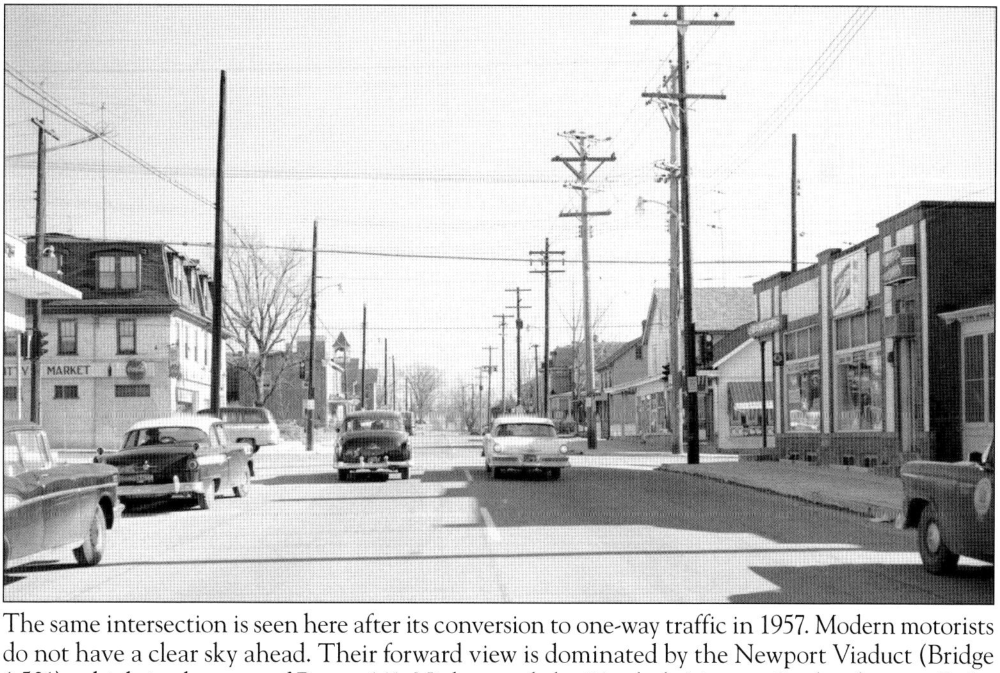

The same intersection is seen here after its conversion to one-way traffic in 1957. Modern motorists do not have a clear sky ahead. Their forward view is dominated by the Newport Viaduct (Bridge 1-501), which is also part of Route 141. Nicknamed the "Asphalt Monster," it has been called a blessing and a curse and dominates the modern downtown.

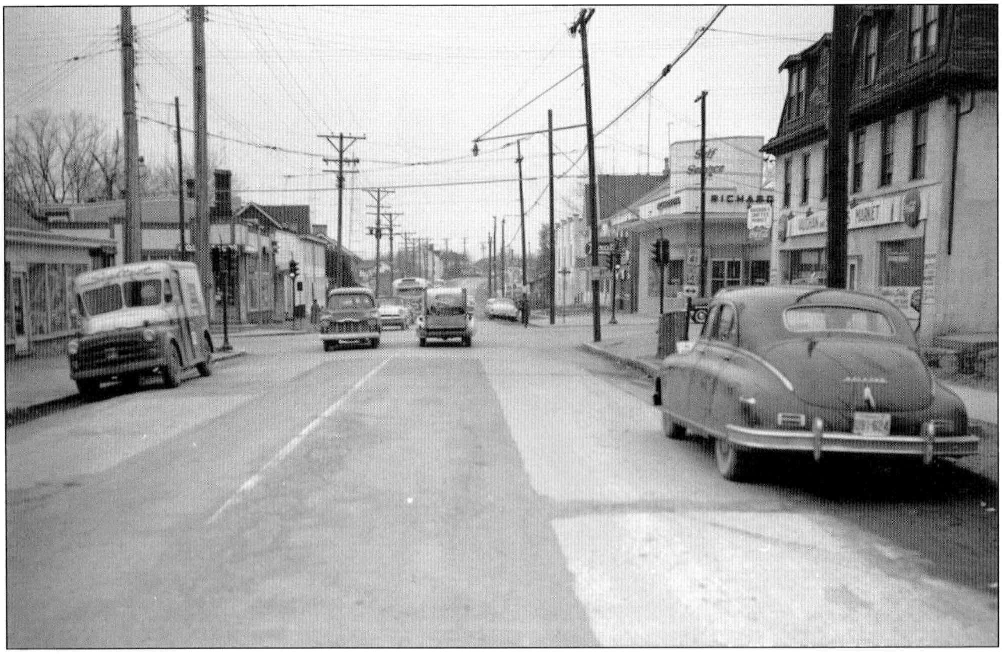

In this westward view of Market and James Streets, Vaughn & Smitty's Market is visible to the right. Joseph Latimer (1719–1897) was a merchant and landowner who became president of the Delaware Convention and signed the ratification of the Constitution in 1787. His residence and store was at this location.

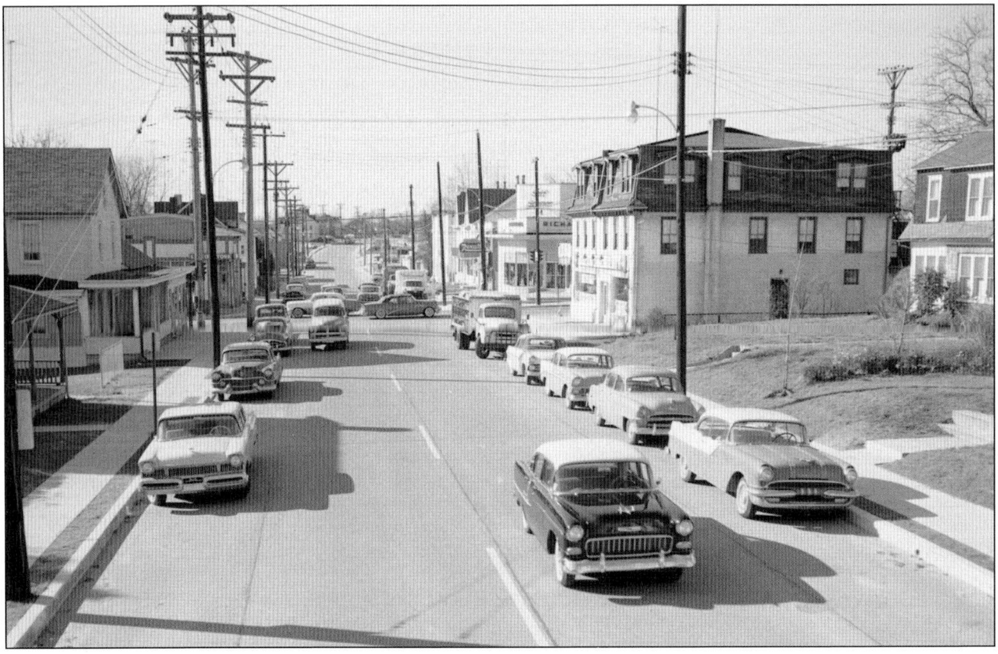

The Newport Viaduct currently occupies this location, and its construction caused the demolition of the houses and buildings in the foreground. Some locals would say that it also led to the end of the area's down-home, downtown feeling. In 1992, a movement to create a historic district that would have protected 10 historical properties failed.

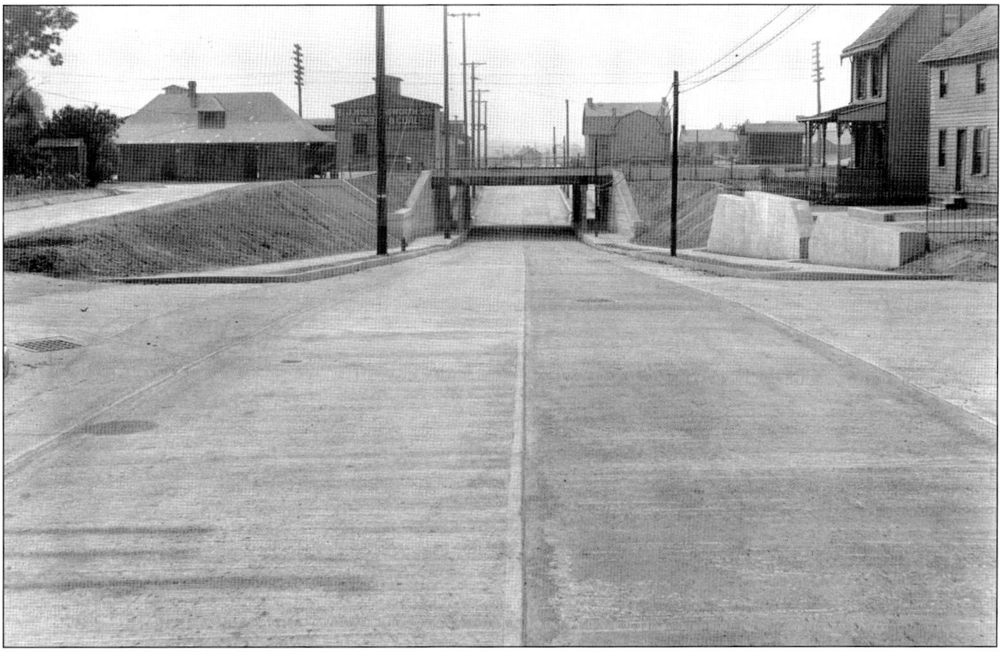

In 1930, an underpass opened to traffic on James Street that eliminated a previous at-grade railroad crossing. This project was one of many throughout the state by the Delaware Highway Department to reduce the danger of car-train collisions. The depot is seen in the upper left. The Philadelphia, Wilmington & Baltimore Railroad laid tracks to Newport in 1837.

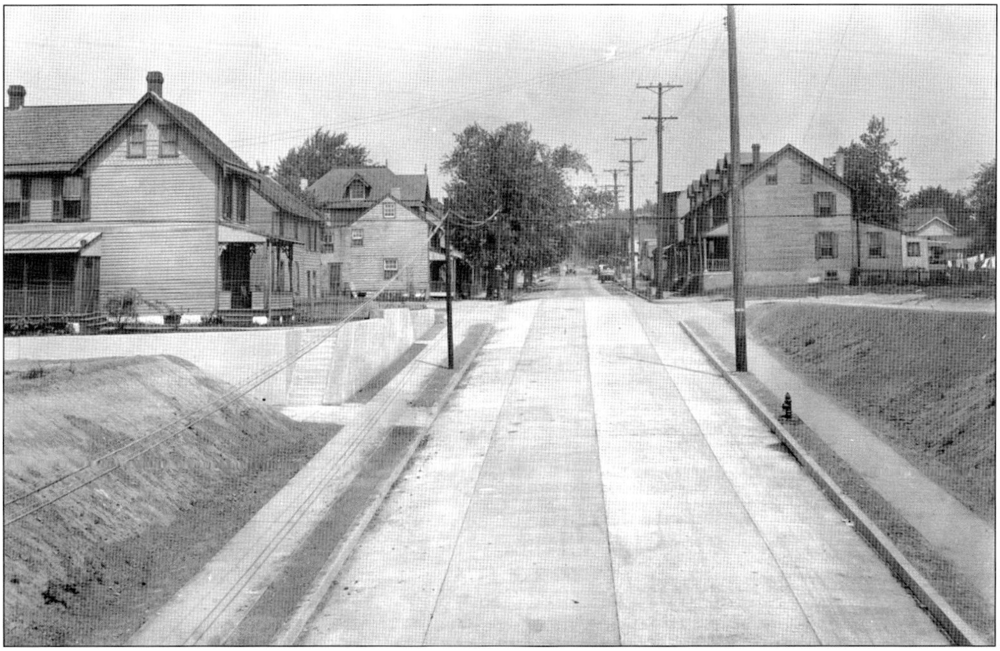

This is the view into Newport from the railroad overpass in 1930. The town's first European settlement dates to 1664, with a 1,200-acre land grant from King Charles II of the United Kingdom to James, Duke of York, who had recently ended Dutch and Swedish rule on the Delaware River with the bloodless takeover of New Amstel (New Castle) and New Sweden (Wilmington).

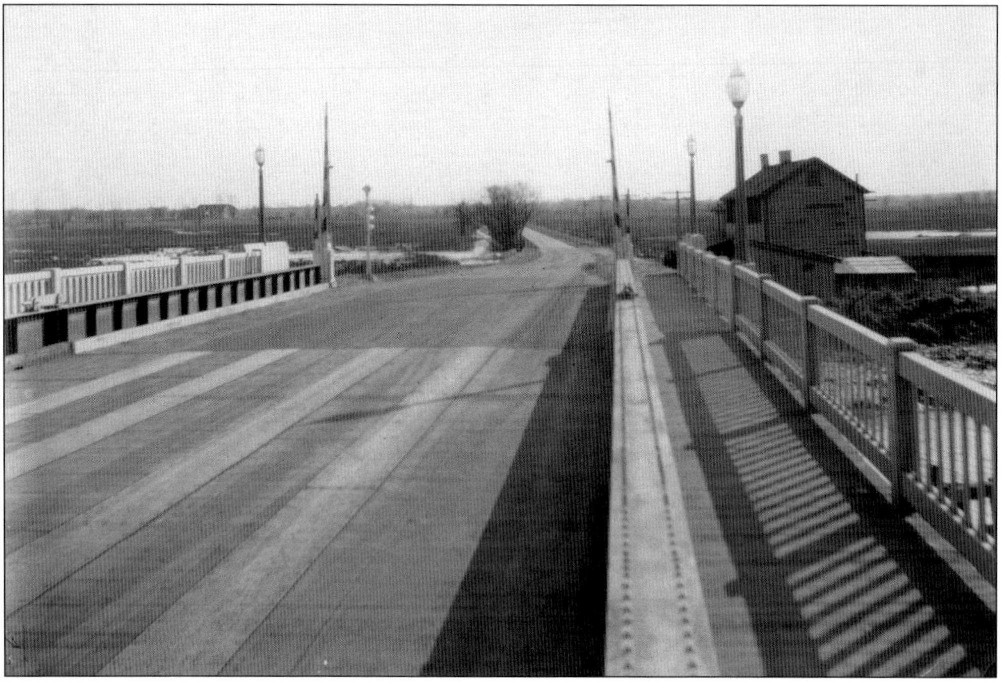

On January 21, 1800, the Delaware General Assembly authorized a ferry operation over the Christina River in Newport in the area later occupied by the James Street Bridge. This 1930 photograph shows the bridge's roadbed and the view south.

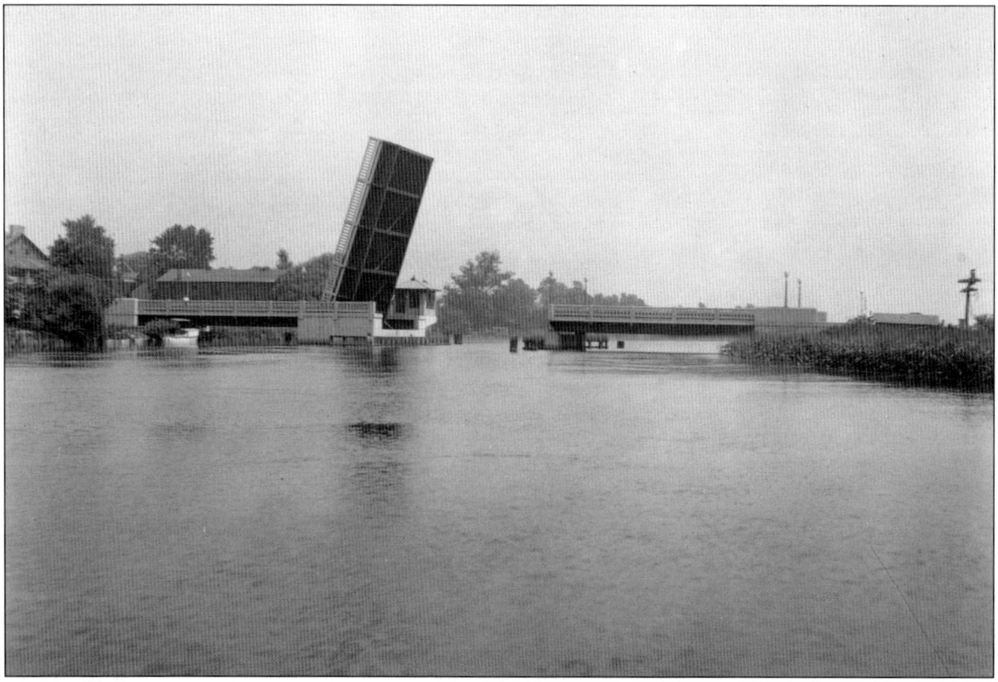

State Highway Bridge 159 is the James Street/Newport Bridge over the Christina River. Designed by Keller and Harrington of Chicago, Illinois, specialists in movable bridges, and with structural steel provided by the Bethlehem Steel Company, the bridge opened to traffic on December 1, 1929.

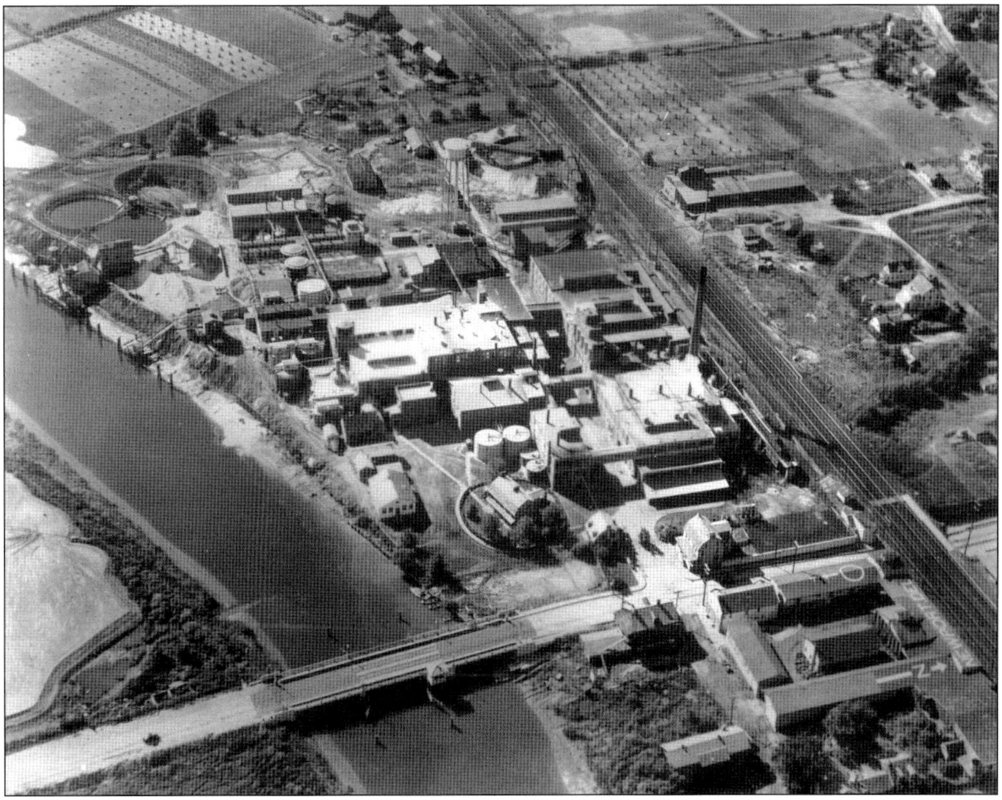

At the start of the 1900s, Newport got new life as a manufacturing center. In 1902, Danish immigrant Henrik J. Krebs opened a plant for the production of lithopones, or white pigments. By the time of his death in 1929, the facility covered seven acres and produced 150,000 pounds per day. The plant was then acquired by E.I. du Pont de Nemours & Co. and was later purchased by BASF Corporation in 1984. This aerial photograph was taken in 1932. (Courtesy of Delaware Historical Society.)

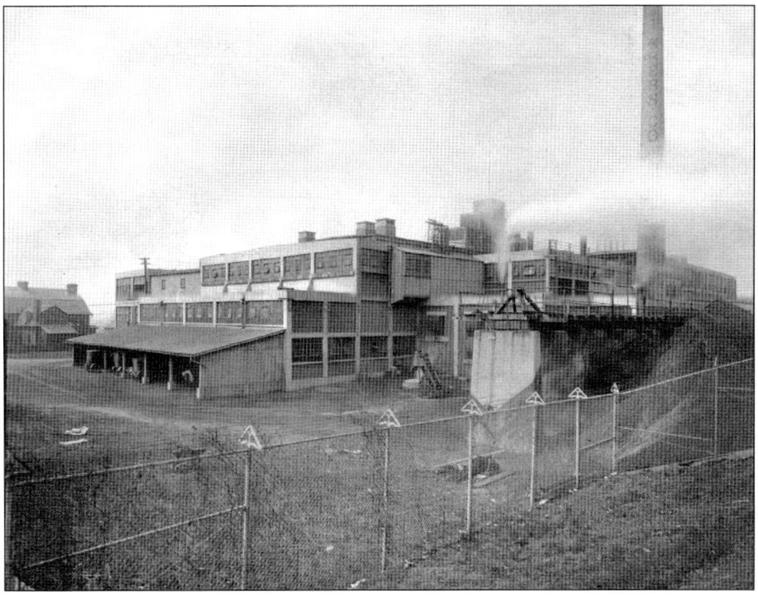

This ground-level view of the Krebs Plant dates to 1933. The historic Joseph Tatnall House is part of the property. It is also called the Oliver Evans House to honor the town's 18th-century inventor, but there is no justification for this as Evans's birthplace was a stone house at the southeast corner of Christian and James Streets and has not survived.

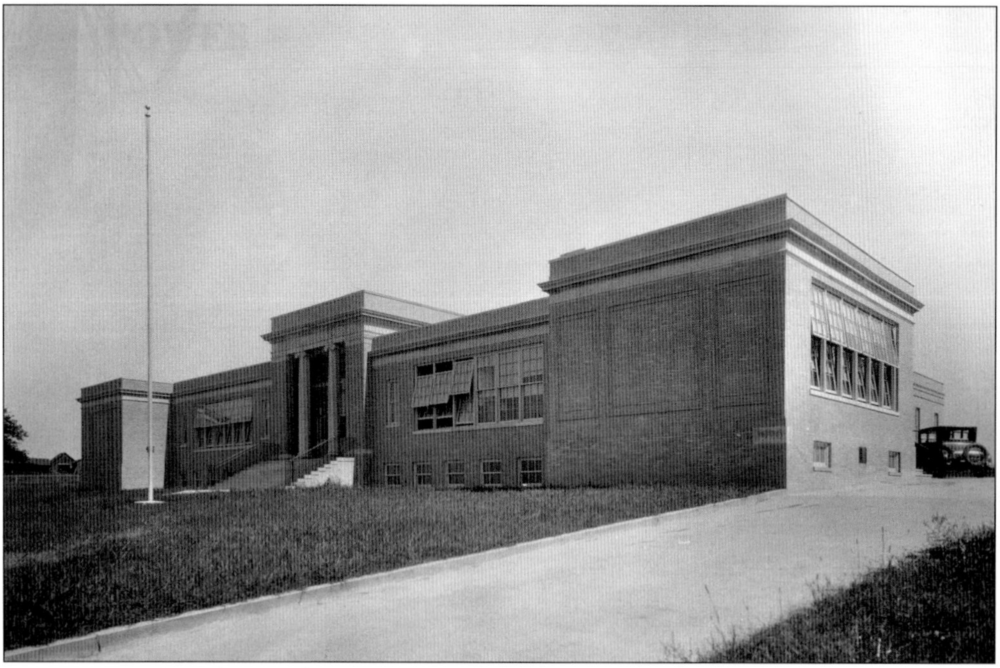

In 1926, Henrik Krebs gave $150,000 toward the construction of an eight-classroom school on the occasion of his 50th wedding anniversary. Built by Pierre Samuel du Pont's Delaware School Auxiliary Association at 234 North James Street, the original Krebs School opened September 7, 1927. Besides classrooms, it had administrative offices, a kitchen and cafeteria, and a 500-seat auditorium. The facility at various times served grades one to nine until it closed in 1981. The location was a high point in Newport that overlooked the entire town and the Christina River, and it had been popular with sightseers. The location is currently the Tower Office Park.

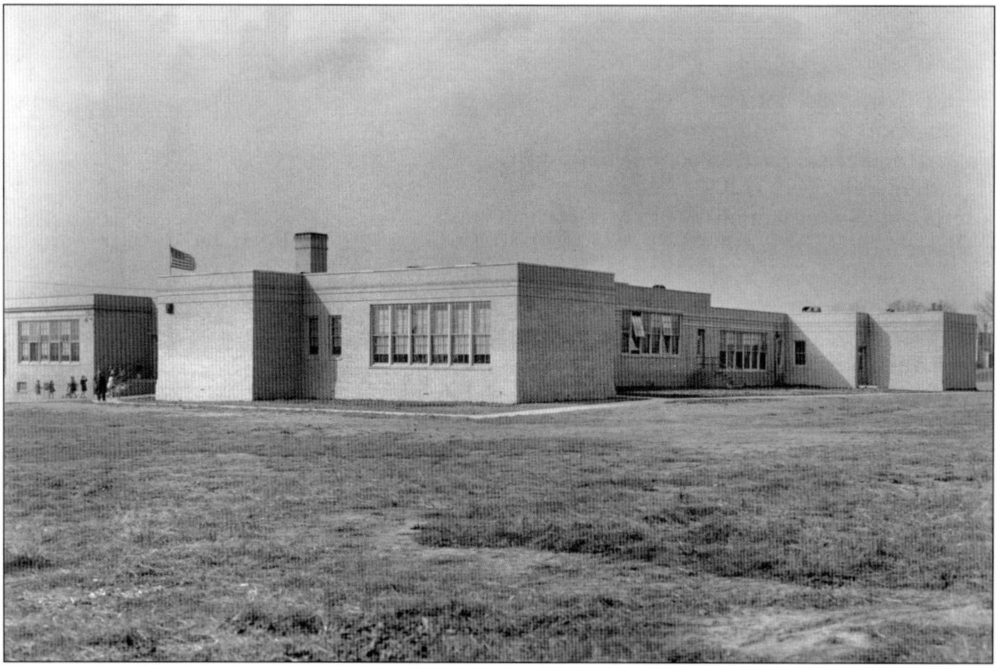

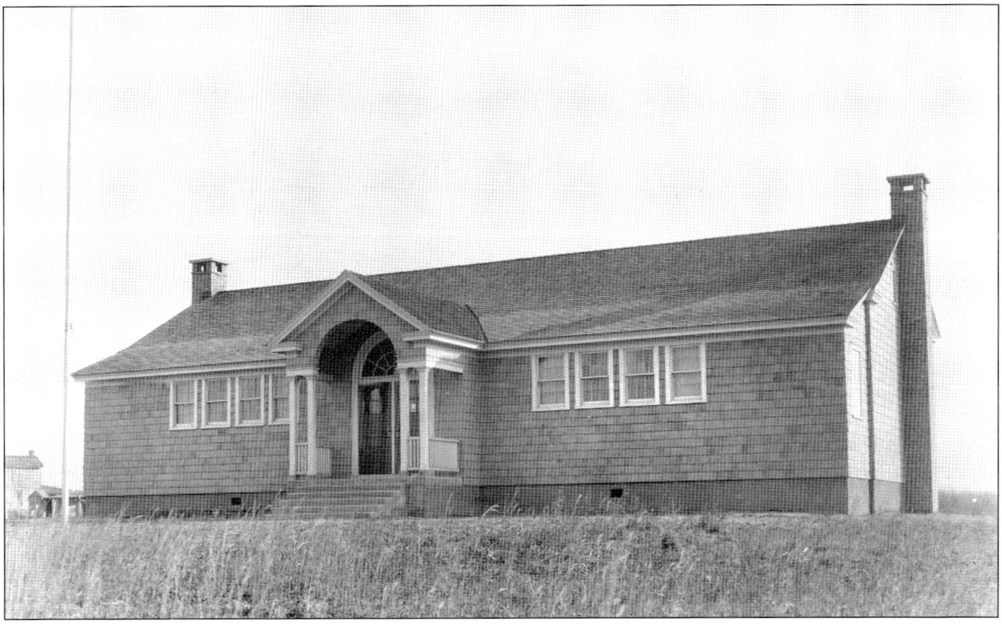

The two-room Newport Colored School was completed in 1922 by P.S. du Pont's Delaware School Auxiliary Association at a cost of $14,140.60. The Belvedere/Cedar Heights area is a historically African American community. In 1875, Delaware passed legislation allowing African Americans to tax themselves for the support of their schools. However, funding was woefully inadequate, and so were the schools.

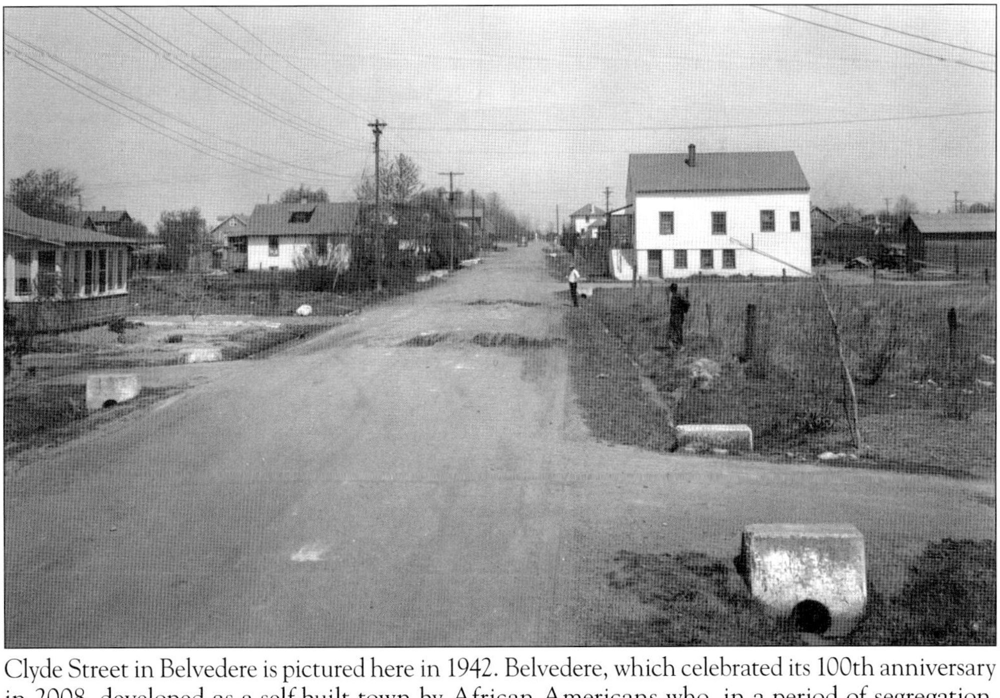

Clyde Street in Belvedere is pictured here in 1942. Belvedere, which celebrated its 100th anniversary in 2008, developed as a self-built town by African Americans who, in a period of segregation, were denied housing in other parts of the county. Its citizens created their own fire company in 1949 because white fire companies refused to service the area.

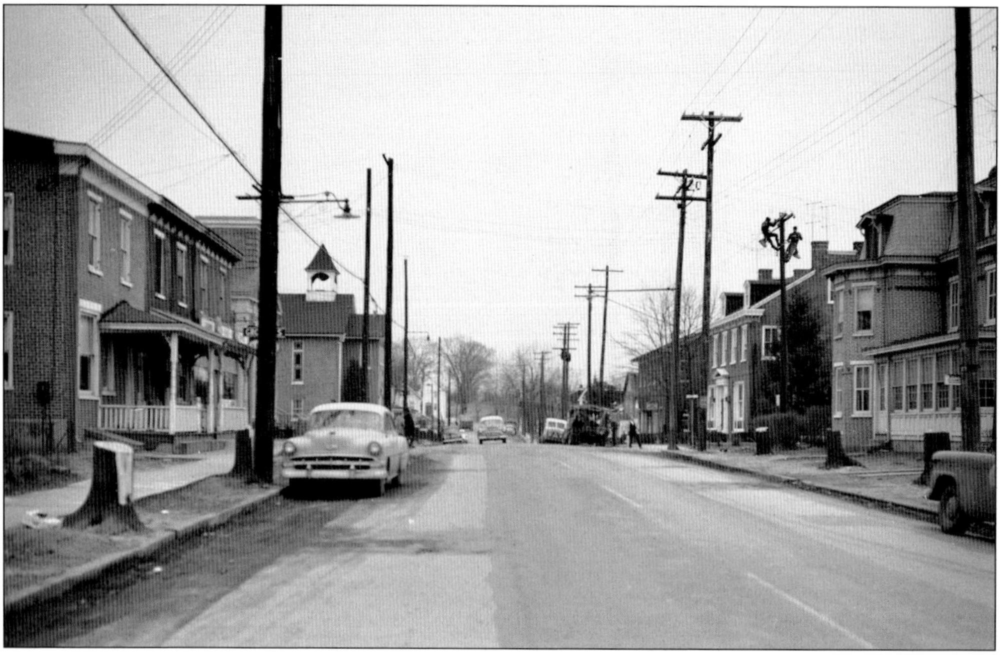

This February 1957 view looks toward Market Street's intersection with Marshall Street. As evidenced by the stumps, trees were being cleared and telephone polls moved, prior to the road construction that would widen the street. By 1971, the houses in this photograph would be demolished to make way for the viaduct.

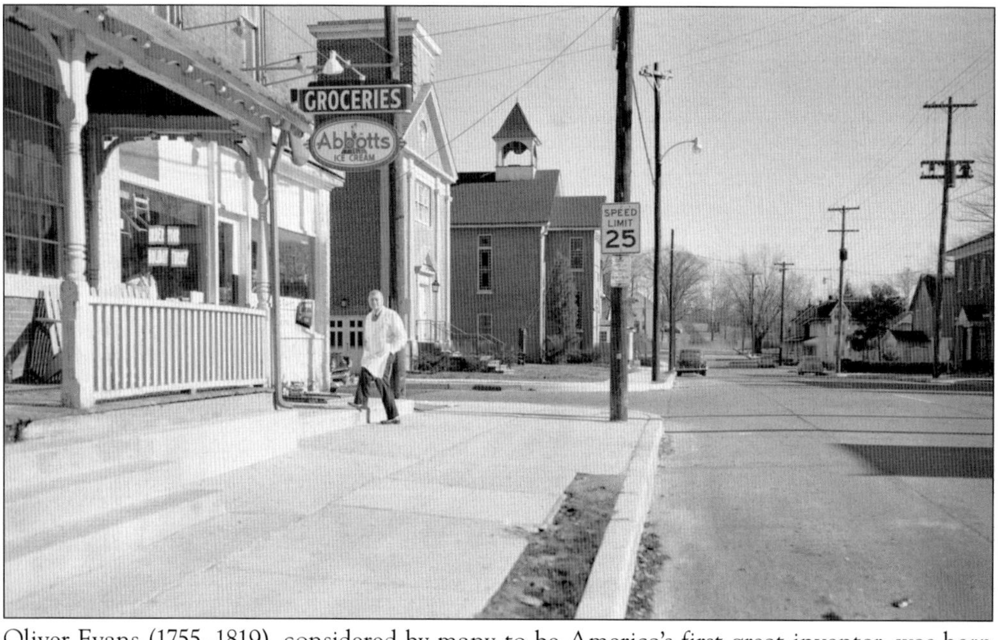

Oliver Evans (1755–1819), considered by many to be America's first great inventor, was born in Newport. He revolutionized grain production and built a steam-driven vehicle that General Motors later credited as the forerunner of the modern automobile. Newport is also the hometown of Dallas Green, a major-league baseball pitcher from 1960 to 1967 who would later manage the 1980 World Series Champion Philadelphia Phillies.

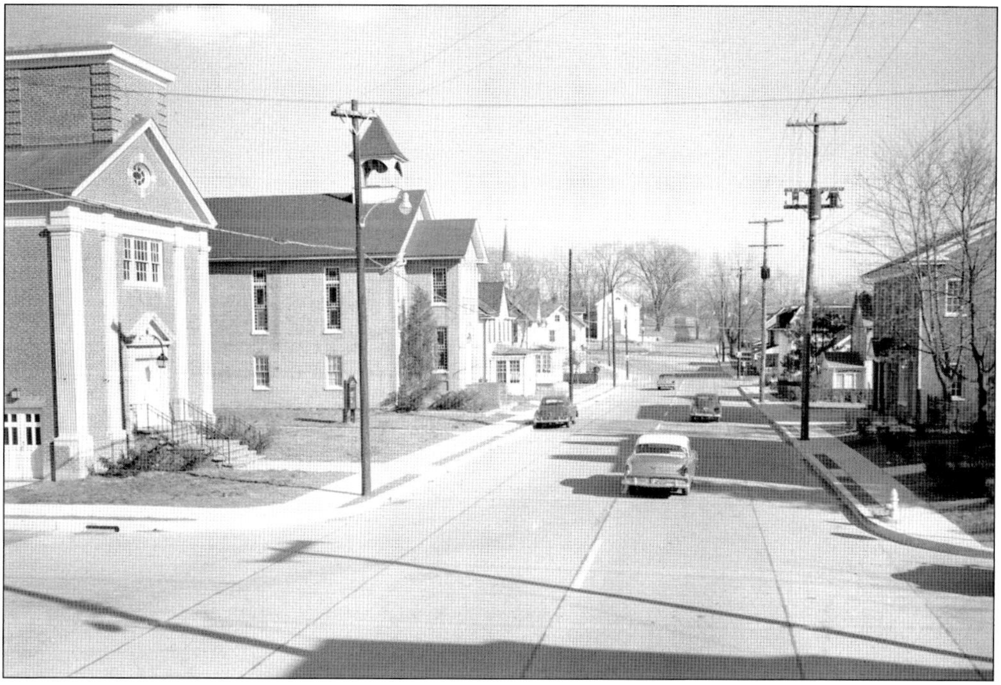

On the left of this photograph are the two buildings of the Peniel United Methodist Church at 115 East Market Street. The name Peniel means the "face of God." The older structure with the bell tower was built 1865. The church on the far left, then minus its steeple, was dedicated in 1954.

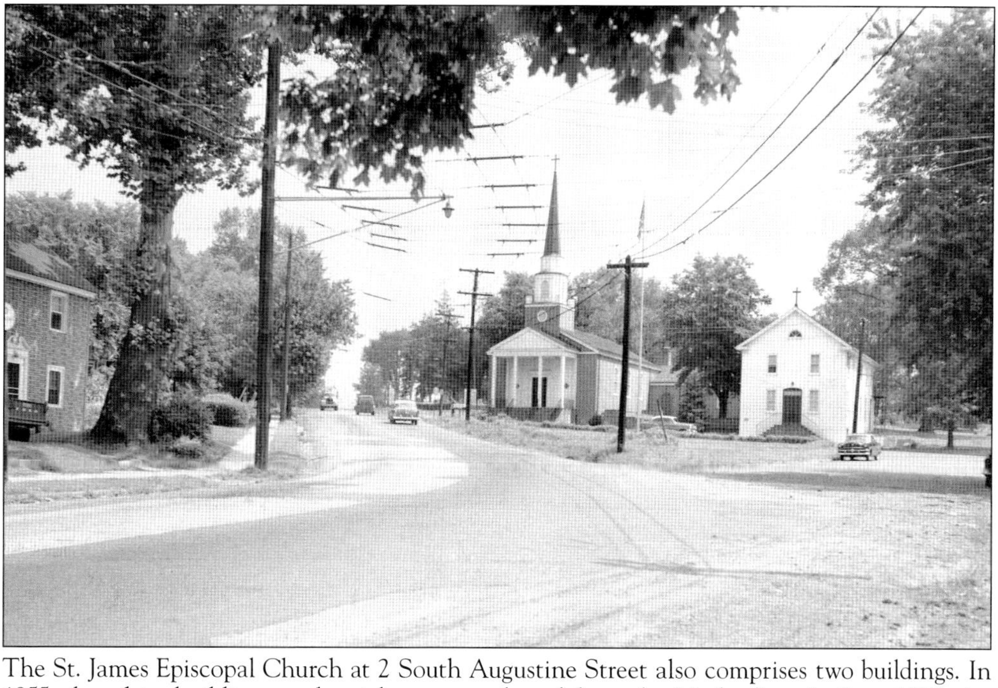

The St. James Episcopal Church at 2 South Augustine Street also comprises two buildings. In 1855, the white building on the right was purchased from the Methodists. In June 1875, the cornerstone for the brick church was laid. An even earlier church at Market and British Streets was taken over by Delaware Revolutionary forces and used as a headquarters in 1776.

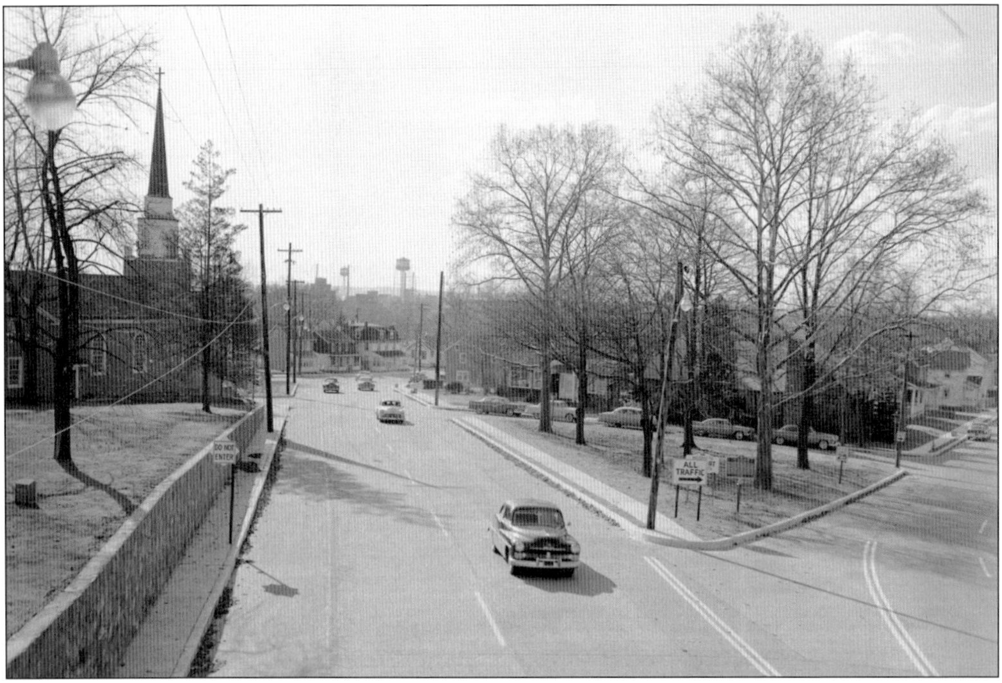

The eastbound traffic pictured here is leaving town via Market Street and entering East Newport Pike in November 1957. Newport, incorporated April 17, 1873, was created as a commission form of government, with five elected commissioners. This form of government continues.

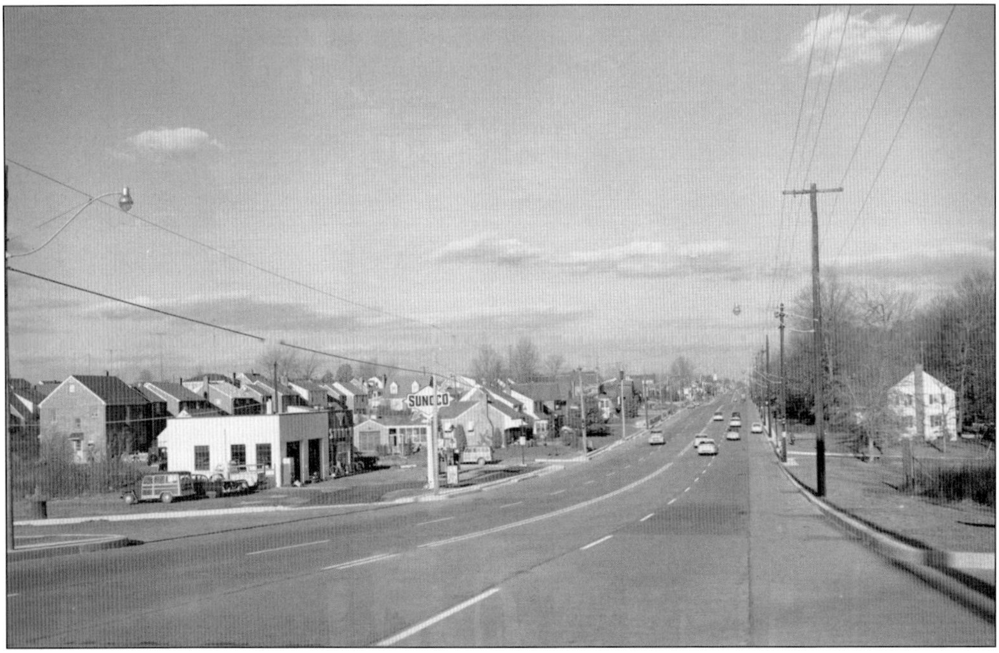

East Newport Pike in 1957 looked very similar to how it does today. Like Christiana, the pike is part of the 620-mile Washington-Rochambeau Route. Continental troops camped along Newport Pike in 1777; they marched through town again on September 5, 1781, on their way to Yorktown, Virginia.

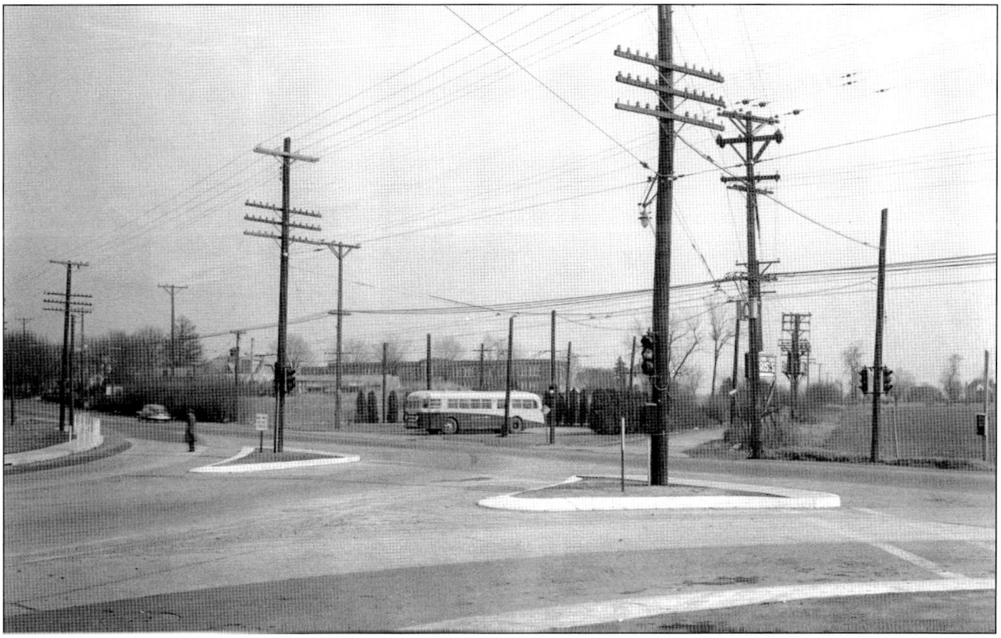

The East Newport Pike, Maryland Avenue, Boxwood Road, and Middleboro Road intersection is pictured here in 1948. Henry Latimer, a prominent banker, had an estate on Middleboro Road called Woodstock. Today, it is the 156-acre Banning Park. John Richardson II, whose father had bought the land from a Swede in 1687, created a milling community called Middleboro. In 1789, descendant Ann Richardson married Henry Latimer, an active participant in the American Revolution and Delaware politics. Woodstock became the center of society along the Christina River and eventually passed to James Latimer Banning. Today, New Castle County's Banning Park has Lewis and Folly Ponds, baseball and softball fields, two soccer fields, eight tennis courts, hiking trails, a playground, and several picnic pavilions.

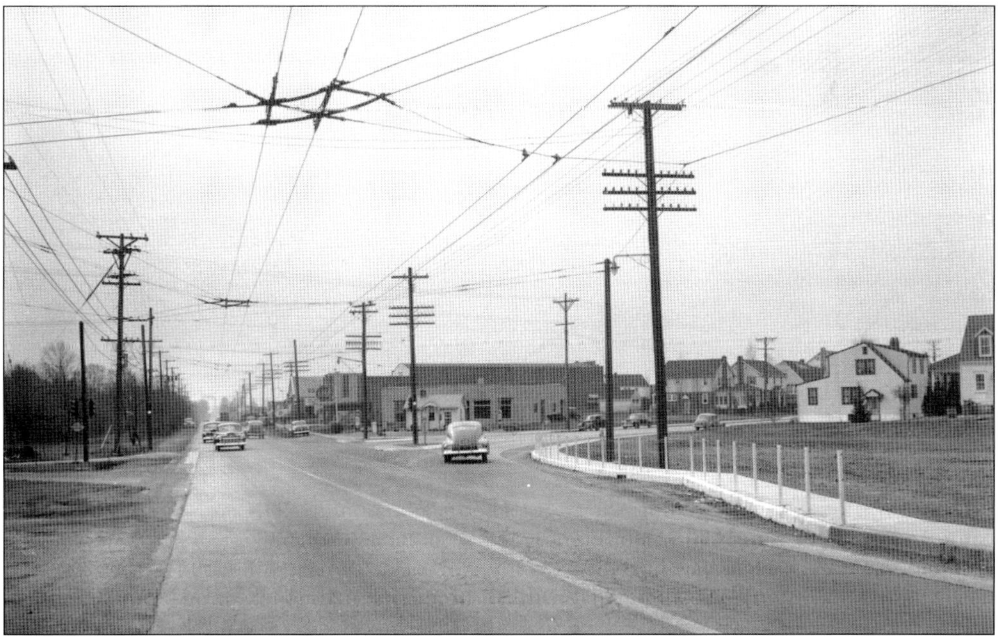

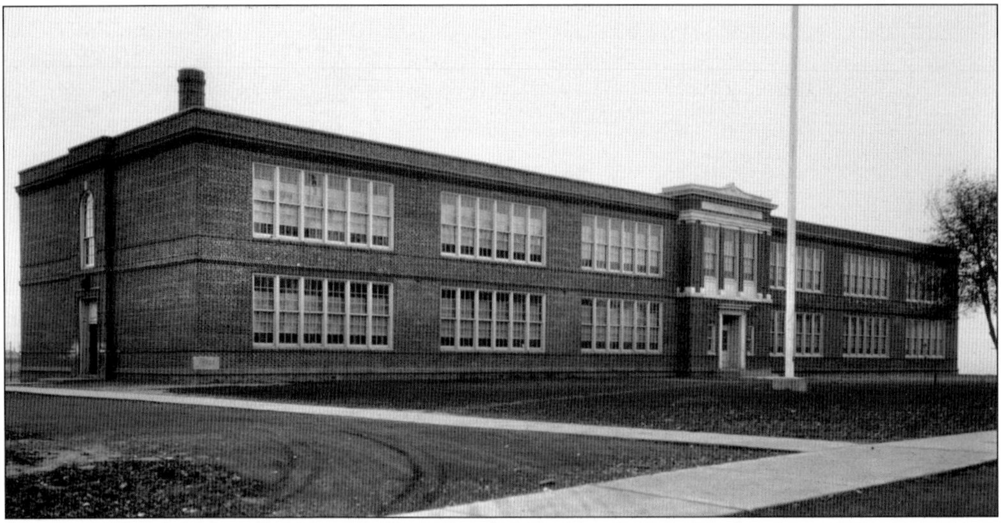

Pierre S. du Pont purchased 11.443 acres for the construction of Richardson Park School. Its original 10-room section was built in 1924 at a cost of $103,803, and it served as an elementary school for 297 pupils. It would be converted into a junior high during the 1940s, with the ninth grade added in 1945. Currently, it serves as an elementary school.

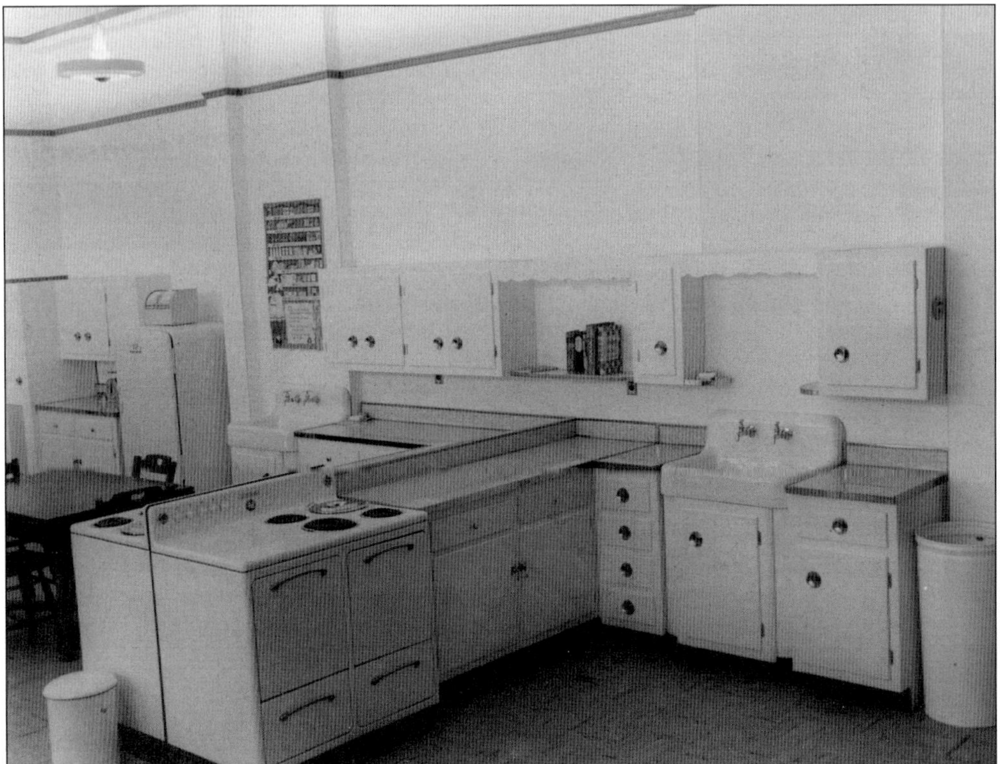

A Richardson Park Junior High School home economics classroom is shown in 1952. In an era of gender-specific education, home economics was for girls only, as the wood and metal shop were for boys only. The original Richardson Park School was built on DuPont Road on land donated by Quaker Richard Richardson in 1780, and that facility served until 1924.

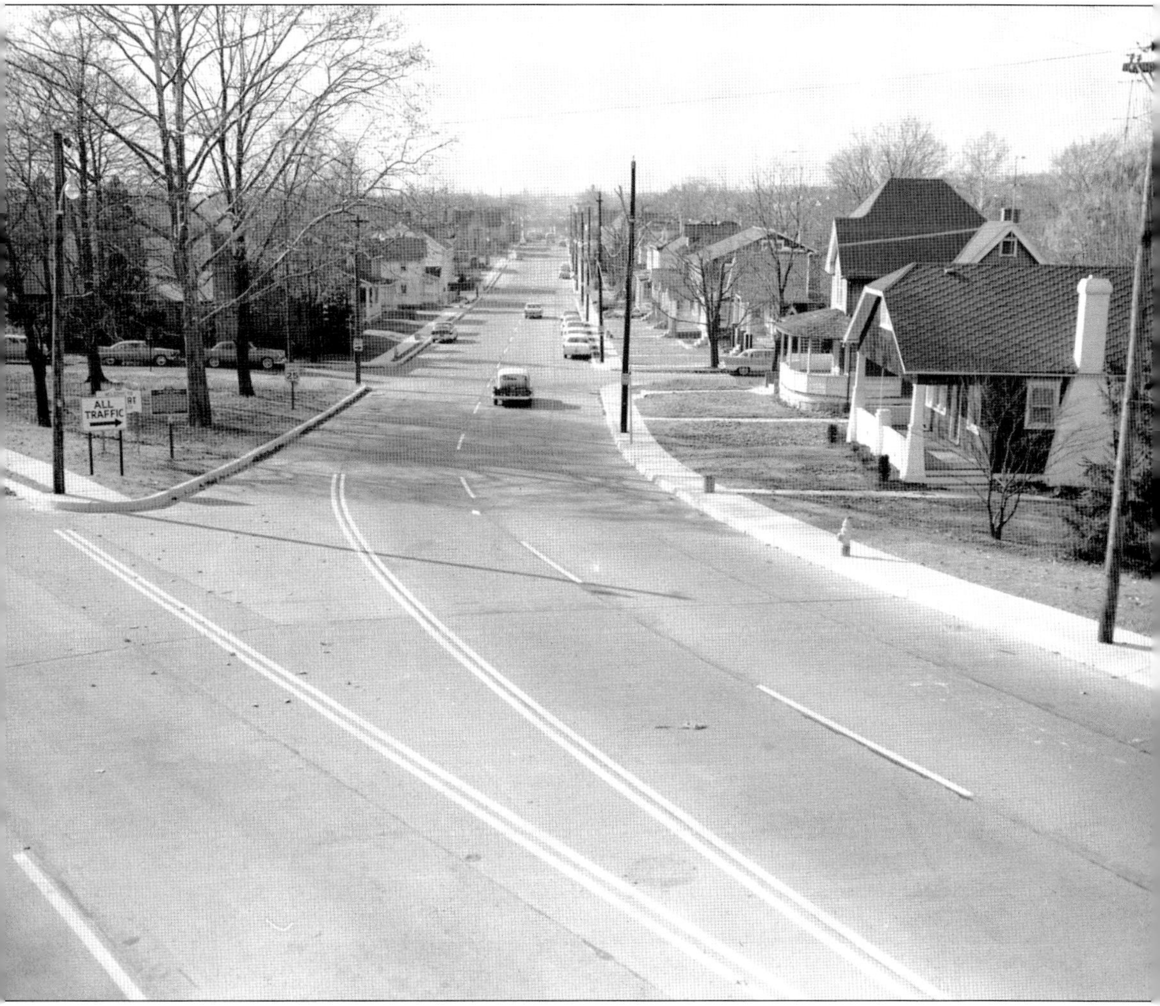

This is the view upon entering Newport on East Justis Street, also part of Route 4, and heading west. Delaware State Route 4 currently runs between its connection at Elkton Road in Newark and its connection to Route 48 in Wilmington. Newport's proximity to various main highways has allowed the town to develop commercial real estate and warehouse-type industrial parks. The additional needs of the community and businesses compelled Newport to amend its charter in 1984 to include a full-time, professional town manager to be appointed by the town commissioners and responsible for the day-to-day operations. But Newport is not all work. The town boasts four public parks as well as a boat ramp and nature preserve along the Christina River.

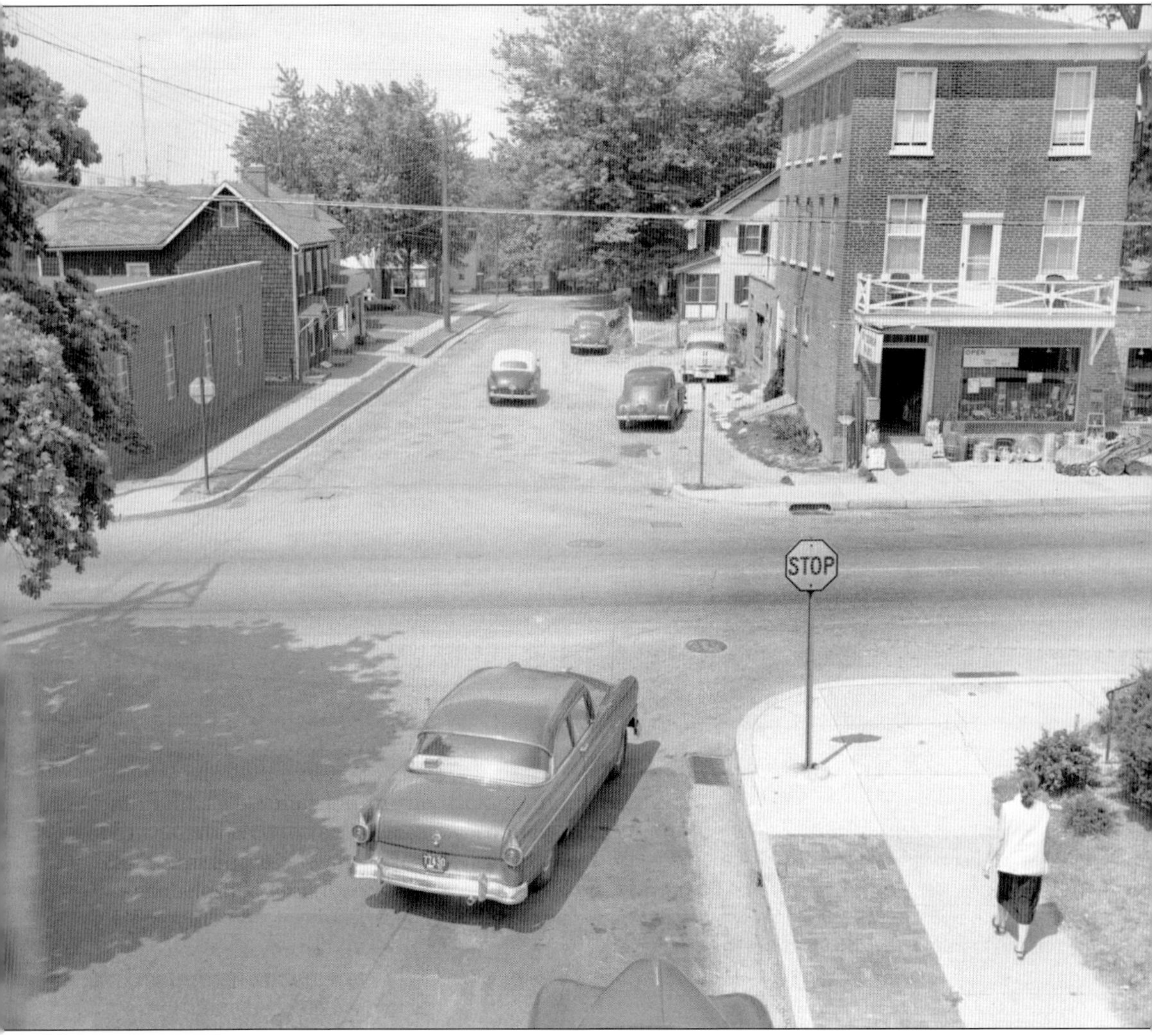

Killgore Hall at 101 North James Street contains the Wroten's Paint & Hardware Store on its first floor in this photograph from 1956. Built in 1883 by John Killgore, a Mason of the Armstrong Lodge No. 26, Killgore Hall provided commercial space on the ground floor and meeting rooms on the second and third floors. The Armstrong Lodge paid an annual rent of $60 for the third floor, where it held meetings until 1913. Prior to Killgore Hall, the family operated a small shop at this location, and their house was next door at 107 North James Street. The home, a two-story frame building that faced east, had a central entrance flanked by six-over-six windows and sheltered by a small porch. Smaller two-over-two windows were on the second floor, and the building's simple, gabled roof had two chimneys. Efforts to save the house and hall were unsuccessful, and the location is currently a vacant lot.

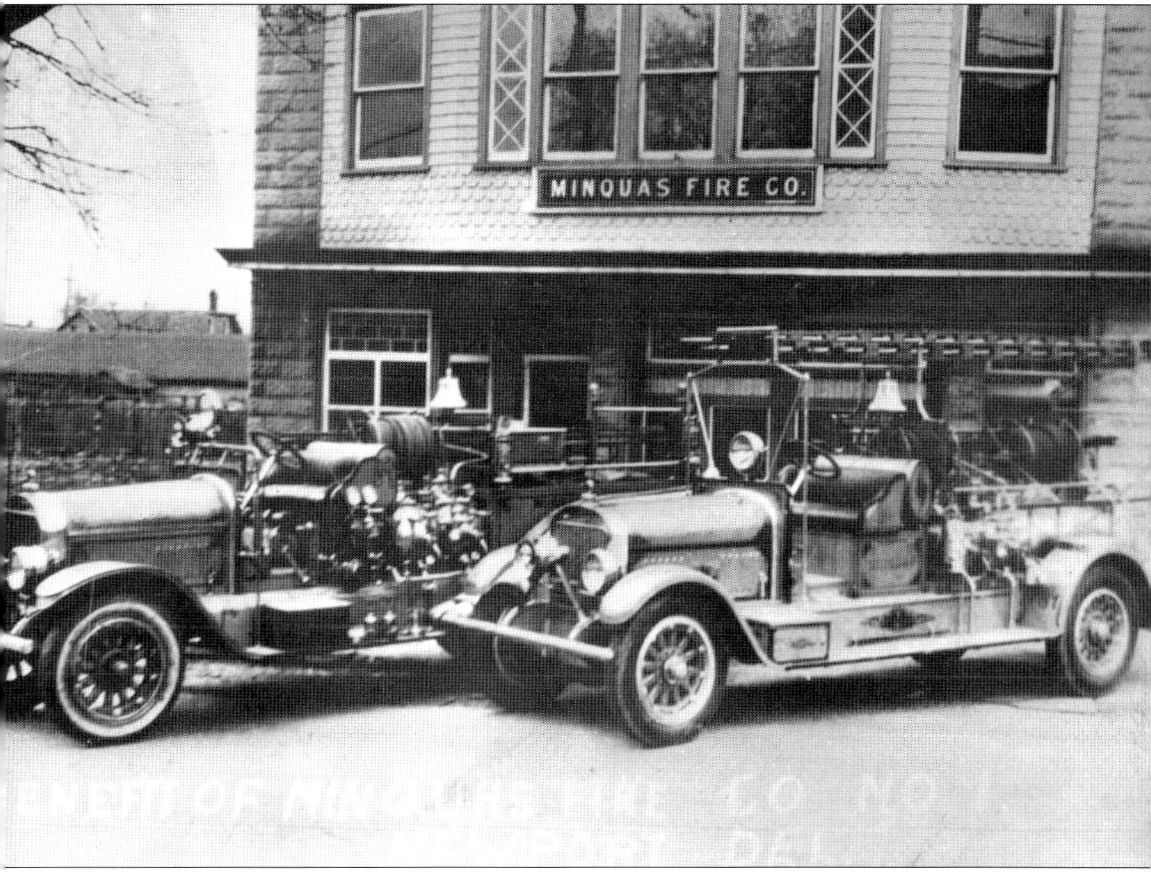

The Minquas Fire Company No. 1 was organized on May 21, 1907, as the Nonesuch Fire Company (after nearby Nonesuch Creek). Lt. Gov. John M. Mendinhall suggested Minquas after the Native Americans that had settled along the Christina River, and so the name was changed. The original firehouse, built in 1907 and pictured here, stood at the same location as the current one—21 North James Street. The company's first piece of equipment was a horse-drawn chemical wagon equipped with two 60-gallon tanks from the Radnor Fire Company of Wayne, Pennsylvania. The $1,000 cost of the equipment was raised by subscription. The wagon was motorized in 1917 and served until 1925. The Minquas Fire Company has renovated and expanded its firehouse over the years, and the current 24,000-square-foot firehouse was erected in 2005. (Courtesy of the Minquas Fire Co. No. 1 of Newport.)

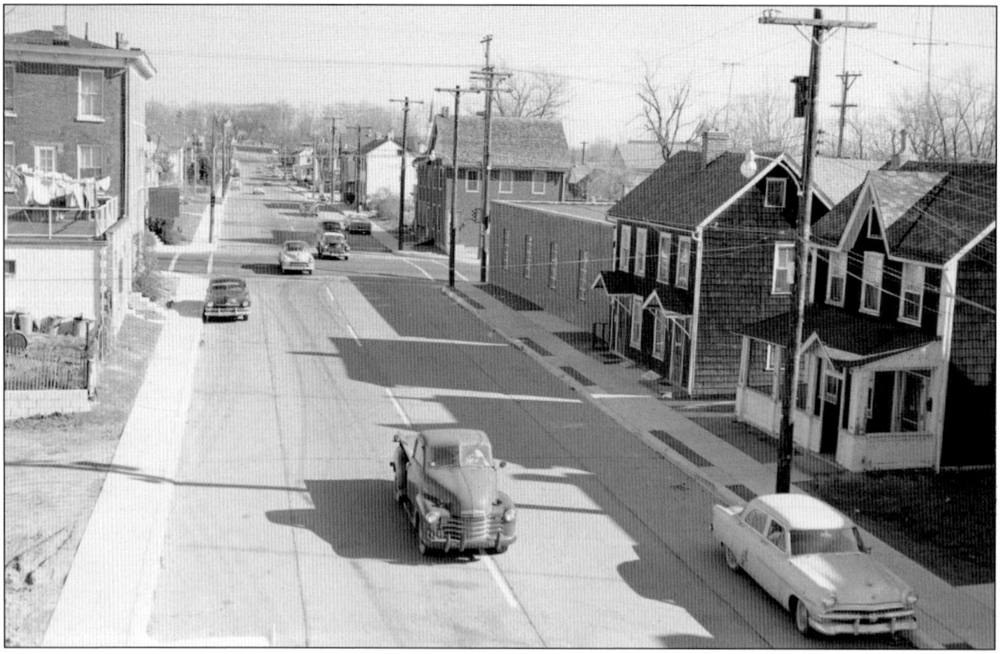

This is a view of Justis Street, looking east in 1957. The opening of the Chesapeake and Delaware Canal in 1829 was expected to benefit communities such as Newport. Instead, the canal led to the economic decline of Newport, Christiana, Stanton, and New Castle. Their heyday as shipping centers had gone, so the towns stayed relatively small.

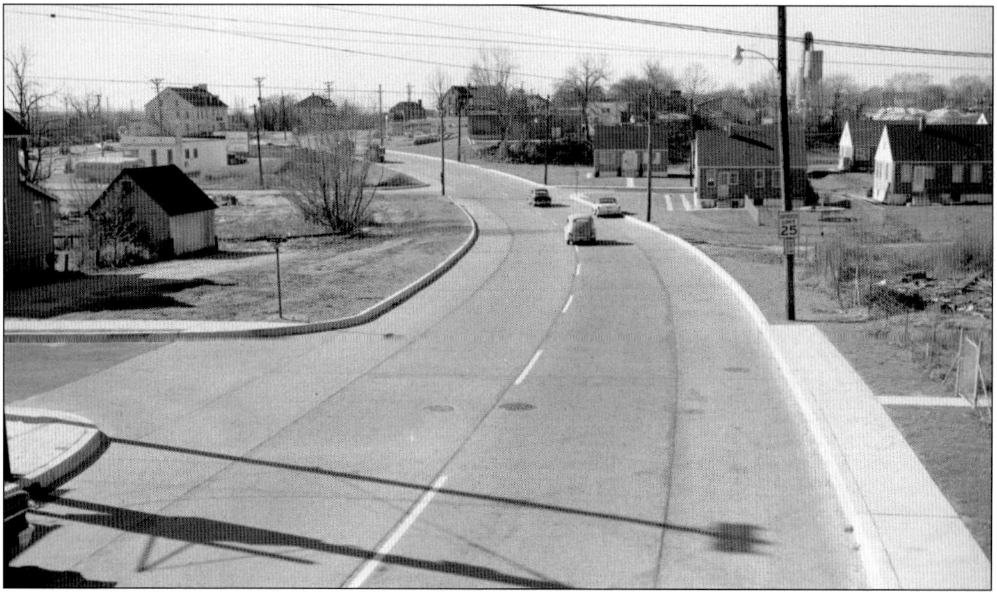

In this westward view of West Justis Street, traffic leaves town on Route 4 and heads toward Stanton. The town of Stanton was originally called Cuckoldstown, and the source of this name is debatable. Some maintain that the origin is scandalous, given that a cuckold is a man whose wife has committed adultery. Another explanation is that the area was once abundant in cockles, a type of clam. The town is currently named for Stephen Stanton, once a prominent landowner in the village.

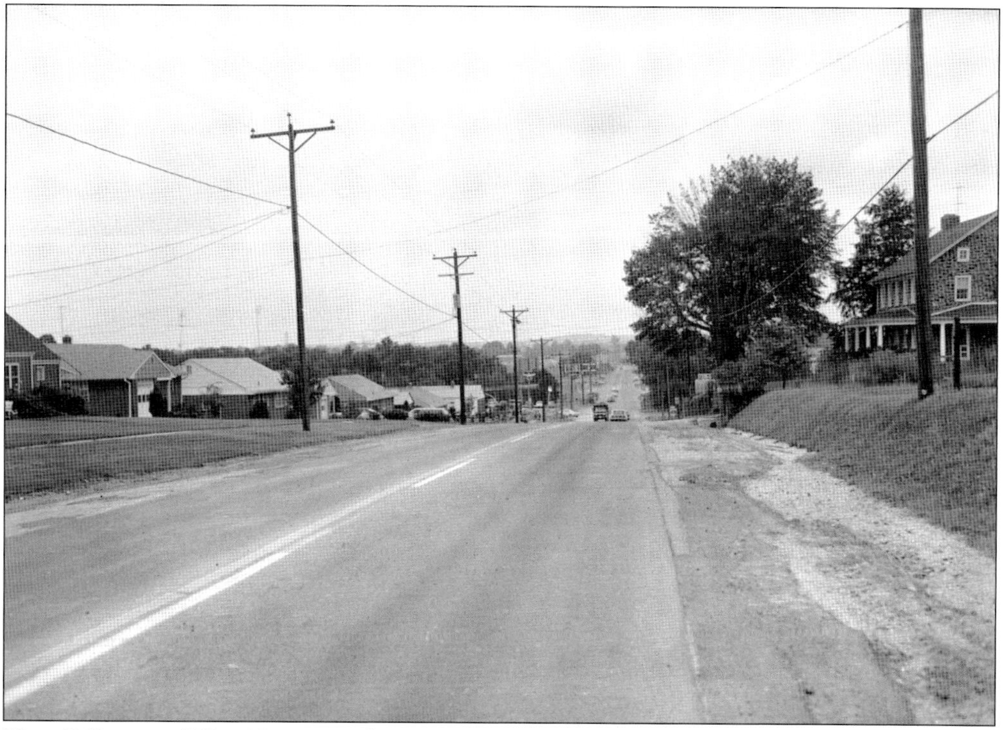

This 1967 view of West Newport Pike, or Route 4, looks toward Stanton. Newport had been part of Christiana Hundred. On October 25, 1682, William Penn directed that Delaware be divided into hundreds—an old English Saxon land division—for the purposes of taxation. These hundreds can still be found on maps or in the local language but no longer serve any purpose.

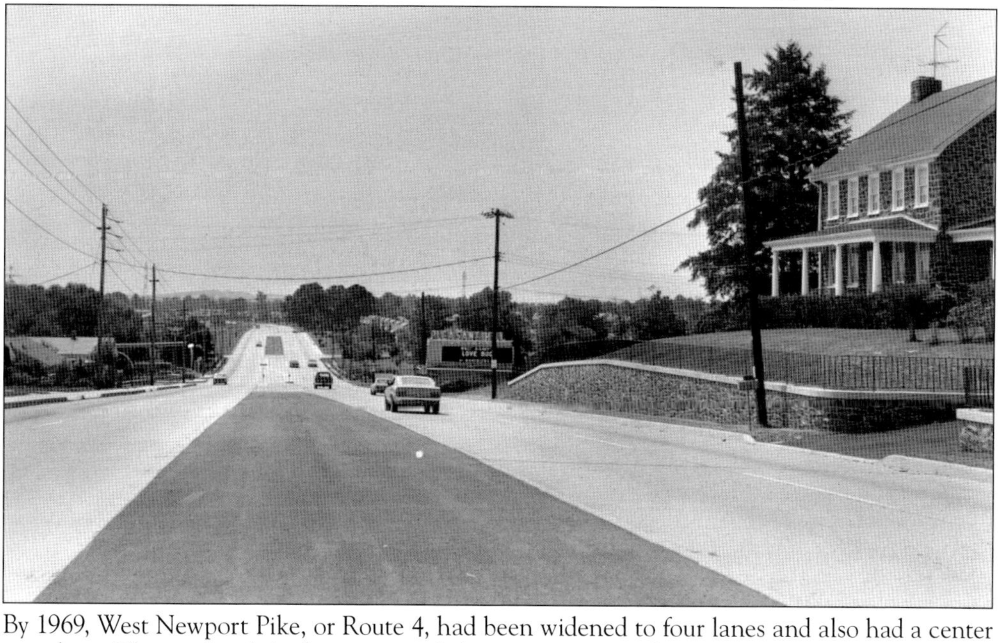

By 1969, West Newport Pike, or Route 4, had been widened to four lanes and also had a center turn lane. The roadwork had necessitated the construction of a retainer wall for the home on the right. This view, minus the drive-in marquee, is virtually the same today.

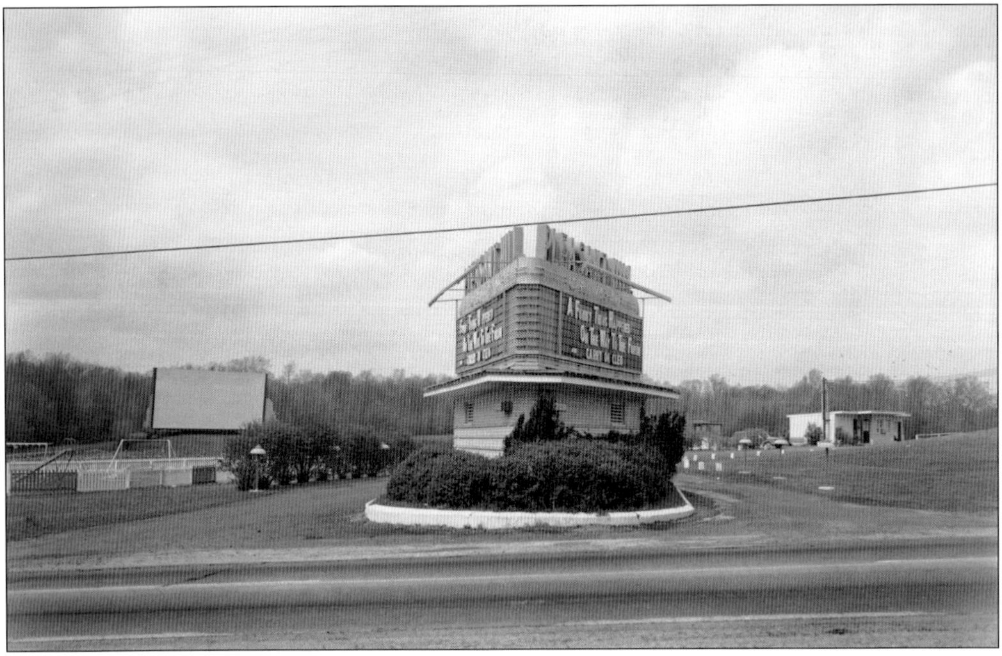

The Pleasant Hill Drive-In at 1317 West Newport Pike (Route 4) was showing a double feature in April 1967: *A Funny Thing Happened on the Way to the Forum* and *Carry On Cleo*. The drive-in held up to 600 cars and operated from 1950 to 1985. Village of Hershey Run currently occupies the property.

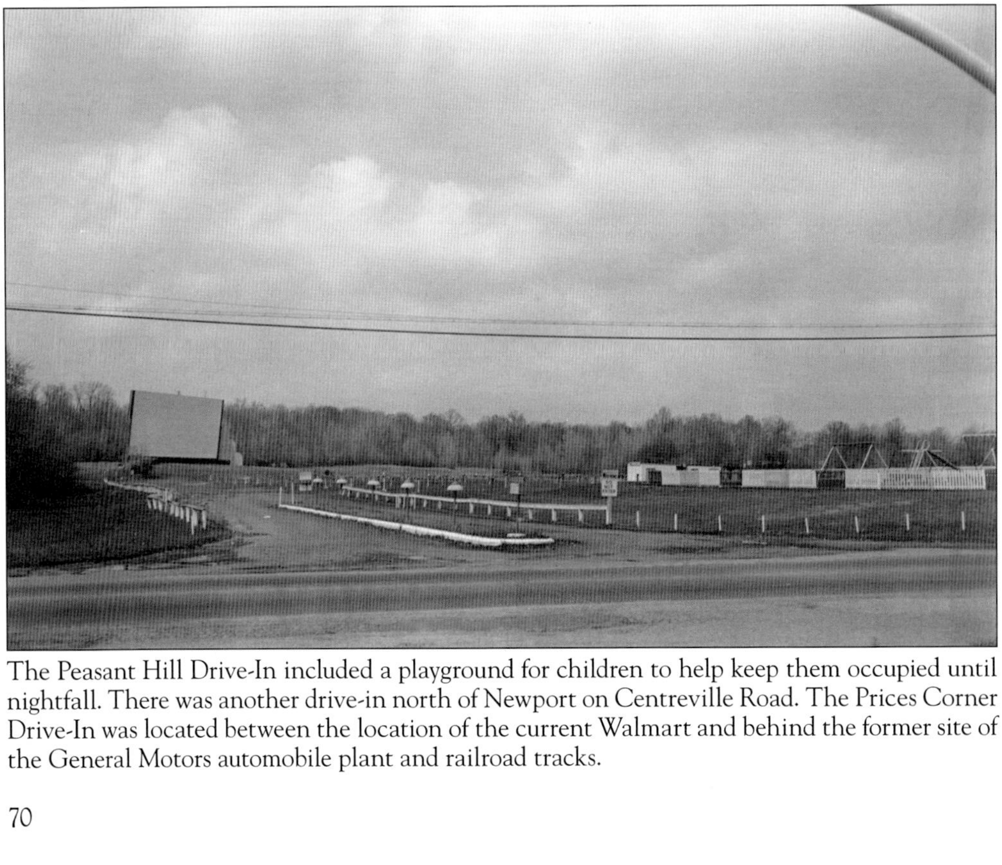

The Peasant Hill Drive-In included a playground for children to help keep them occupied until nightfall. There was another drive-in north of Newport on Centreville Road. The Prices Corner Drive-In was located between the location of the current Walmart and behind the former site of the General Motors automobile plant and railroad tracks.

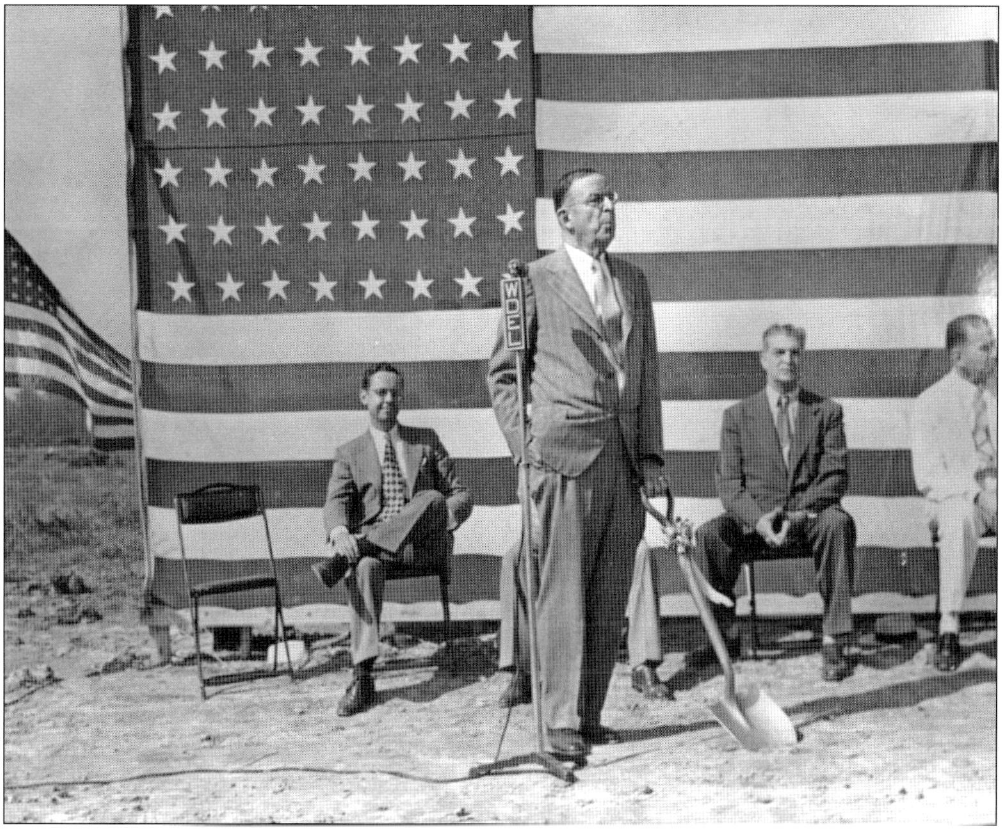

The ground-breaking ceremony for the General Motors Wilmington Assembly plant on Boxwood Road took place on August 28, 1945. Standing at the WDEL radio station microphone is Delaware governor Walter Bacon (1880–1962); seated are, from left to right, Gerrish Gassaway, Robert Ahlers, and Wilmington mayor Thomas Herlihy Jr. (Courtesy of Delaware Historical Society.)

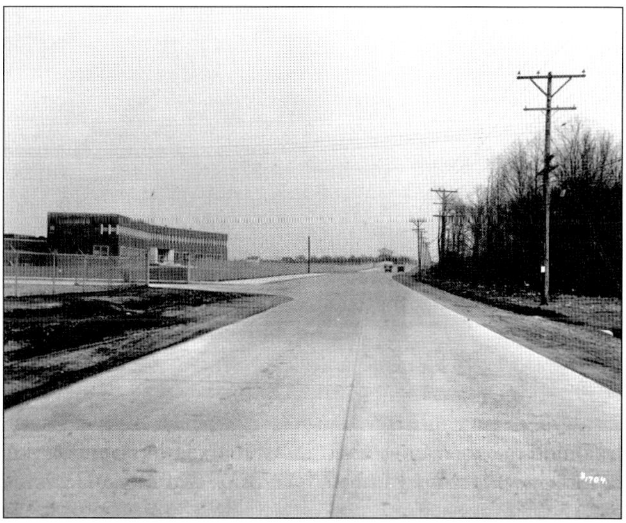

The General Motors plant is seen here shortly after its opening in 1947. The Wilmington Assembly Plant was a 3.2-million-square-foot facility that produced millions of cars during its existence. In the 1950s and 1960s, the Boxwood Road plant was a B-O-P facility, manufacturing Buicks, Oldsmobiles, and Pontiacs. As part of the 2009 bankruptcy and restructuring of General Motors, the Wilmington Assembly closed on Tuesday, July 28, 2009. Its final product was a Pontiac Solstice convertible.

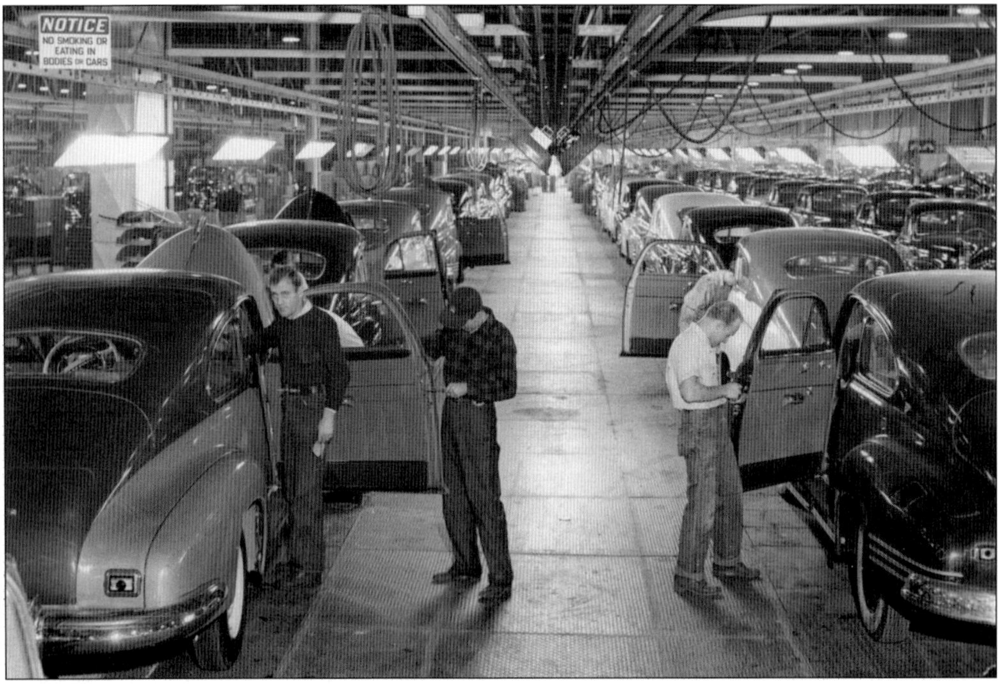

In its first year, the General Motors automobile factory provided employment for 3,500 workers—many of them World War II veterans—and produced 40 automobiles per hour. By 2009, the decision to close the 62-year-old factory affected 550 active employees along with another 500 or so laid-off hourly workers who had hoped to be called back.

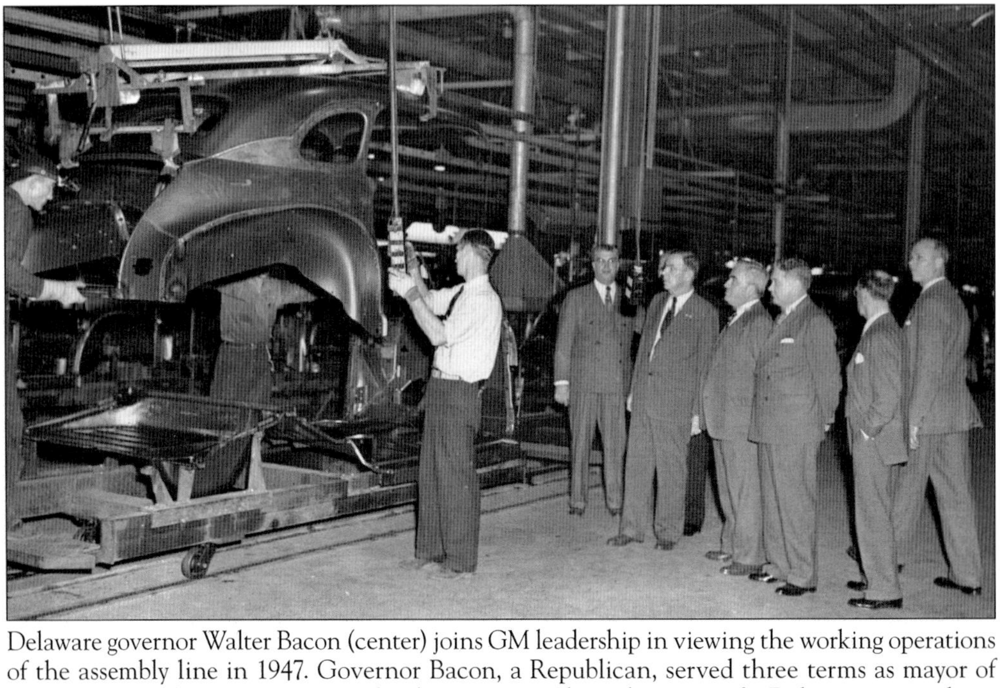

Delaware governor Walter Bacon (center) joins GM leadership in viewing the working operations of the assembly line in 1947. Governor Bacon, a Republican, served three terms as mayor of Wilmington and two as governor of Delaware. He is the only mayor of a Delaware city to have been elected governor.

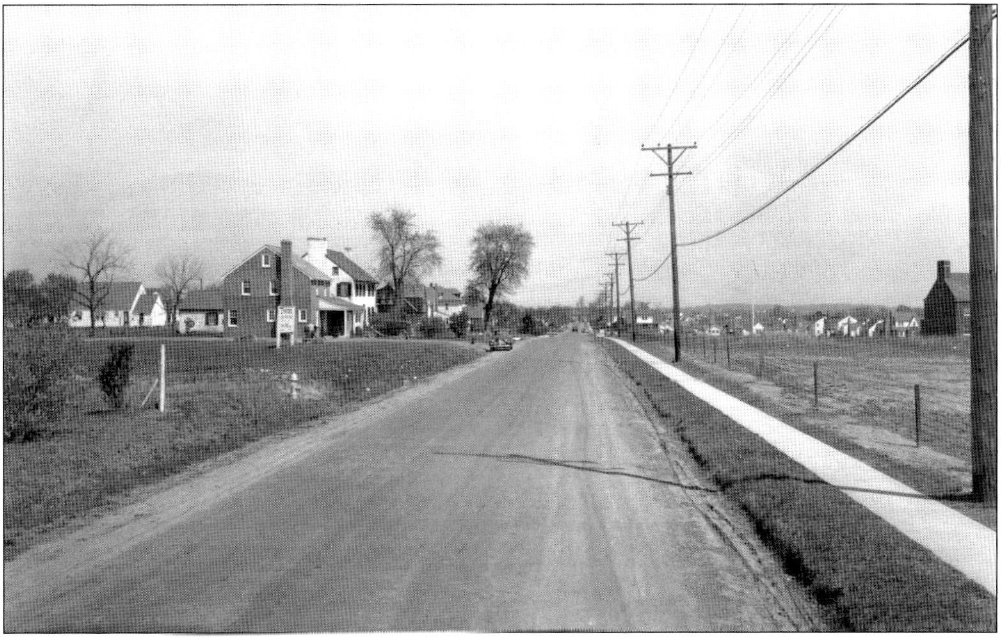

This 1942 image of Boxwood Road, looking toward the Woodcrest development, predates the General Motors plant. Boxwood Road is part of Route 62. When the Route 141 viaduct was completed in 1979, Route 41 was realigned from the Newport Gap Pike to overlap with Kirkwood Highway to the Delaware 141 interchange (Exit 6) at Prices Corner. The pike was renumbered to Delaware 62 in 1980 between Old Capitol Trail and the Delaware 141 Boxwood Road interchange (Exit 5).

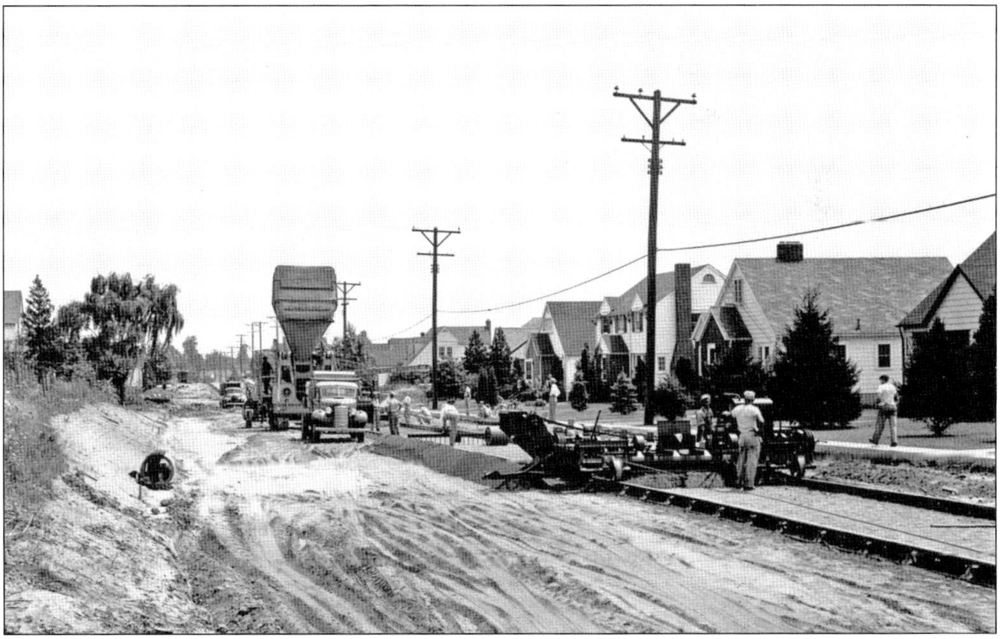

Boxwood Road got a makeover in 1946 in anticipation of the increase traffic in the Woodcrest development from the opening of the General Motors Wilmington Assembly plant. The bungalow-style homes were built by George H. McGovern, Inc., with Liberty Housing Company of Wilmington as the sales agent.

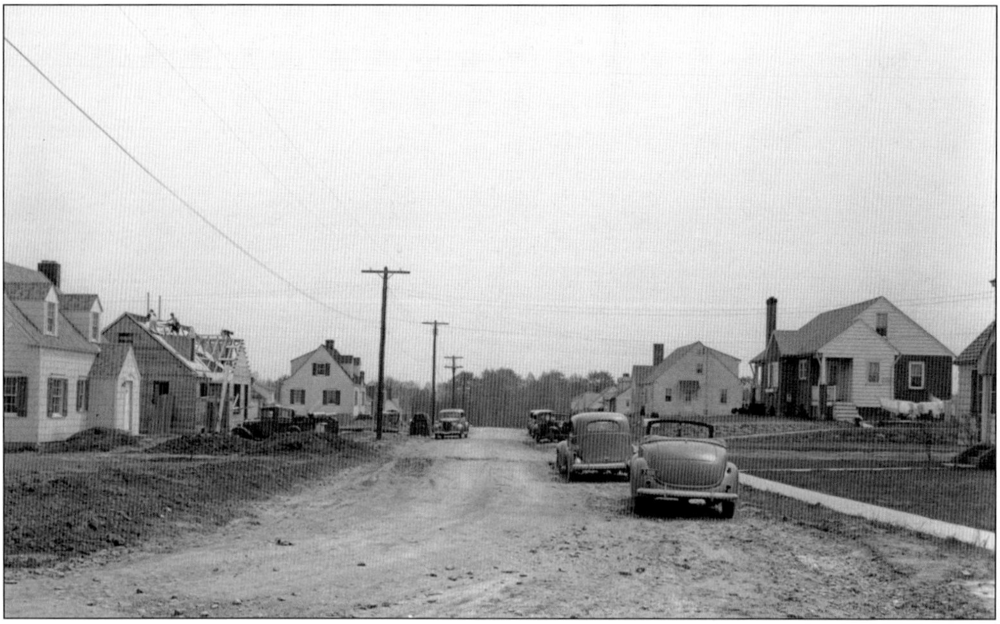

This home construction on Troy Avenue in Woodcrest took place in 1938. Building lots were advertised by Liberty Housing Company in 1934, and the then new Henry C. Conrad High School was used as an incentive to move to the area. Building started in 1936, and in three years, 75 homes had been erected. All home buyers were eligible for Federal Housing Administration–insured mortgages.

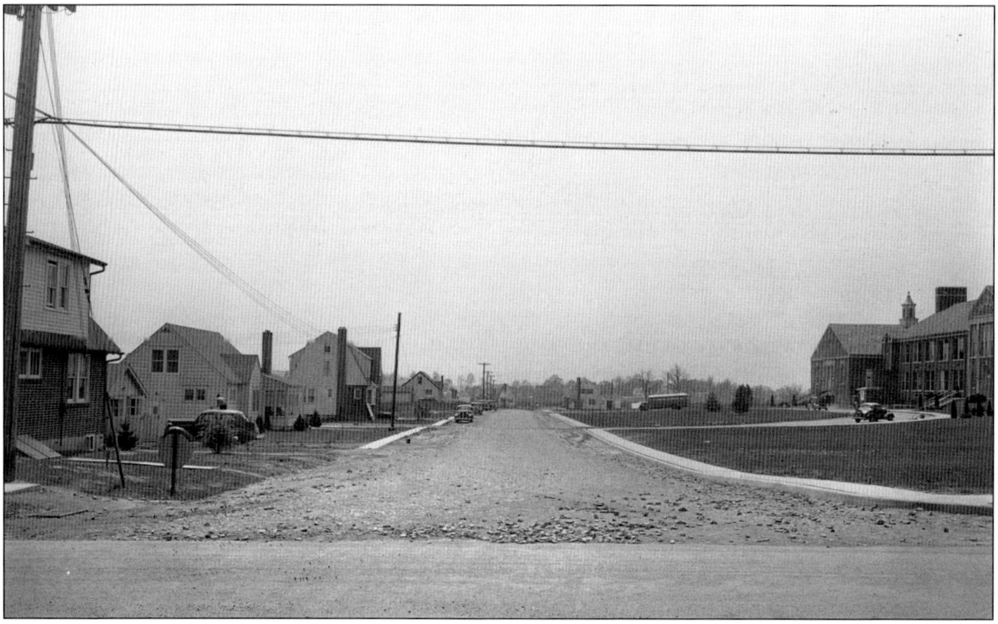

Captured in 1938, these new homes on Jackson Avenue were across from Conrad High School. The school owed its Colonial design to architect G. Morris Whiteside, and it cost $400,000 to build. Conrad opened for grades seven to twelve in 1935. A new auditorium and classroom wing was added in 1954, and by 1956, the school served only the 10th, 11th, and 12th grades. Severe overcrowding led to the construction of John Dickinson High School.

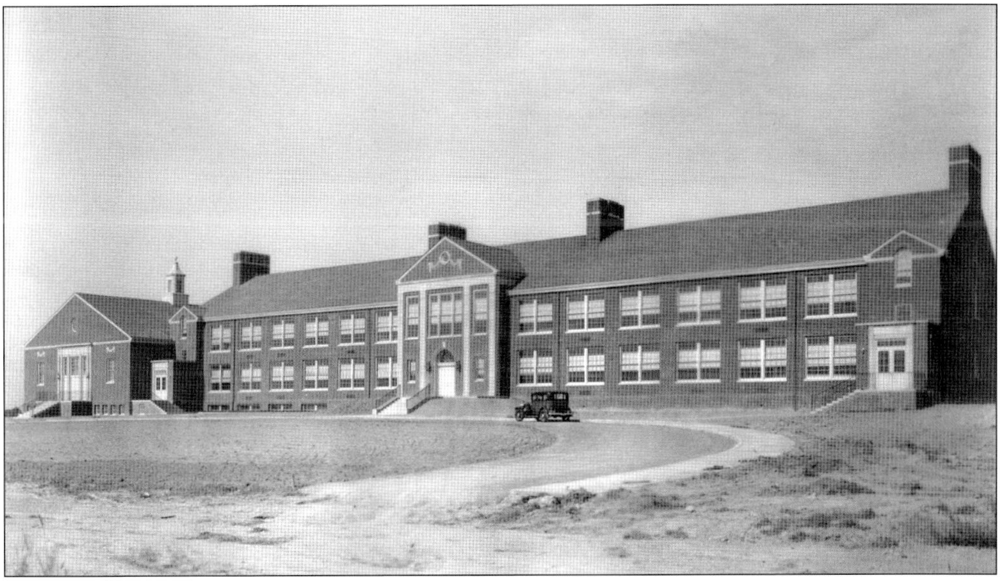

Conrad High School became a junior high in 1978 as part of the federal desegregation order to create a more balanced racial mix among the students of Delaware. Most Conrad students went to Wilmington High, while inner-city students came to suburban institutions like Conrad. The school then closed from 2005 to 2007, reopening as Henry C. Conrad School of Science. (Courtesy of Delaware Historical Society.)

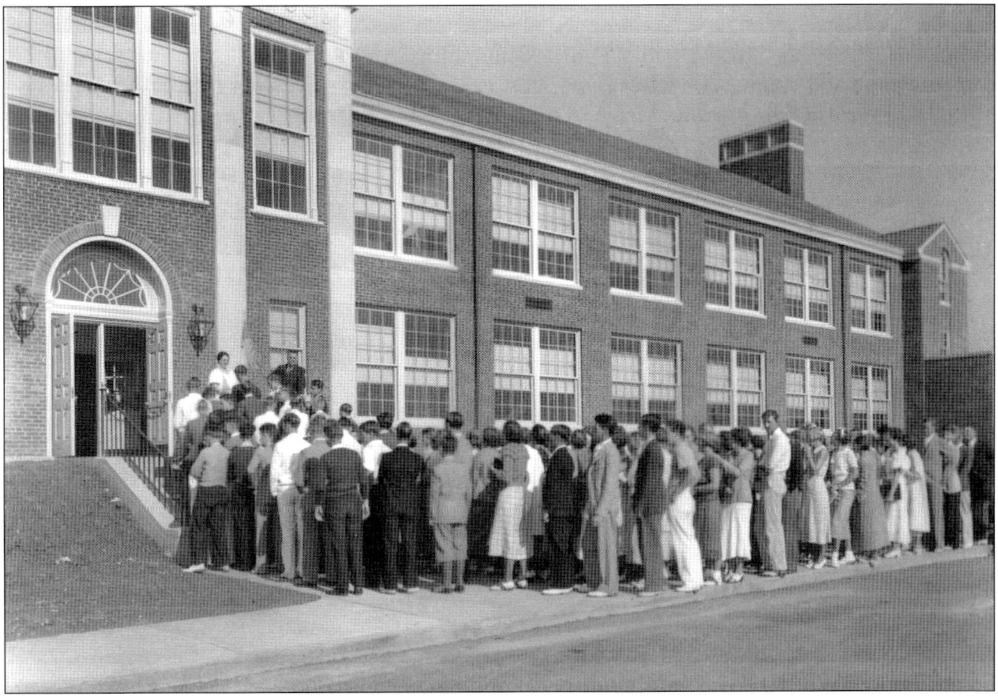

In 1935, there were a total of 400 students in grades seven through twelve along with 28 faculty members. The first yearbook, the *Conradian*, was published in 1937. The school was named after Henry C. Conrad (1852–1930), a Wilmington attorney, judge, public-office holder, and newspaper owner who wrote a three-volume history of Delaware. (Courtesy of Delaware Historical Society.)

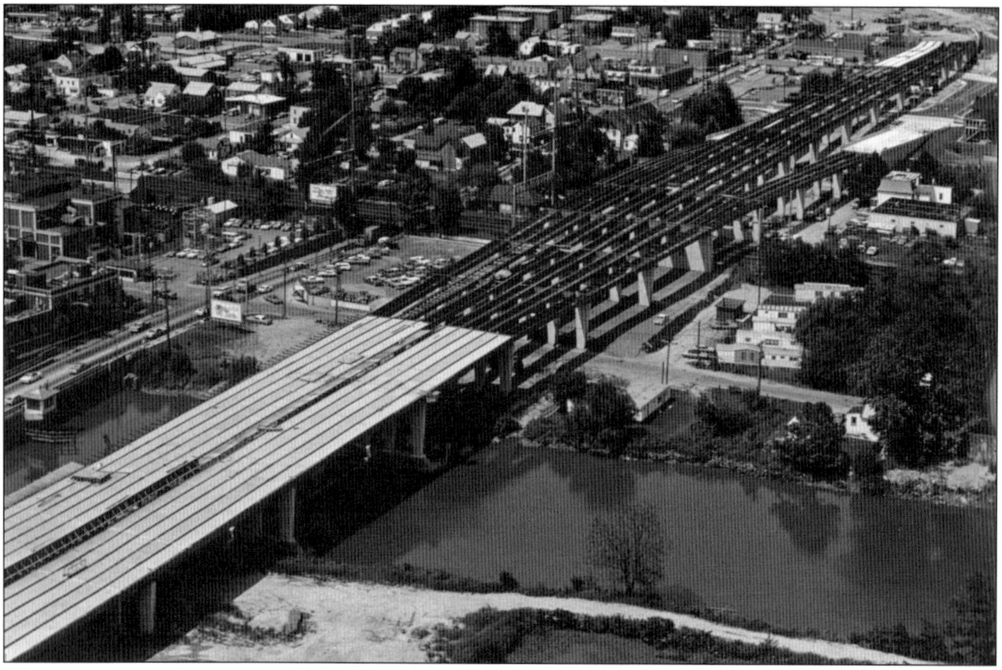

The opening of Interstate 95 and its interchange with Route 141 south of Newport created a need to alleviate through traffic downtown. Started in 1971 and completed eight years later, the 2,000-foot-long viaduct, which crosses over the Christina River and Market and Justis Streets, averages 87,000 vehicles a day. (Courtesy of Delaware Historical Society.)

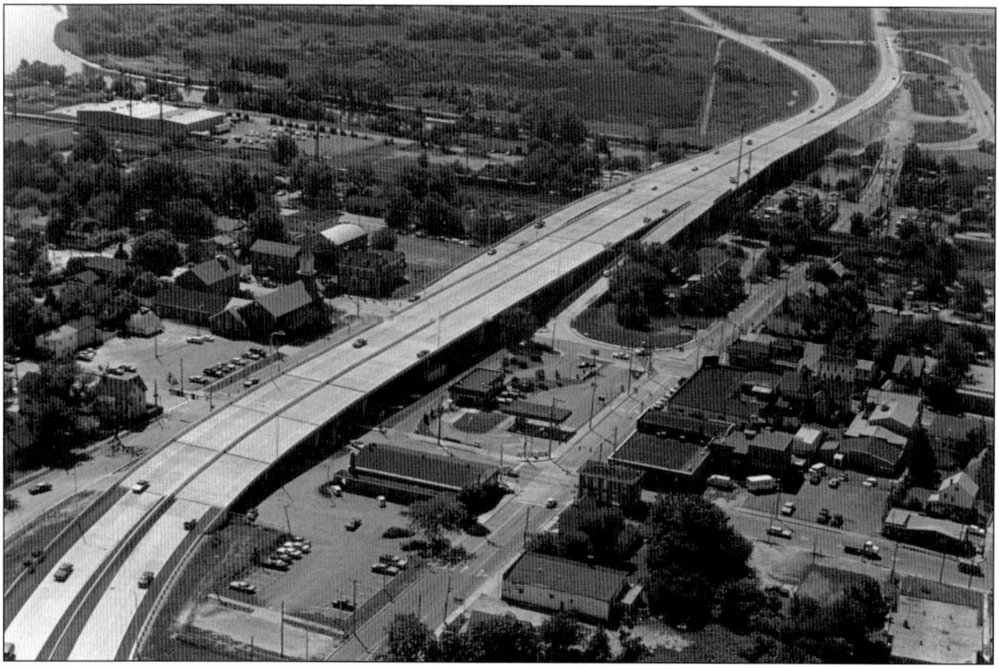

Construction of the viaduct, referred to as "the Asphalt Monster," caused the displacement of homes and businesses and split the town. This aerial view is looking toward the Christina River. James Street and its bridge over the river run parallel off the viaduct's right side.

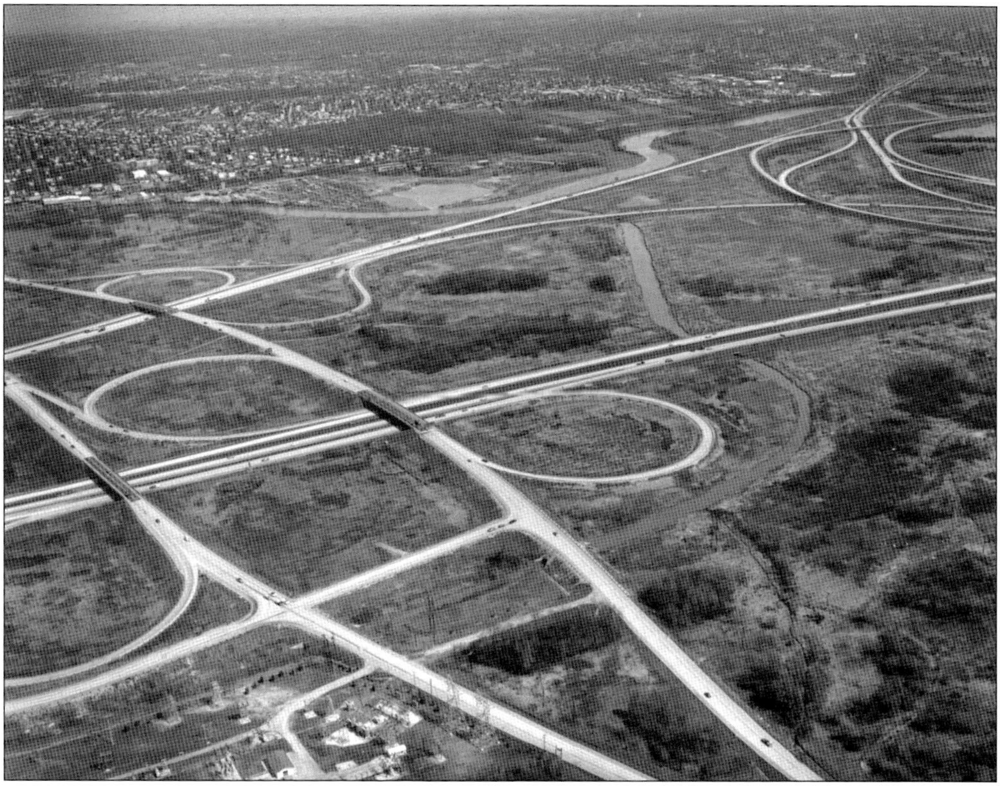

Interstate 95 was completed through Delaware in 1968. The aerial photograph above shows the Christina River flowing alongside the interstate's southbound lanes in the upper portion of the image. The crossroads in the lower left of the photograph are both directions of Route 141. The Nonesuch Creek is also seen flowing vertically in the photograph, linking to the Christina. The view below shows both directions of Interstate 95 crossing the Christina on the left and connecting to the city of Wilmington in the distance. The unfinished portion of Interstate 495 is visible on the right. (Both, courtesy of Delaware Historical Society.)

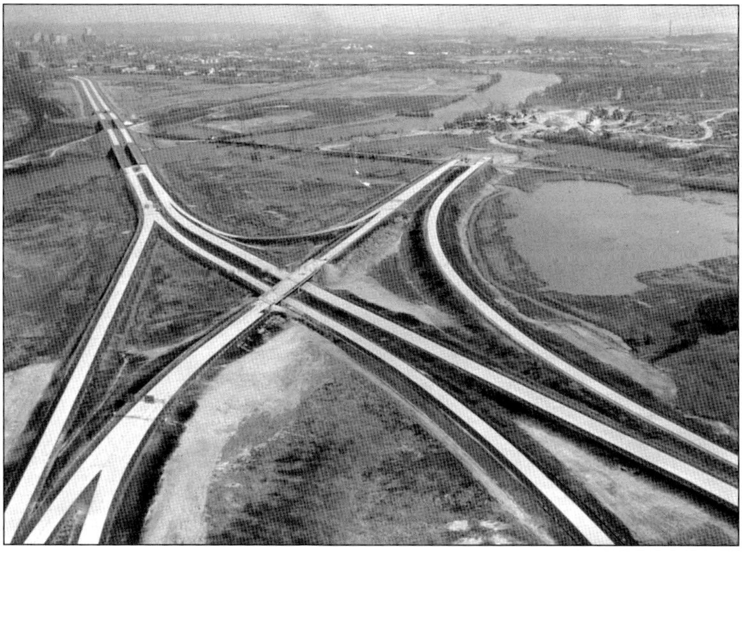

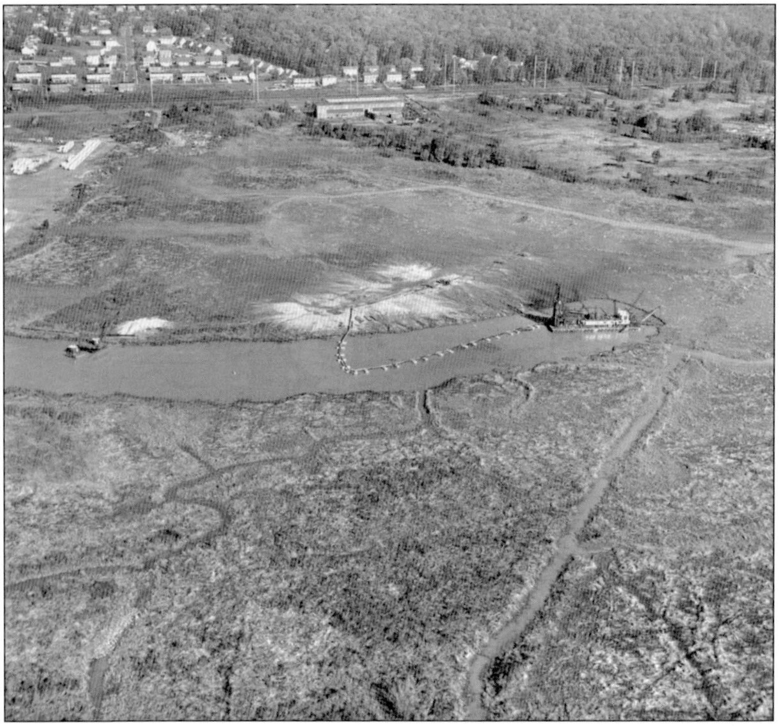

In 1961, before any construction began on Interstate 95 between Newport and Wilmington, the Christina River was rerouted and straightened just east of Route 141, eliminating a loop in the river seen in the photograph below. The old course was filled in, and the construction of the north- and southbound lanes of Interstate 95 proceeded without the need for two more bridges.

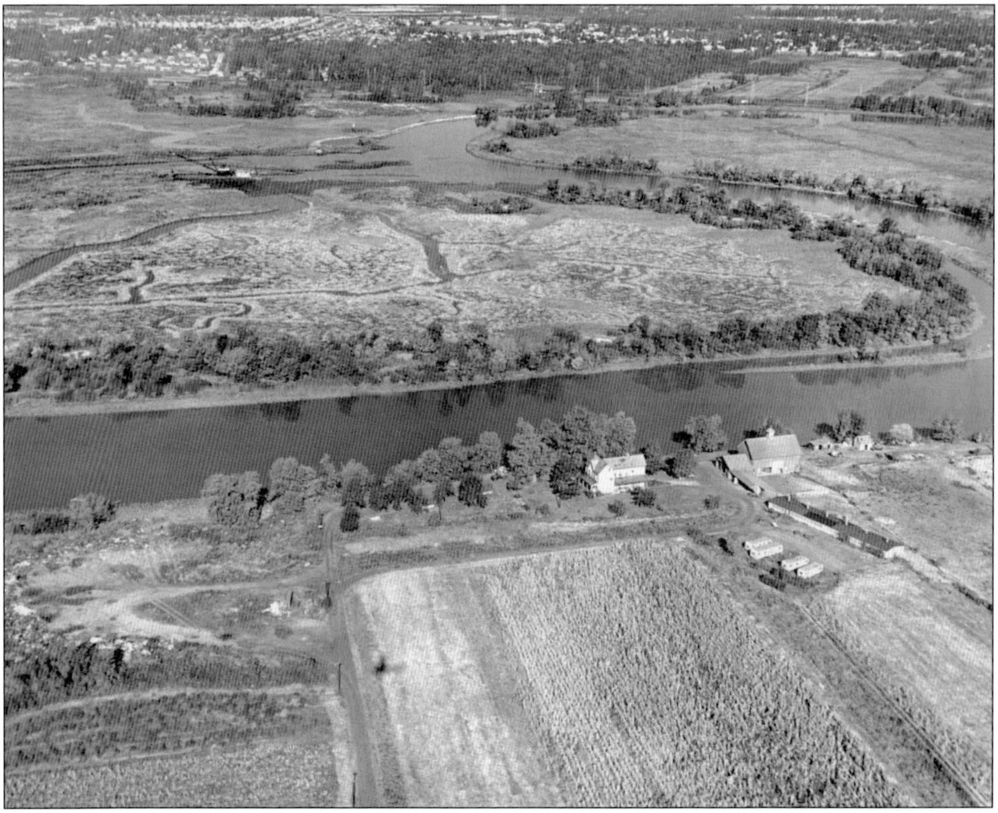

Four

WILMINGTON

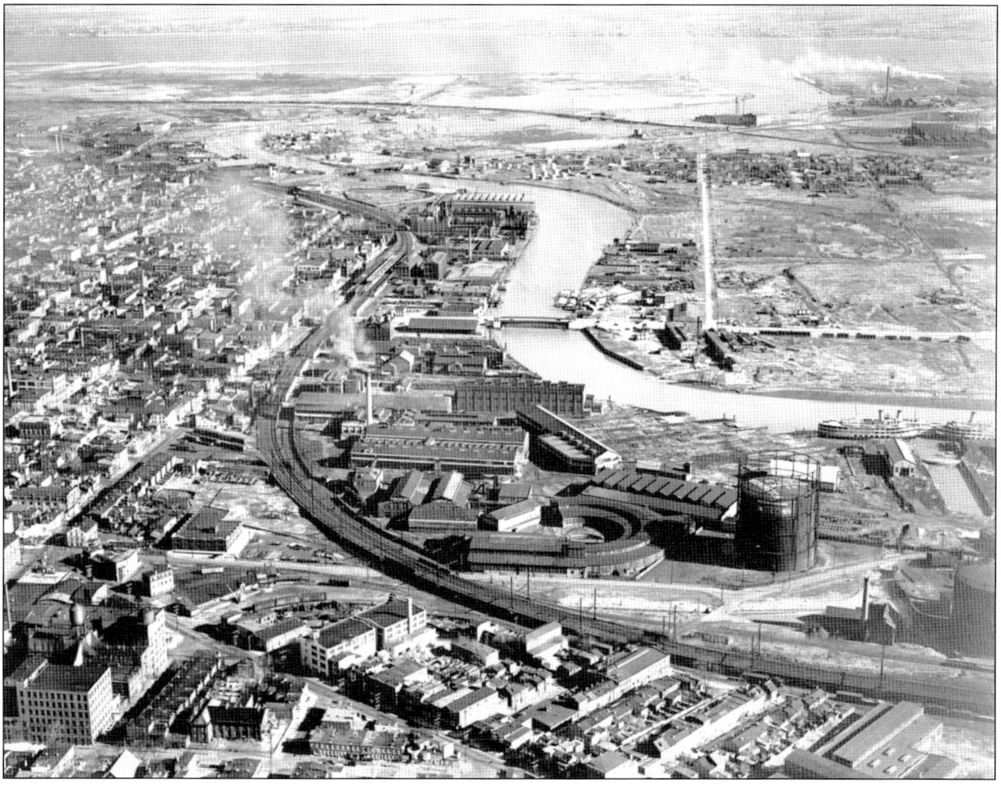

Heavy industry is the historical legacy along the Christina River in Wilmington, and it can be attributed to the arrival of the Philadelphia, Wilmington & Baltimore Railroad in 1837. A horseshoe-shaped roundhouse belonging to the company is seen in the photograph. Between the river and railroad tracks were railcar manufacturers and shipbuilders, their support businesses, and passenger service such as the Wilson Line.

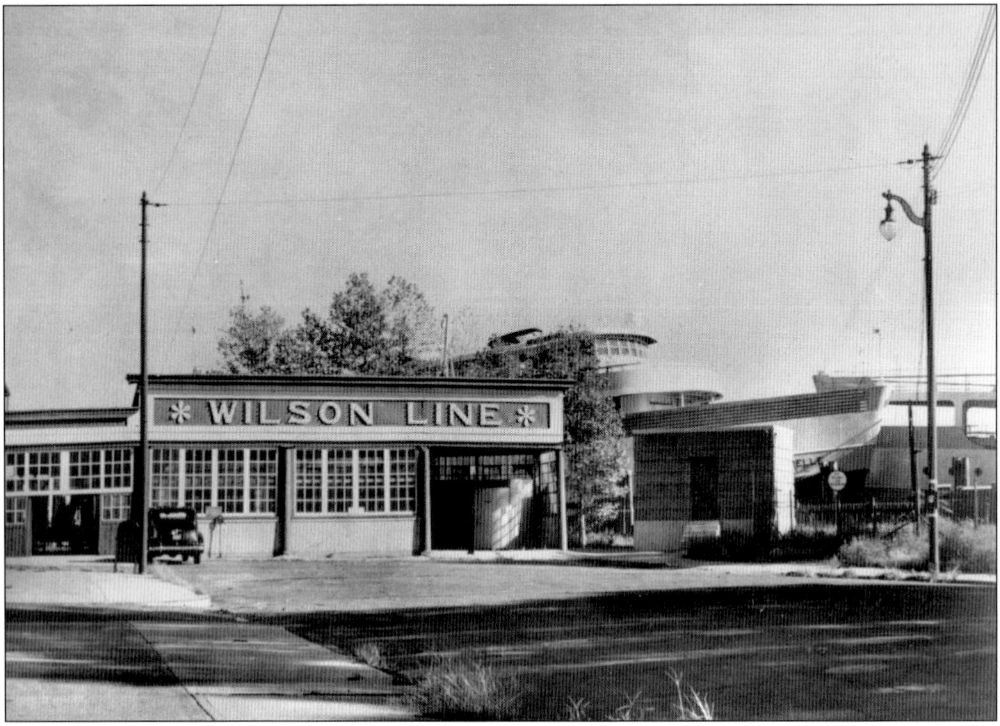

Before the proliferation of automobiles, goods and people moved by train or boat. The Wilson Line was an excursion company that began in 1820 as the Wilmington Steamboat Company. It had its wharf at East Fourth Street along the Christina River. This photograph is from 1955. The firm ended passenger service five years later. (Courtesy of the Hagley Museum and Library.)

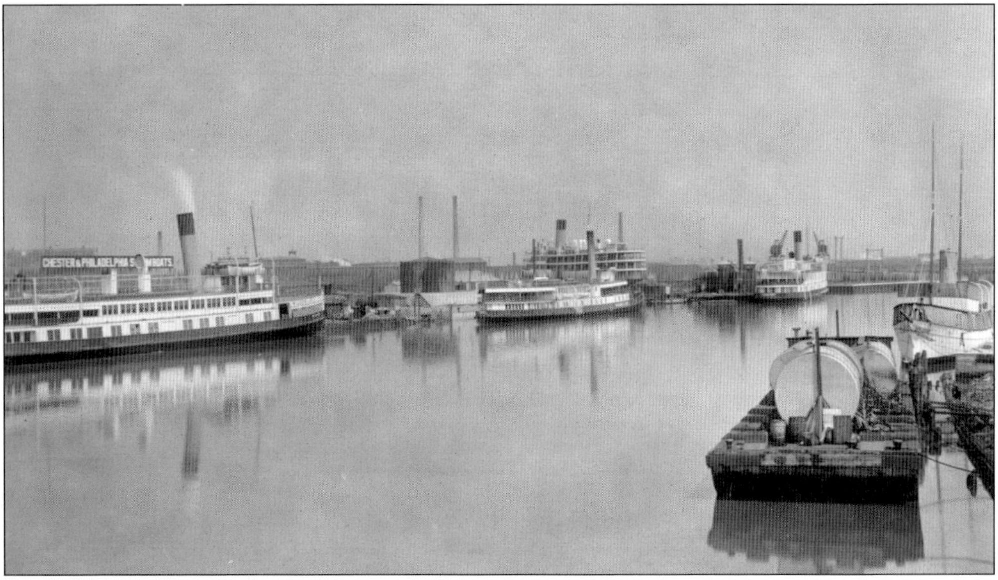

This is the Wilson boat landing as seen from the Christina River. The Wilson Line operated boats between Wilmington; Philadelphia; and Chester, Pennsgrove, and Riverview Beach, New Jersey. It was not unusual for Wilmington families to board a boat to Philadelphia, spend the day in that city, and return home in the evening.

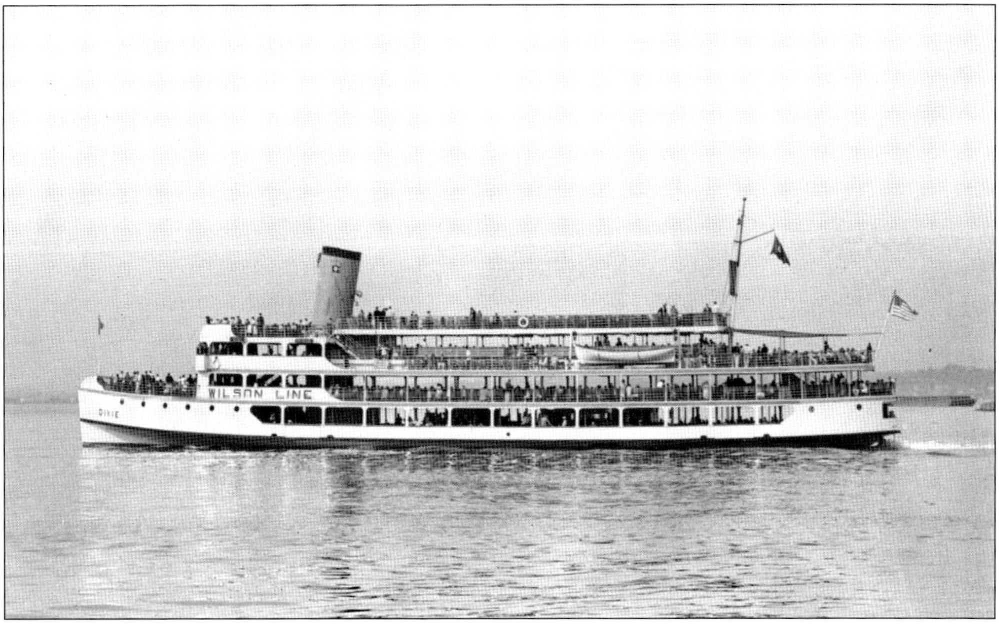

The Wilson Line's *Dixie* was originally named *Brandywine* and was later called *Pilgrim Belle*. The Wilson Line steamers, with the exceptions of the *State of Delaware* and the *State of Pennsylvania*, were built at Wilmington's Harlan & Hollingsworth shipyard on the Christina. The *State of Delaware* and the *State of Pennsylvania*, capable of holding 4,000 passengers, were built at another shipyard—Pusey & Jones—in 1922 and 1923. (Courtesy of Delaware Historical Society.)

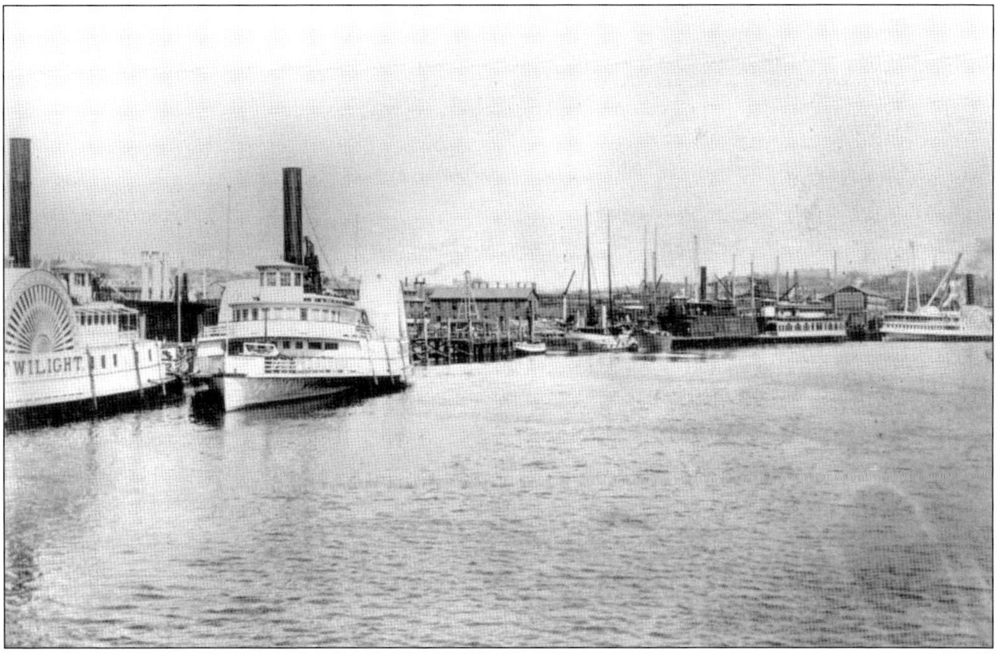

Passenger boat lines between Wilmington and Philadelphia began as early as 1774 with G.W. Bush & Sons, founded by Samuel Bush. The steamships in the foreground belonged to the Warner Company, a service founded by John and William Warner at the base of Market Street in 1794. The company lasted over a century.

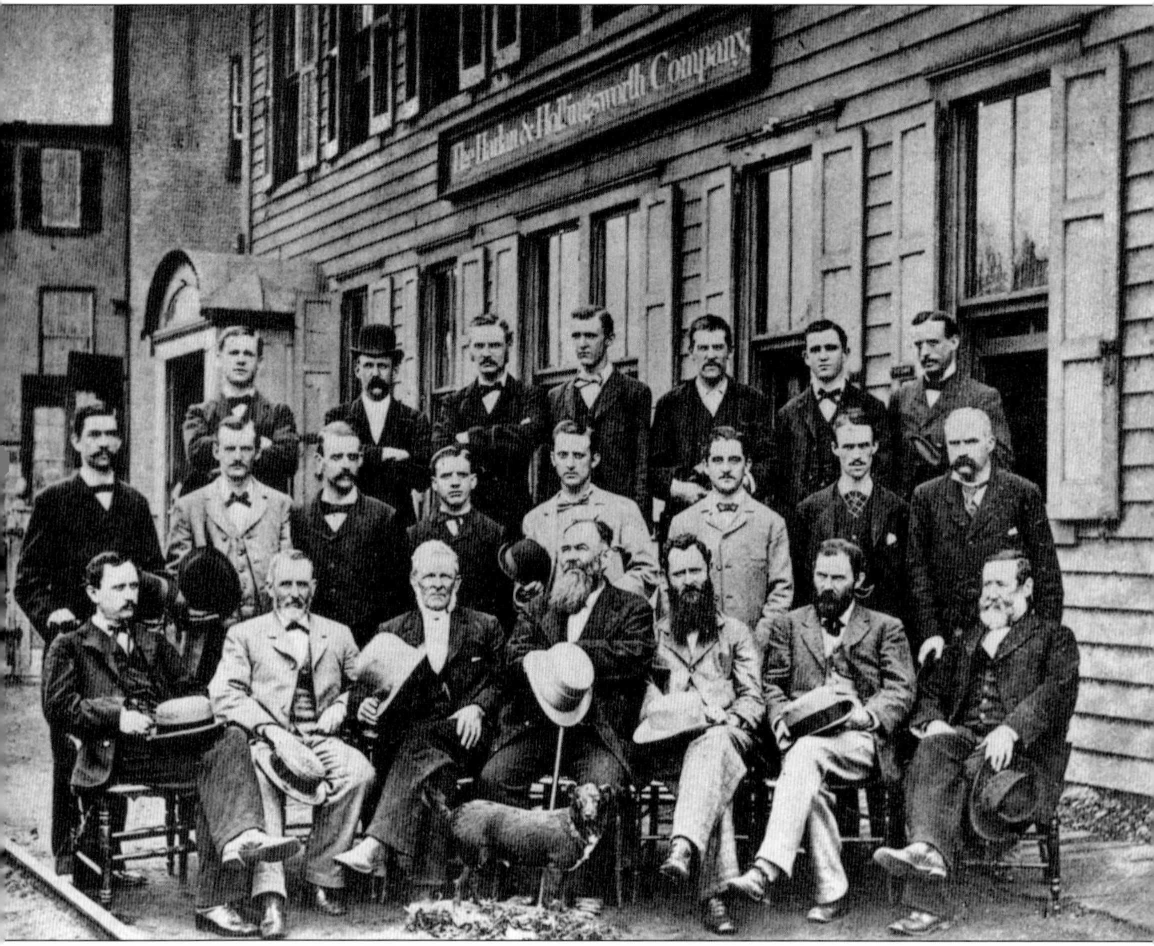

The Harlan & Hollingsworth Company management oversaw the manufacturing of railcars and ships. The company started as the Harlan & Hollingsworth Railcar Company in 1836 at Front and Tatnall Streets. It moved to the waterfront between Tatnall and Madison Streets and expanded to shipbuilding in 1843. By 1900, the manufacturing facilities spread out over 70 acres and 60 buildings on both sides of the Christina River. Harlan & Hollingsworth sold its interest in the shipyard to Bethlehem Steel in 1904. The Dravo Company of Pittsburgh bought most of the shipyard and resumed operations, and with the outbreak of World War II, Bethlehem Steel opened its remaining property and, together with Dravo, produced several types of vessels for the US Navy. (Courtesy of Delaware Historical Society.)

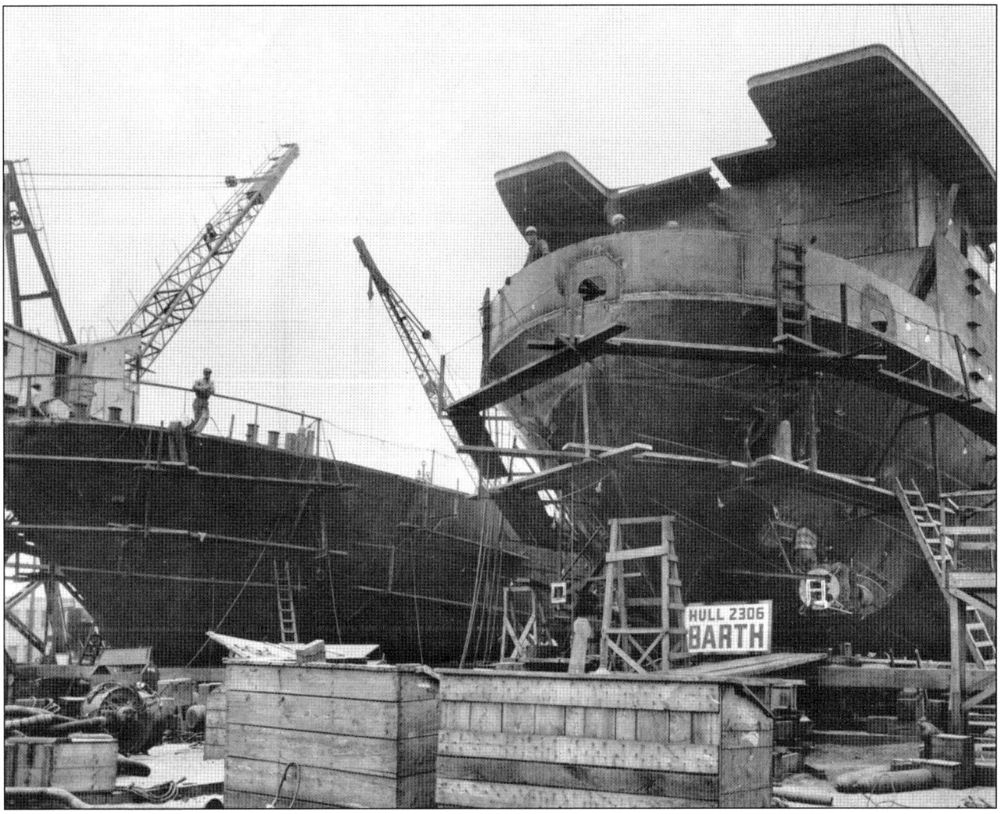

In this view of the Dravo Corporation Shipyard from September 28, 1944, the seagoing hopper dredge *Barth* is under construction for the US Engineers Department. The company employed both men and women during the war years, reaching a total of 11,000 workers. The wage was 52¢ per hour, which was then considered a good salary. (Courtesy of Delaware Historical Society.)

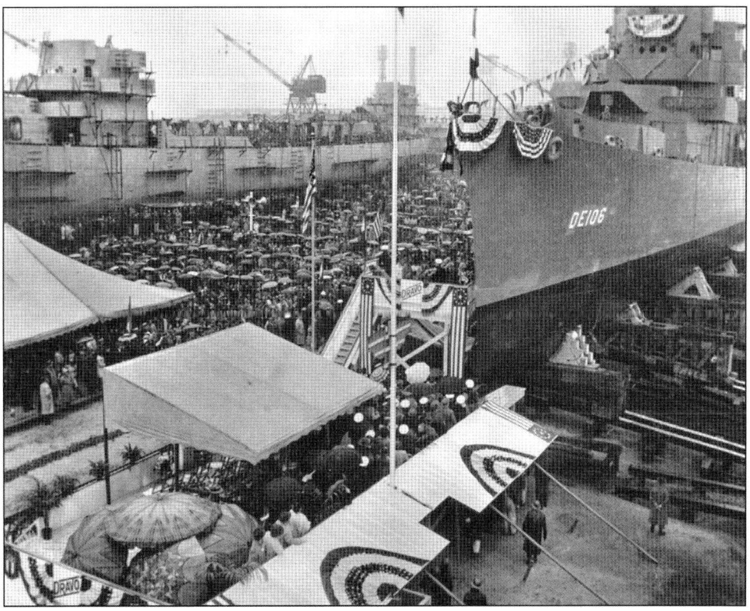

The launching ceremony for this destroyer escort (DE) 106 took place on Armistice Day, November 11, 1943. The vessel was built at Dravo's Wilmington Shipyard for the French navy and was christened the *Senegalais*. (Courtesy of Delaware Historical Society.)

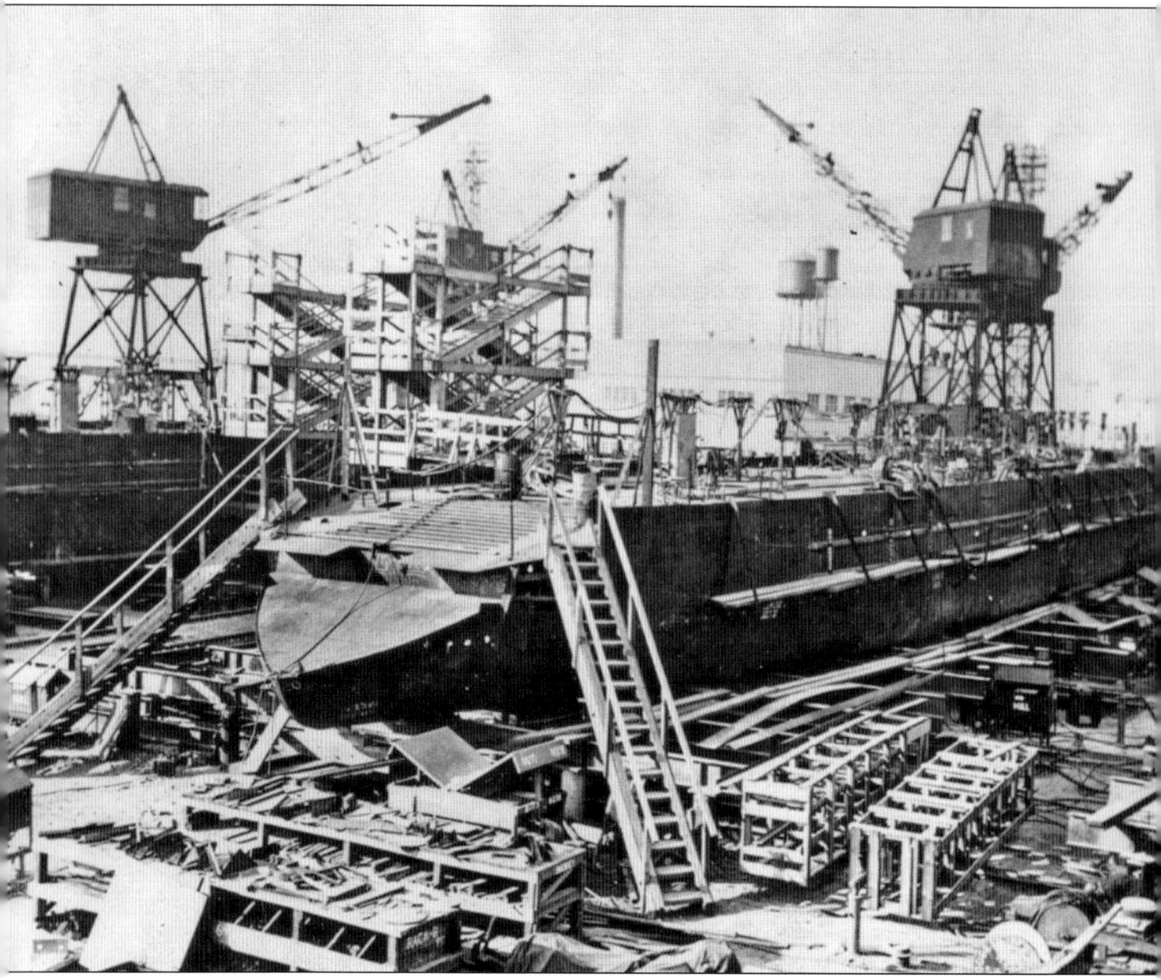

This is one of many Landing Ship Mediums (LSM) built for World War II. Dravo was praised for its production records; over 200 ships were built between 1940 and 1945 (some 48 in 1944 alone, including LSMs and destroyer escorts). The Dravo Corporation shipyards spread out over 120 acres on the old Harlan & Hollingsworth property at the base of Madison Street. Cranes used by Dravo are all that remain of this once giant manufacturer, now incorporated as part of Dravo Plaza, a retail and restaurant area along the waterfront. (Courtesy of Delaware Historical Society.)

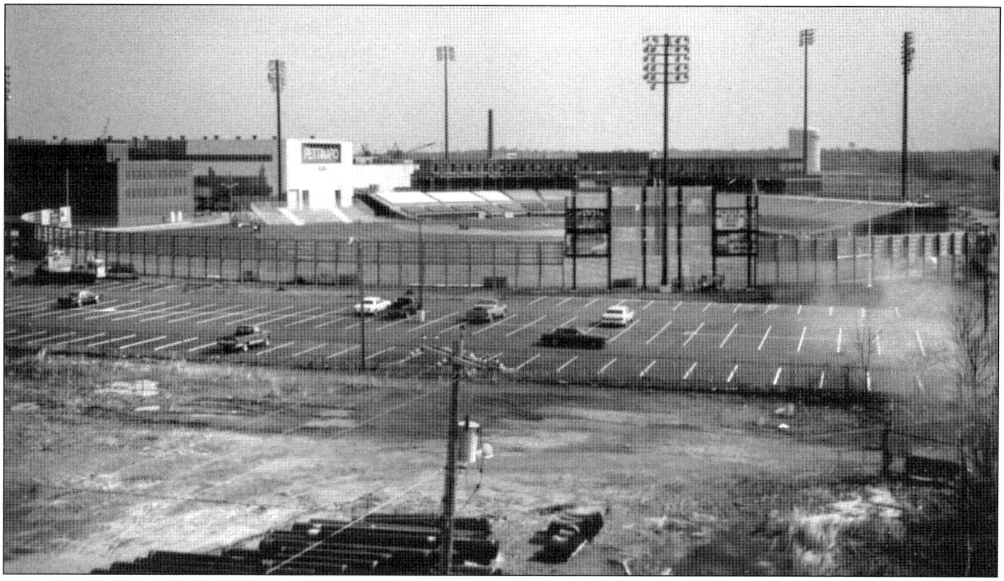

At the site where Dravo ships were once built, Daniel Frawley Stadium was constructed and opened in 1993. The stadium serves the second edition of the Wilmington Blue Rocks professional baseball team, a Class A ball club in the Carolina League that is affiliated with the Kansas City Royals. The original Blue Rocks played at Wilmington Park at Governor Printz Boulevard and Thirtieth Street from 1940 to 1952. Connie Mack and Bob Carpenter Jr. were the team's original owners when the club was in the Interstate League and affiliated with the Philadelphia Athletics. Bob Carpenter Jr. assumed full ownership after the 1943 season and linked the club with the Philadelphia Phillies, a franchise he also owned. In 13 seasons, the original Blue Rocks never had a losing record and won four Governor's Cup titles. The team also served as the training ground for Hall of Fame pitcher Robin Roberts. (Both, courtesy of Delaware Historical Society.)

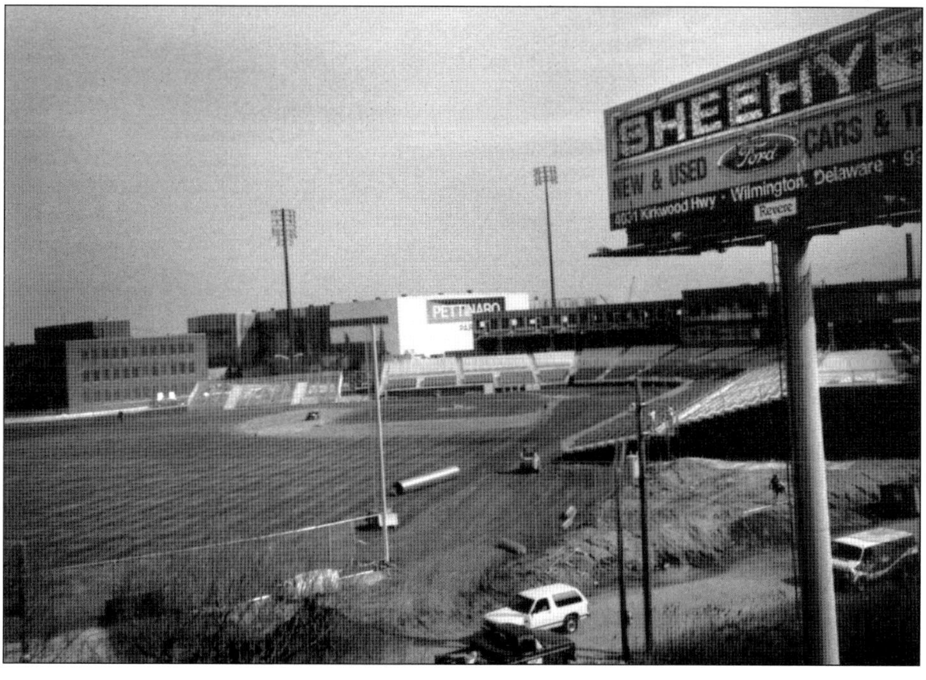

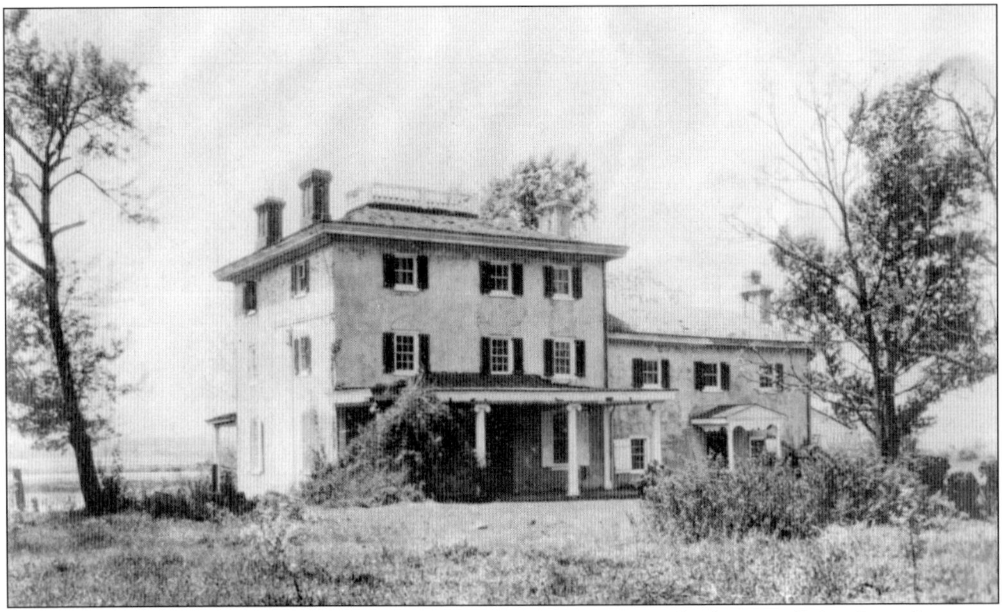

Long Hook Farm, whose original section was built in 1660, was the home of Maj. Peter Jacquett (1755–1834). Jacquett was an officer during the American Revolution and was involved in every engagement under General Washington that took place in Delaware, Pennsylvania, New Jersey, and New York. The property, located 1.1 miles south of the Christina River on the west side of Route 13, burned down in the 1980s. (Courtesy of Delaware Historical Society.)

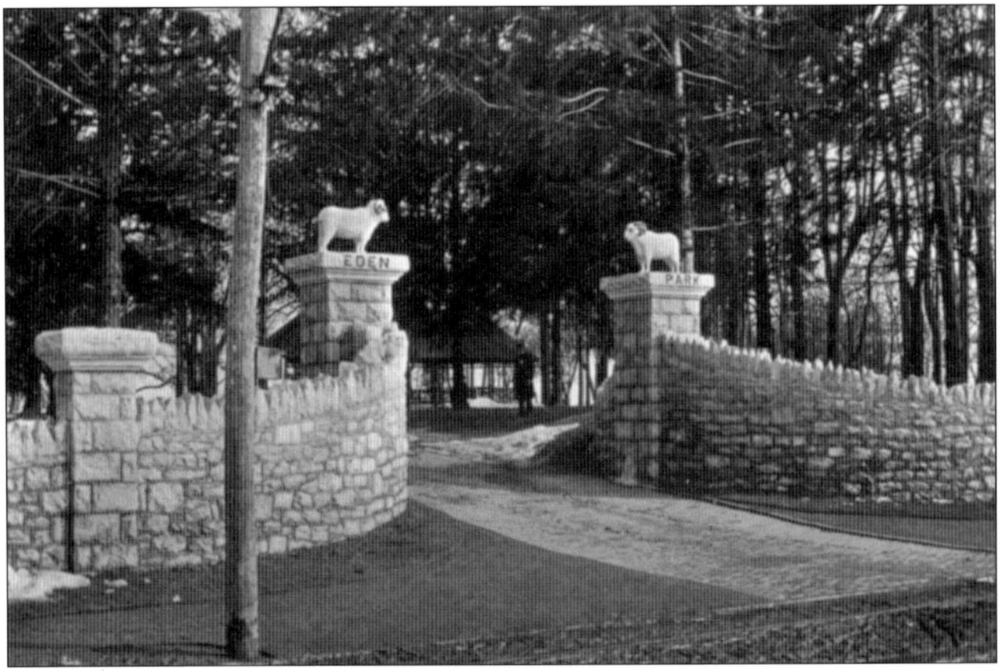

South Wilmington's Eden Park was once owned by Pierre Bauduy. Bauduy had been instrumental in the building of the du Ponts' powder mills along the Brandywine River, but after a personal feud arose, he set up his own powder works in Eden Park. However, a large explosion in 1861 destroyed the plant, and it never reopened. (Courtesy of Delaware Historical Society.)

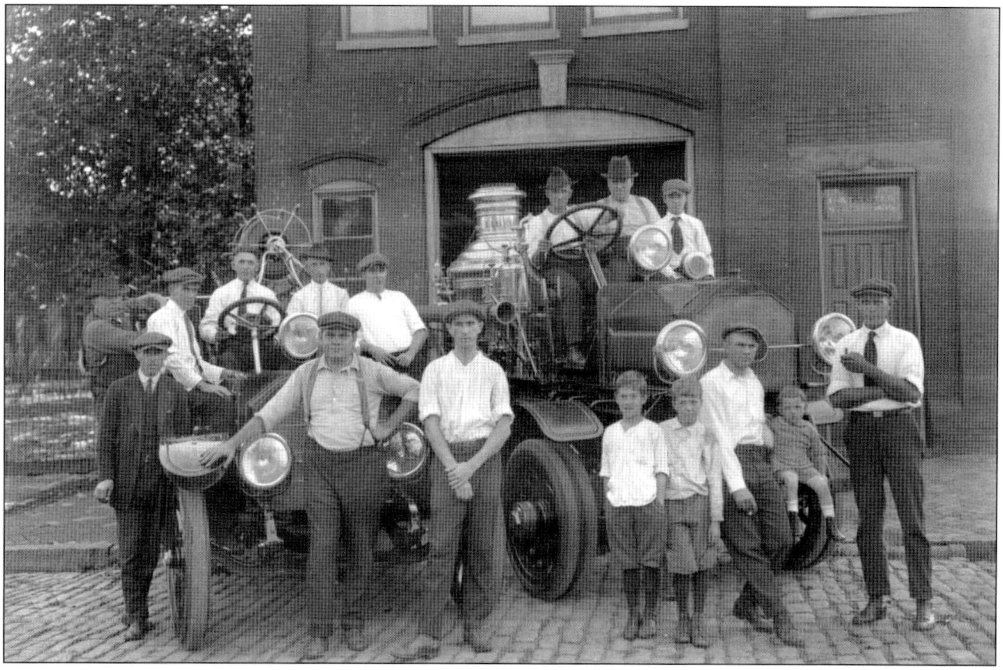

Liberty Company No. 9 of the Wilmington Fire Department is pictured in 1930 at its original firehouse at A Street and New Castle Avenue. The volunteer company was established September 11, 1890, and incorporated February 12, 1891. (Courtesy of Delaware Historical Society.)

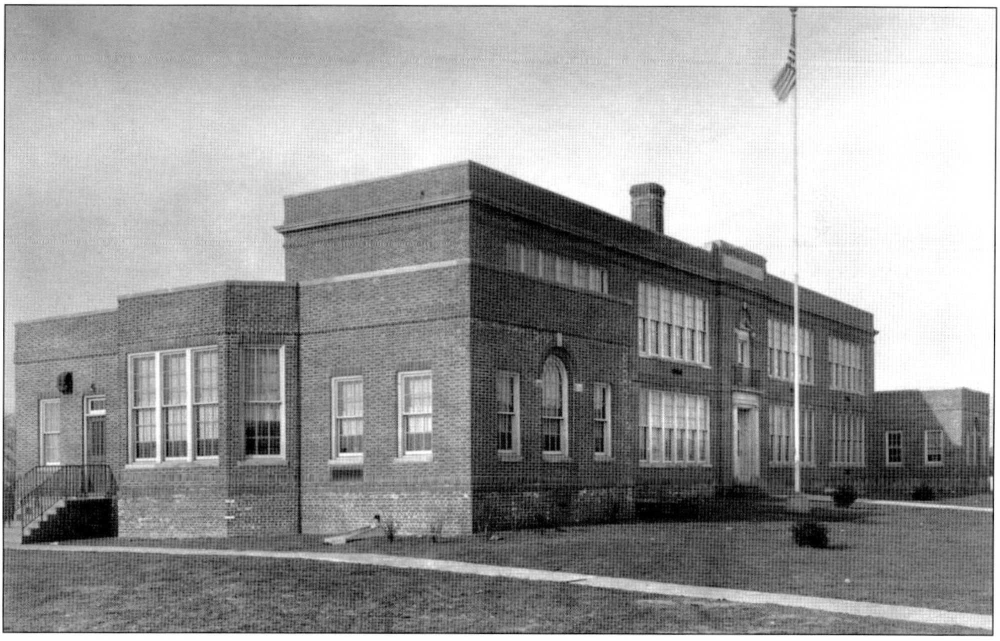

Samuel G. Elbert Elementary School at C and Townsend Streets opened in 1929. Its namesake, Dr. Samuel Elbert (1865–1939), graduated from Howard University with an academic degree and later graduated from its medical school. He worked tirelessly to improve educational opportunities for African Americans in a period of racial segregation. In 1976, Samuel G. Elbert Elementary School combined with John Palmer School to form the Elbert-Palmer Elementary School.

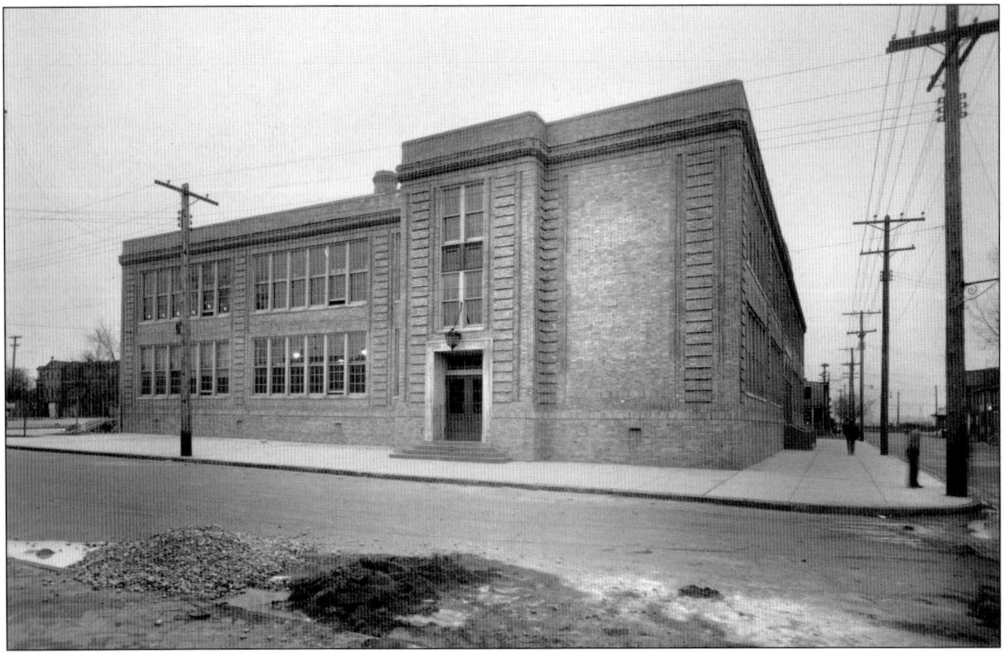

The John Palmer School was located at 1210 Lobdell Street and was named for John Palmer Jr. (1860–1930), who graduated from the University of Pennsylvania with a medical degree. For 38 years, among his many affiliations, he served on the Wilmington Board of Education as a member and as president of the board.

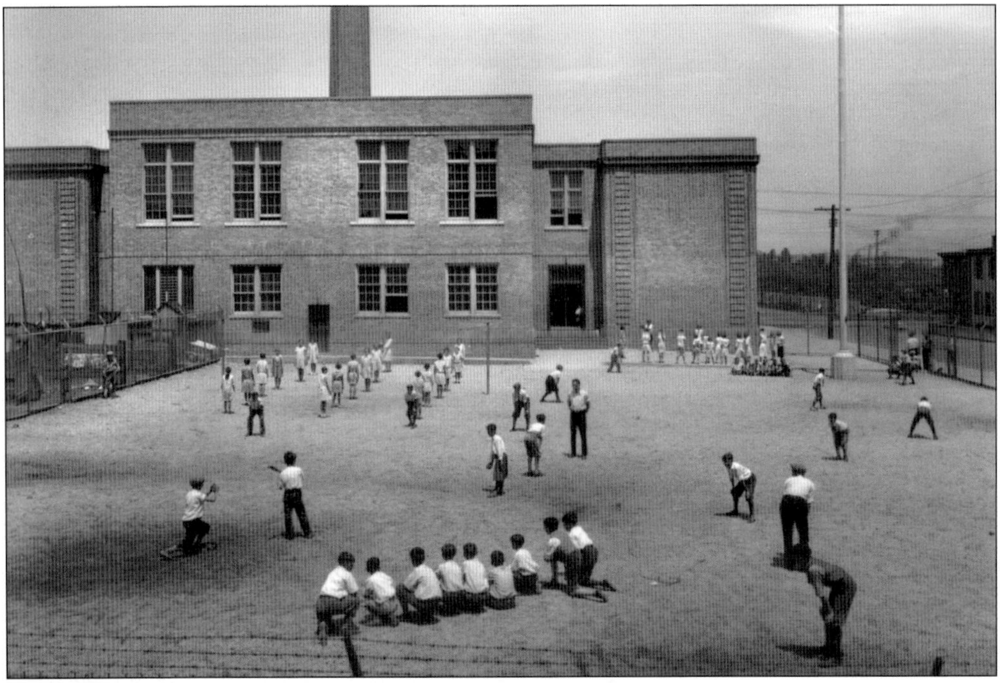

These students are pictured on the playground at the John Palmer School during gym class in 1931. The building is currently the Elbert-Palmer Elementary School. (Courtesy of Delaware Historical Society.)

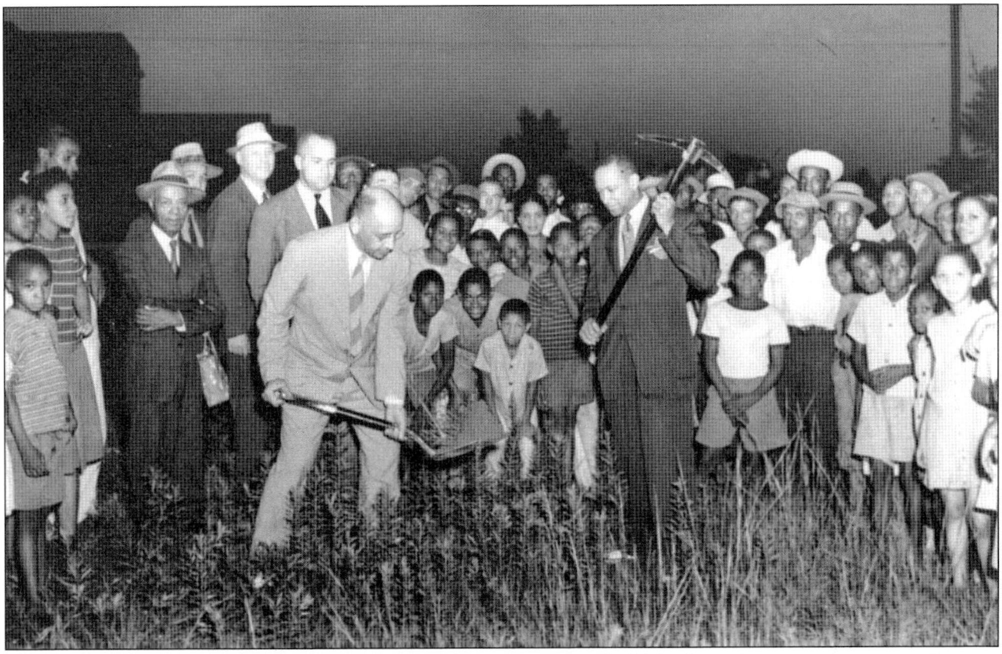

A ground-breaking ceremony during World War II was held before the construction of some emergency housing in the Southbridge community of Wilmington. The first independent African American church in the United States—the African Union Church—was established in Southbridge in 1812. The community had historically been surrounded by manufacturing, commercial, and industrial properties, and its economy remained very dependent on manufacturing. After World War II, as the shipbuilding operations closed, the neighborhood saw steady decline.

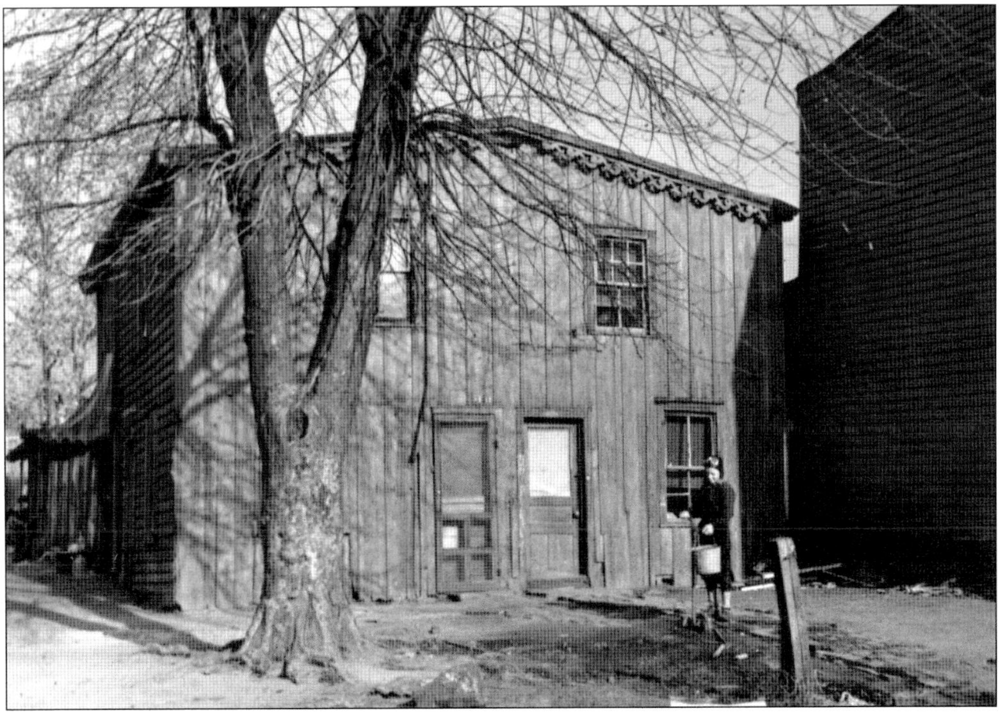

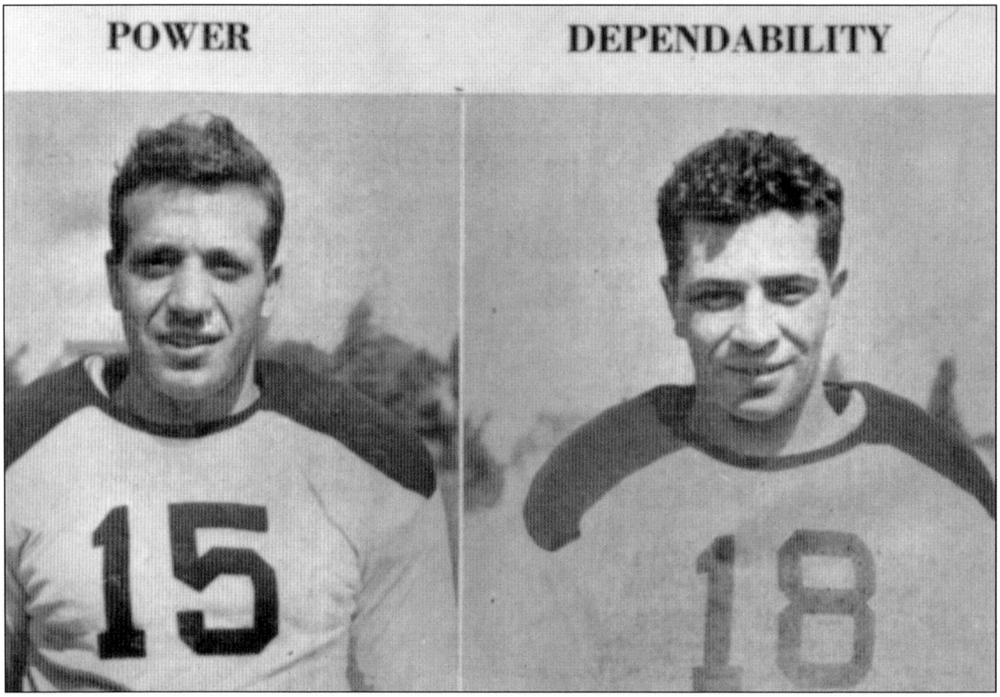

The Wilmington Clippers were a minor-league football team from 1937 to 1941 and then from 1946 through 1949. Prior to the 1940 opening of Wilmington Park on Governor Printz Boulevard, the Clippers played at Pennsy Field along the Christina River at Third and Church Streets. The 1937 team featured a five-foot-eleven-inch, 192-pound guard from Fordham—Vince Lombardi (No. 18)—who would become a National Football League Hall of Fame coach and have his name immortalized on the Super Bowl trophy. (Courtesy of Delaware Historical Society.)

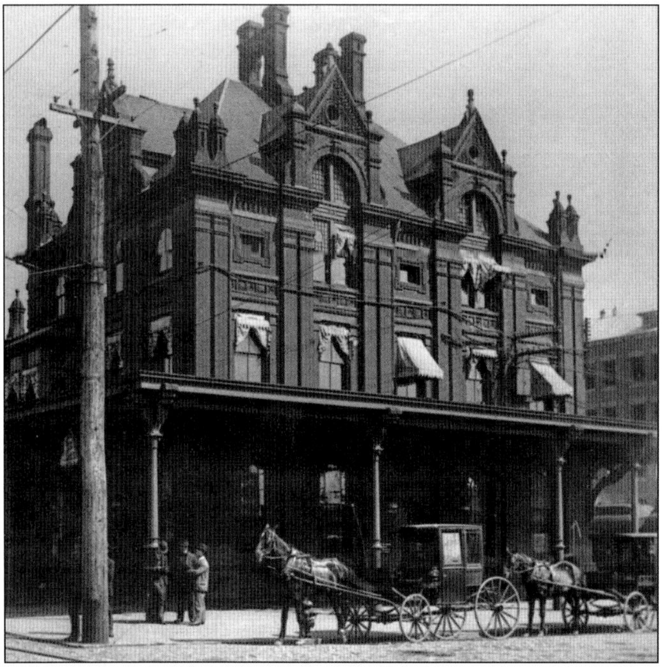

The city of Wilmington developed from the Christina River around Front Street and up Market Street. Pictured here in 1901 is the Philadelphia, Wilmington & Baltimore Railroad station on French Street, with the tracks at grade. The current Wilmington Station at 100 South French Street elevated the tracks onto a viaduct and replaced this structure on June 29, 1908. The station is also called the Joseph R. Biden Jr. Railroad Station, a designation given in a ceremony on March 19, 2011, in honor of the vice president of the United States.

The Hotel Merritt stood across from the train station on the northwest corner of North French Street and East Front Street. Seen here in 1940, it was originally operated by Tobias Merritt and known as the European Hotel. Merritt also operated the Wilmington Hotel before retiring in 1890.

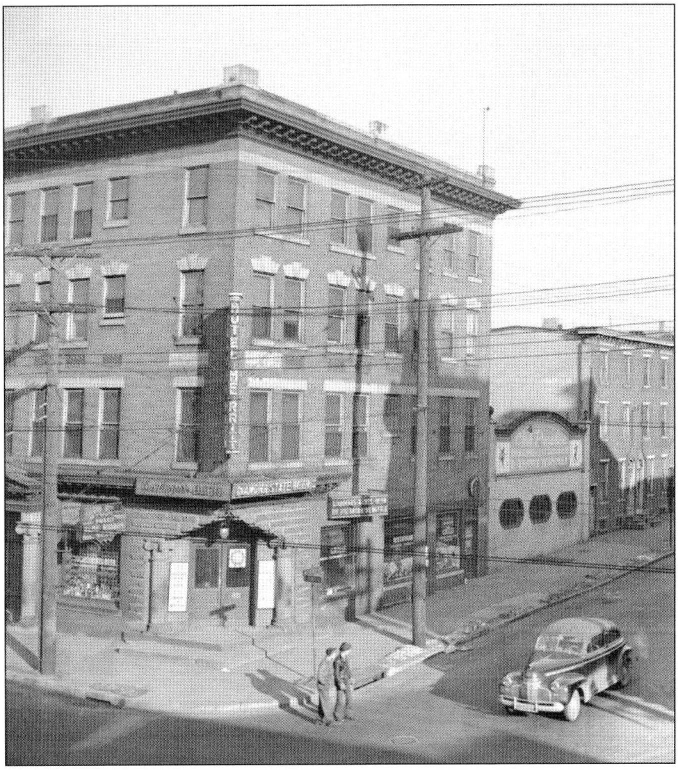

On the northeast corner of the same intersection was the Hotel Grande, formerly the Grand Union Hotel, built in 1886 and operated by Henry Blouth, a German immigrant. Blouth operated a brewery in the hotel and was president of the Wilmington Brewing Company. His hotel was a popular spot for the city's German immigrants and people of German descent.

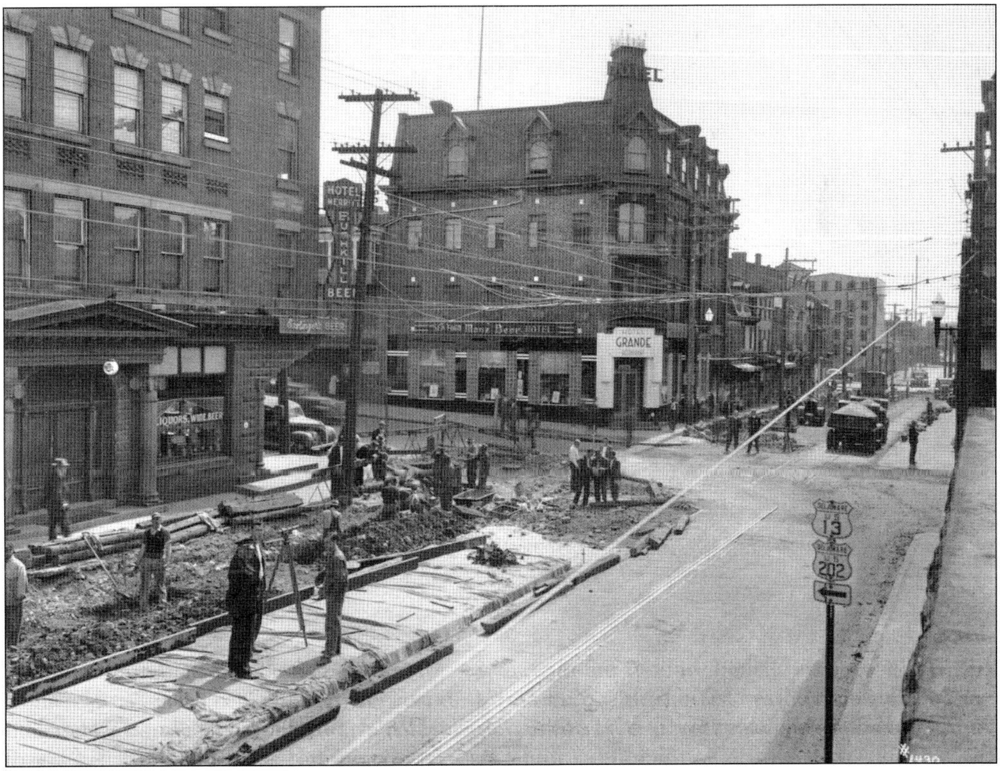

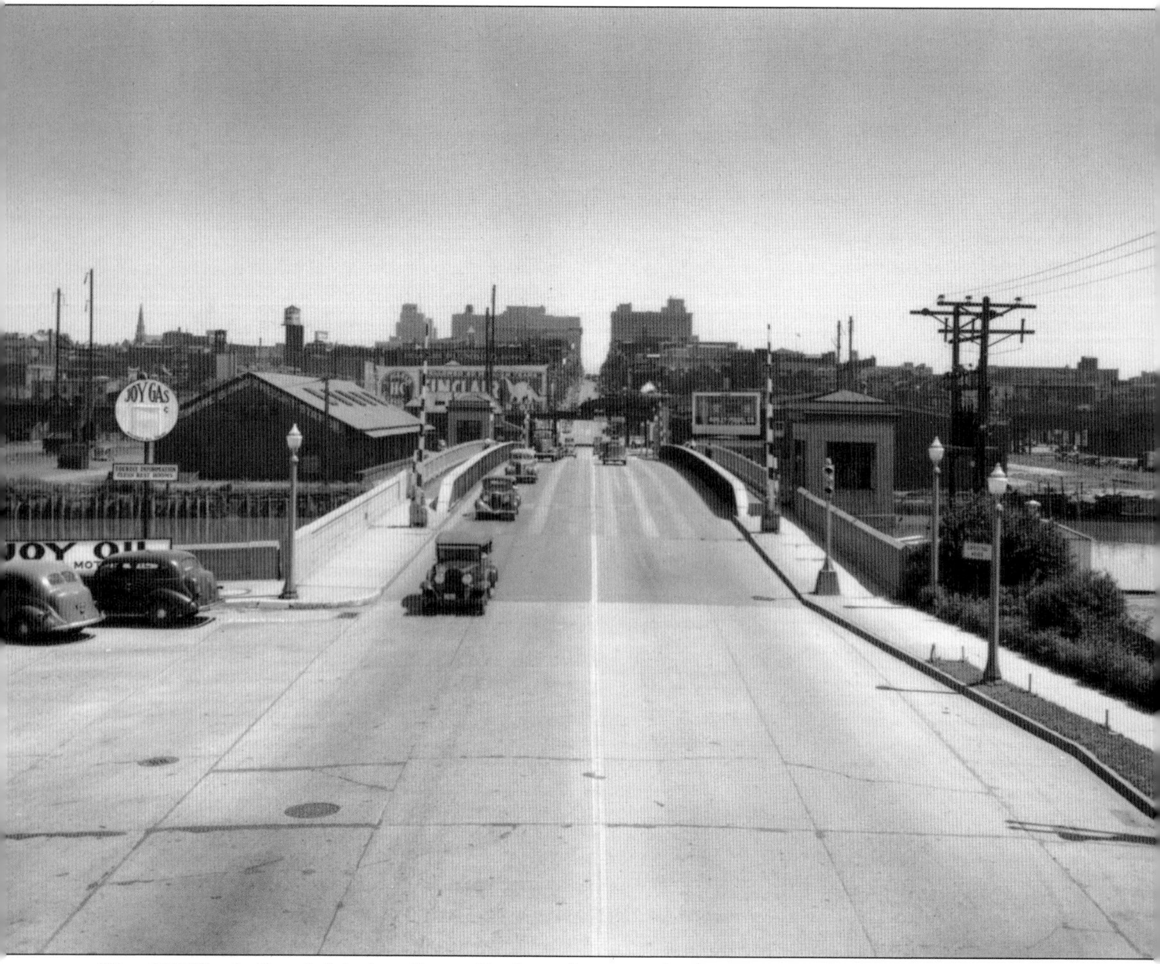

The 1927-built South Market Street Bridge, photographed in 1939 with the city of Wilmington in the background, is still in use. It was renamed the John E. Reilly Sr. Bridge in 1983 after a former state senator. The bascule bridge is 208 feet long and is one of only three trunnion bascule highway bridges predating 1957 that are still in operation. The structure underwent extensive repairs in 1982 and again in 2005. A bridge has spanned the Christina River in this area since 1808, starting with a wooden turn bridge that was replaced in 1883 by a metal truss structure.

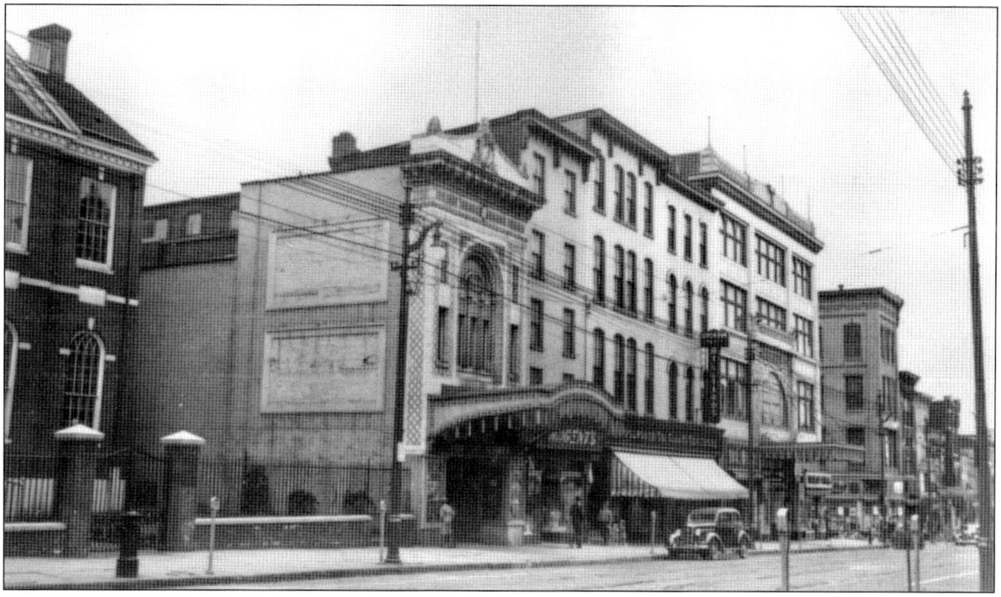

Market Street had its share of theaters. By 1913, five movie houses were operating—the Pickwick, the Lyric, the Palace, the Majestic, and the Victoria. The Arcadia Theater at 510 North Market Street is seen here in 1939, with the Old Town Hall on the left. The Queen is also in this block. In the 1920s, the Garrick, the Majestic, the Queen, and the Arcadia were sold to Warner Bros. (Courtesy of Delaware Historical Society.)

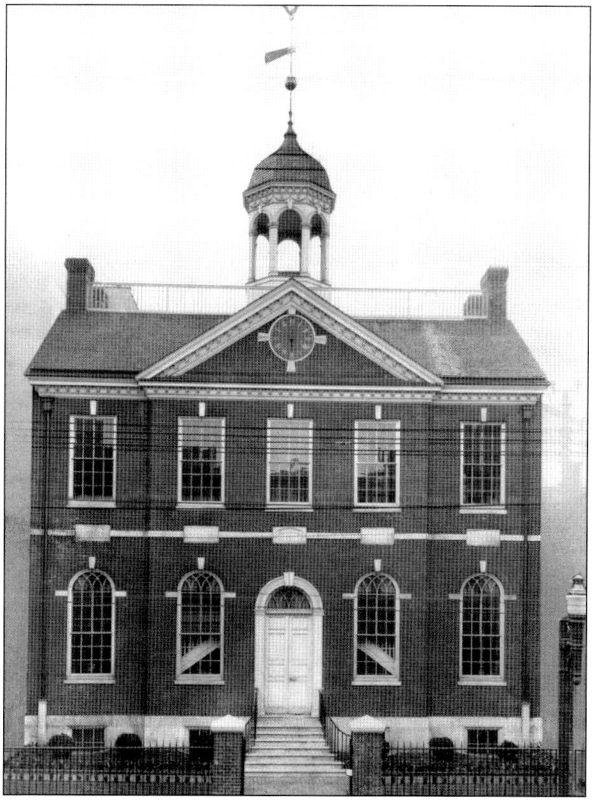

Old Town Hall in the 500 block of Market Street was designed by Frenchman Peter Bauduy and built in 1798 to house the city's civic business and jail. It has also held reception dinners for the Marquis de Lafayette and Pres. Andrew Jackson. Henry Clay's body was laid in state there in 1851. The building also served as home to the Delaware Historical Society, founded in 1864, and remains in the society's care as an exhibit hall.

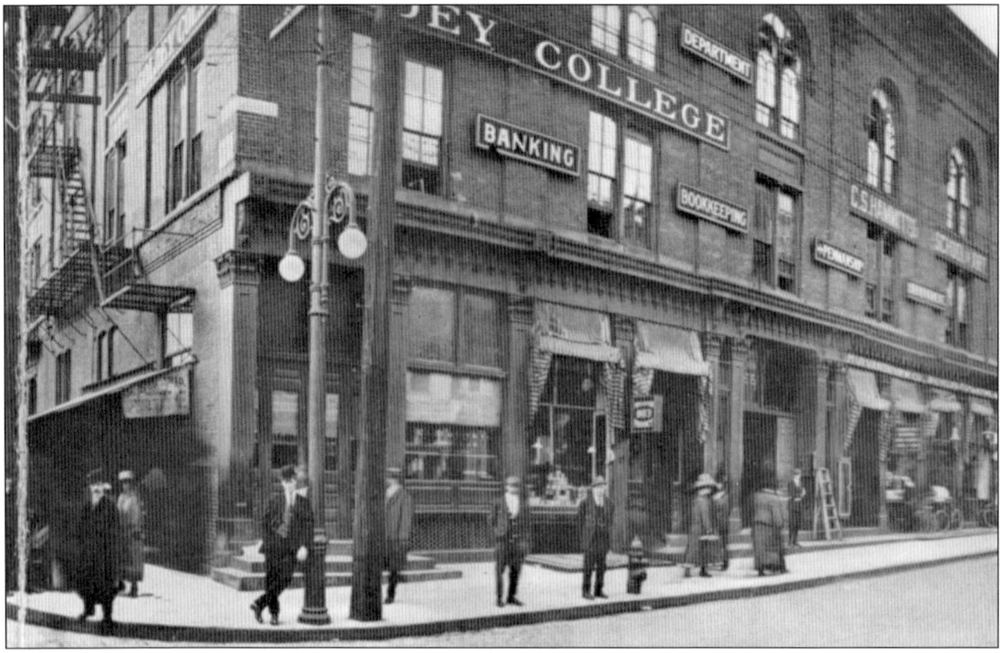

Goldey College is pictured in 1903 at Eighth and Market Streets before its move to Ninth and Tatnall Streets in 1923. Beacon Business College was at Tenth and King Streets, and the two schools merged to form Goldey-Beacon College, on Limestone Road in Pike Creek. (Courtesy of Delaware Historical Society.)

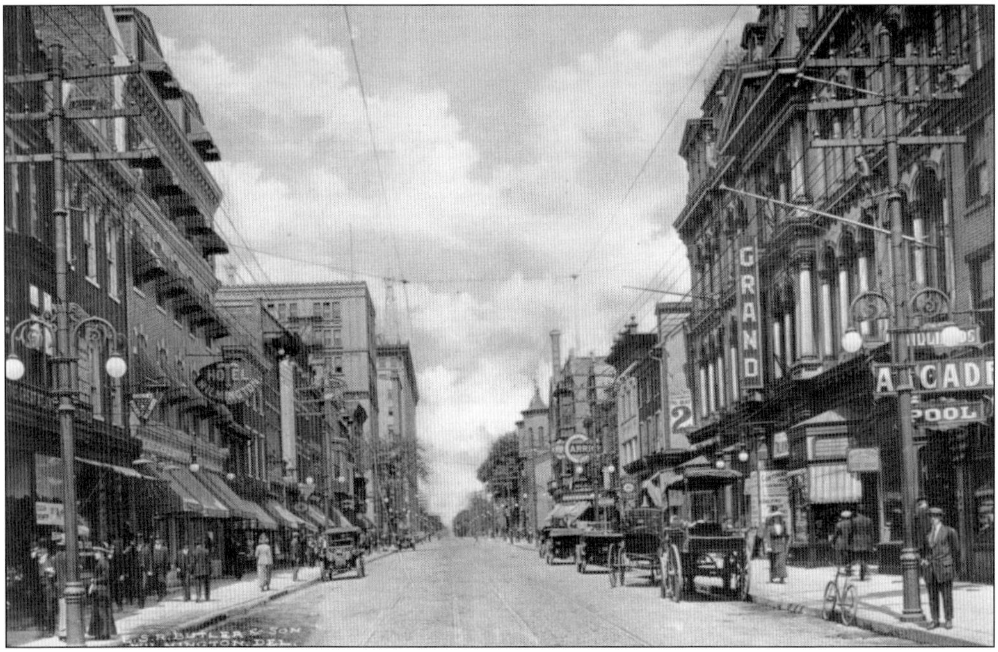

The view in this image looks north up Market Street from Eighth Street and toward Rodney Square in 1903. The Grand Opera House is seen on the right. Built by Masons in 1871 and with a cast-iron facade, it was the first theater in the city to host live performances. (Courtesy of Delaware Historical Society.)

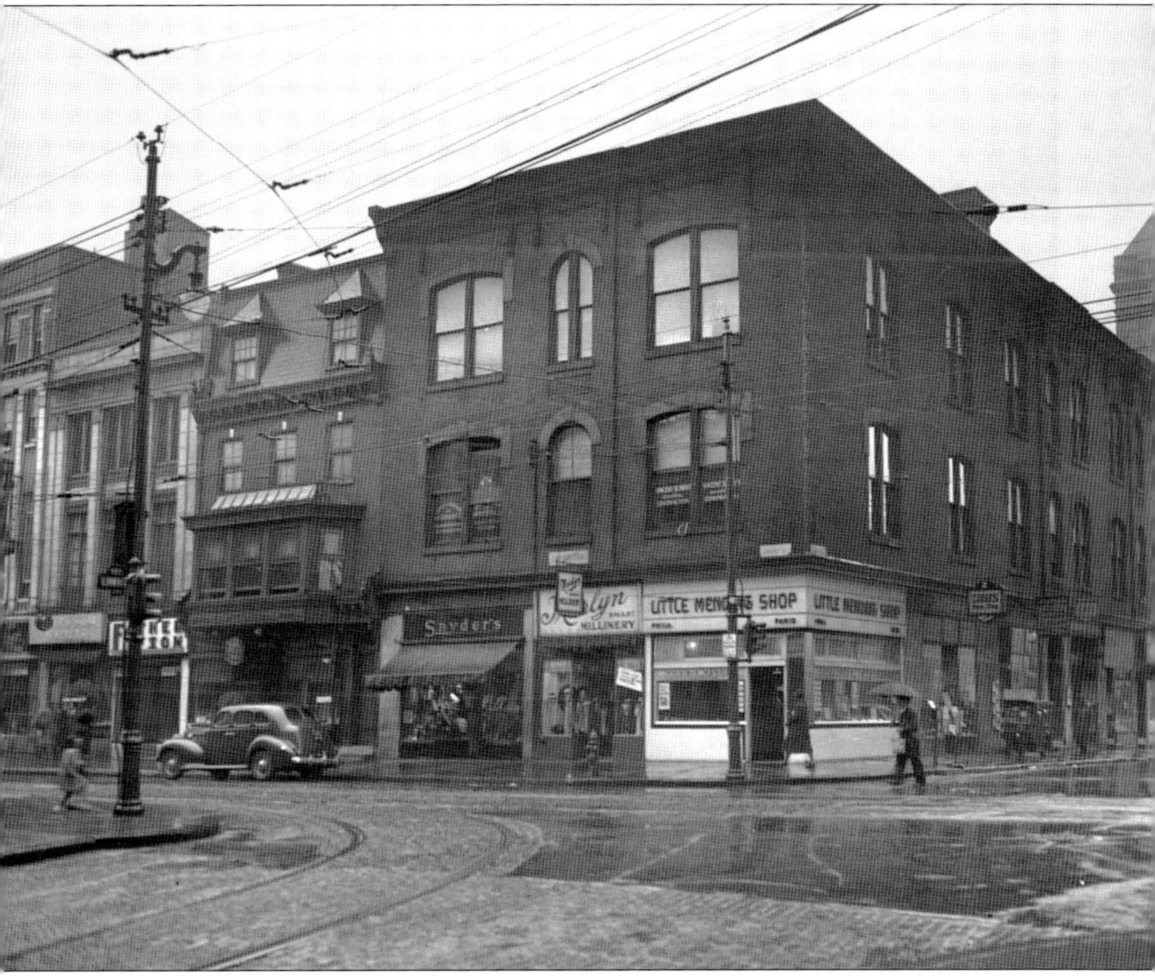

Note the trolley tracks in this view of Ninth and Market Streets from 1939. Trolley service from the Railroad Station up Market Street to Tenth Street began in 1864 with the Wilmington City Railway Company. Horse- and mule-drawn cars were used until electric-run trolleys arrived by 1892. In 1936, the company that started mass transportation in Wilmington merged with the Delaware Electric Power Company, but track service would give way to bus transportation. The area of the first trolley line, which included Delaware Avenue to Rising Sun Lane and the Middle Depot on Delaware Avenue at the corners of DuPont Street and Clayton Street, has become the vibrant Wilmington neighborhood of Trolley Square. The Trolley Square Shopping Center was built in 1978 where the trolley barns once stood.

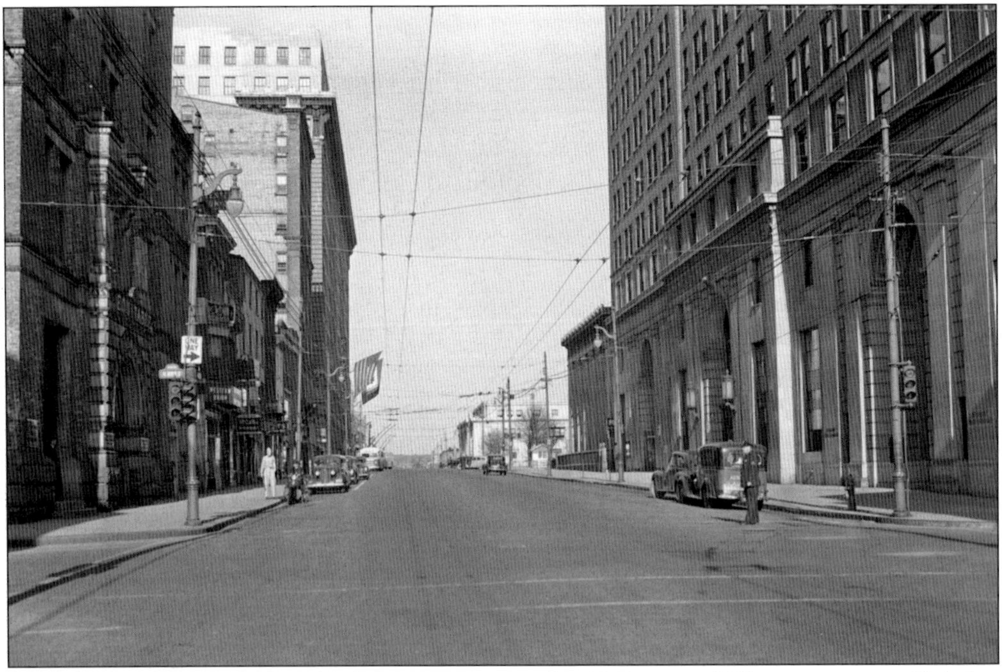

A quiet Market Street above Ninth Street is seen in this 1942 image. Wilmington, east of Market Street and along both sides of the Christina River, is on flat, low-lying ground. West of Market Street, the land rises to a point that marks the watershed between the Brandywine and Christina Rivers. This watershed runs along Delaware Avenue westward from Tenth and Market Streets. The hilly side saw the development of the city's original residential areas.

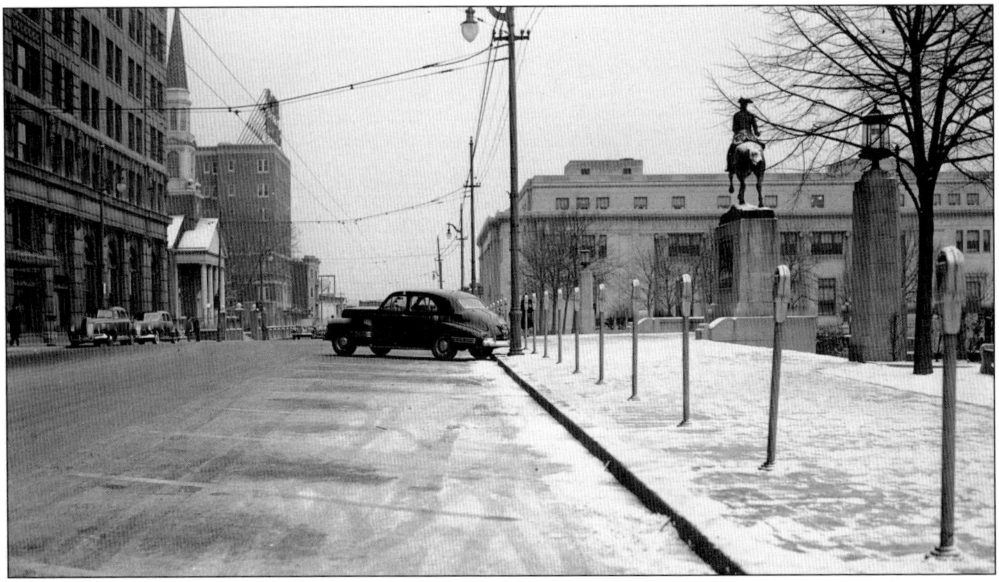

Market Street is sandwiched between the DuPont Building on the left and Rodney Square on the right. The equestrian statue of Caesar Rodney was sculpted by James Edward Kelly and placed here on July 4, 1923, to honor Rodney's perilous ride from Dover to Philadelphia in one night to cast Delaware's deciding vote in the Continental Congress debate over the Declaration of Independence.

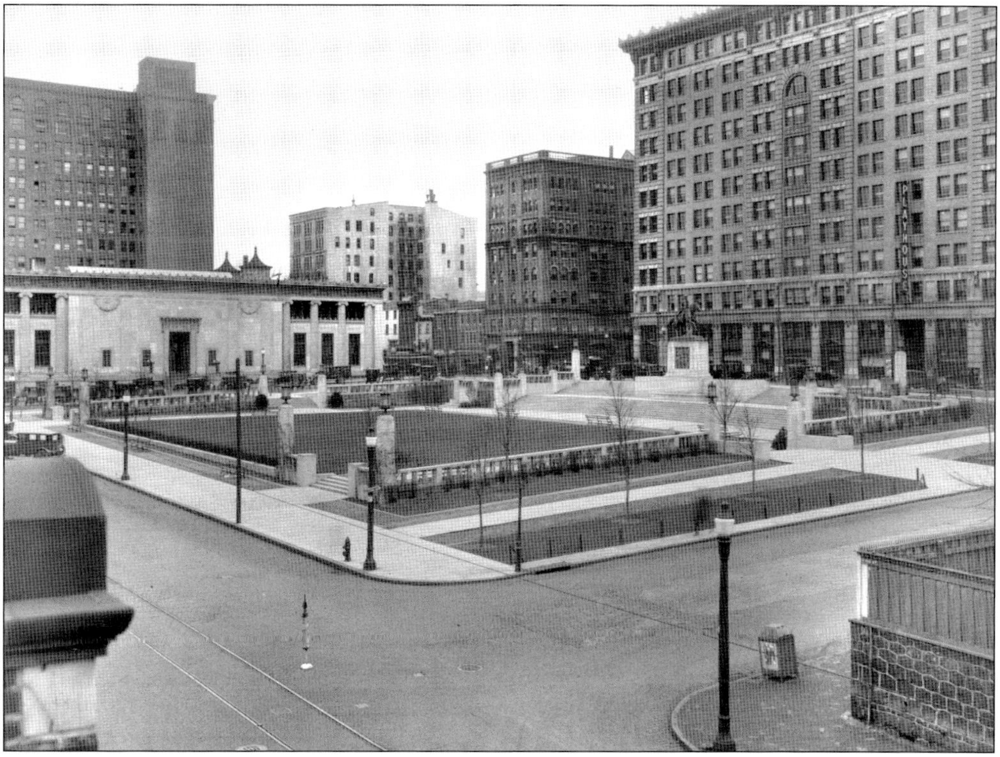

Rodney Square is pictured here in the late 1920s. Once the city's first reservoir, the area had been drained in 1878 for the construction of the original New Castle County Courthouse. With the courthouse demolished, the creation of a parklike square can be credited to DuPont executive John J. Raskob (1879–1950), who was inspired by the City Beautiful movement, a reform philosophy spreading across the country in the late 19th and early 20th centuries to beautify American cities. (Courtesy of Delaware Historical Society.)

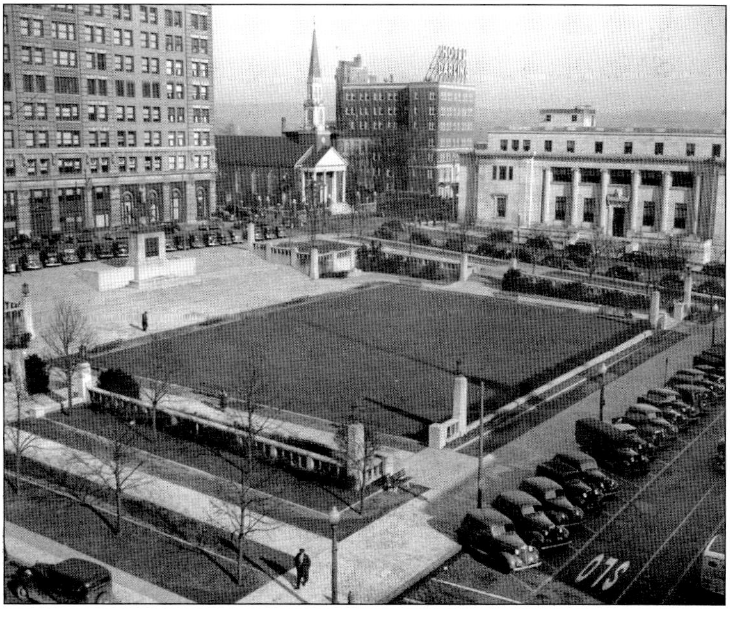

Here, Rodney Square is seen in 1937 shortly after the completion of the US Post Office, Courthouse & Customhouse (right). This building would be converted into the headquarters for Wilmington Trust in 1973. Also visible are the spire of the First & Central Presbyterian Church at Eleventh and North Market Streets and the Hotel Darling in the distance.

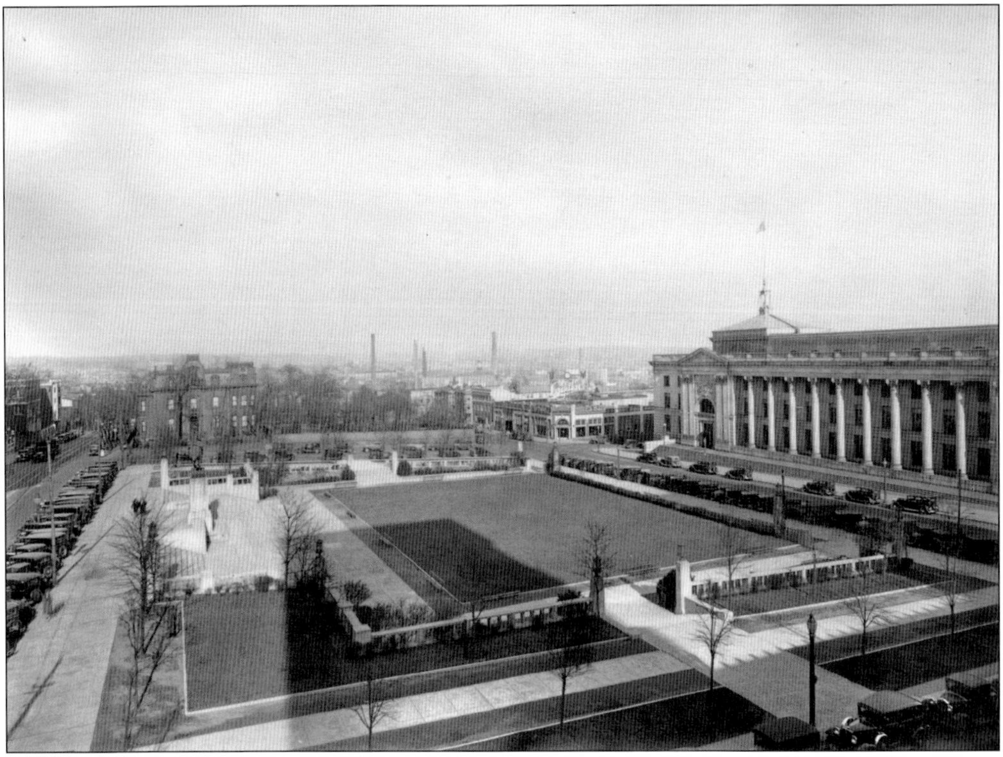

Rodney Square is seen in 1932, before the US Post Office, Courthouse & Customhouse had been built. The mansion in the background is the McComb-Winchester estate. The owners sold the property to the federal government for $500,000. The US Post Office, Courthouse & Customhouse was a symmetrical building designed in the Classical Revival style, and its facade was embellished with Ionic pillars and topped with ornate cornices.

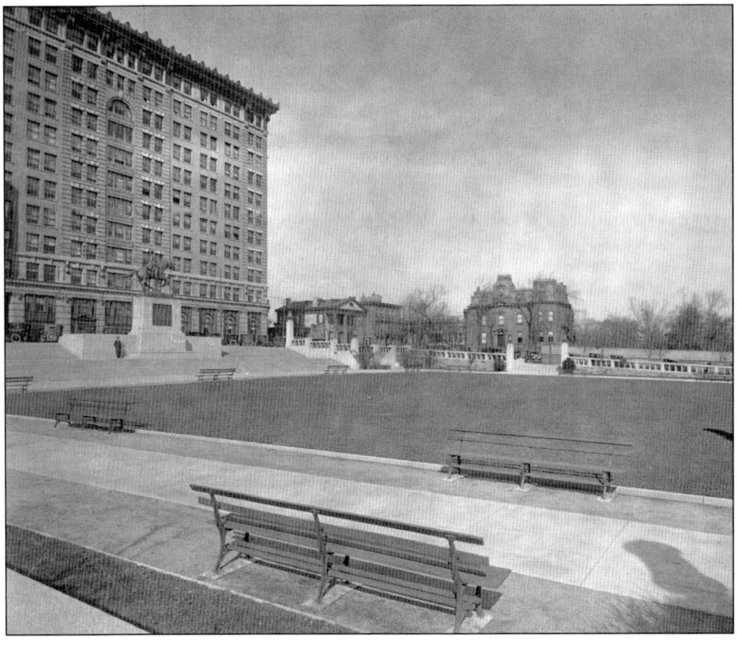

Rodney Square, pictured in 1925, was designed by the Philadelphia firm of Zantinger, Borie & Medary. The National Park Service has designated Rodney Square Historic District in the National Register of Historic Places. Caesar Rodney (1728–1784) was an early advocate of American independence, a member of the Continental Congress, and president of the state of Delaware.

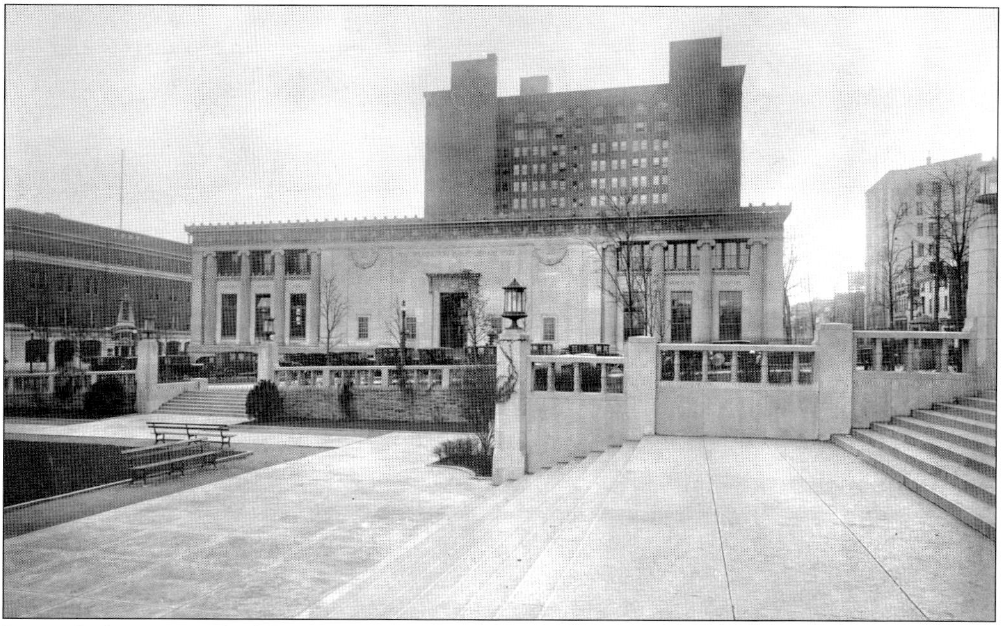

Pierre S. du Pont pushed for the creation of the Wilmington Institute Free Library and assisted by buying the lot at Tenth and Market Streets to donate to the city. New York architect Edward Lippincott Tilton (1861–1933) designed the building, which cost $750,000 to construct.

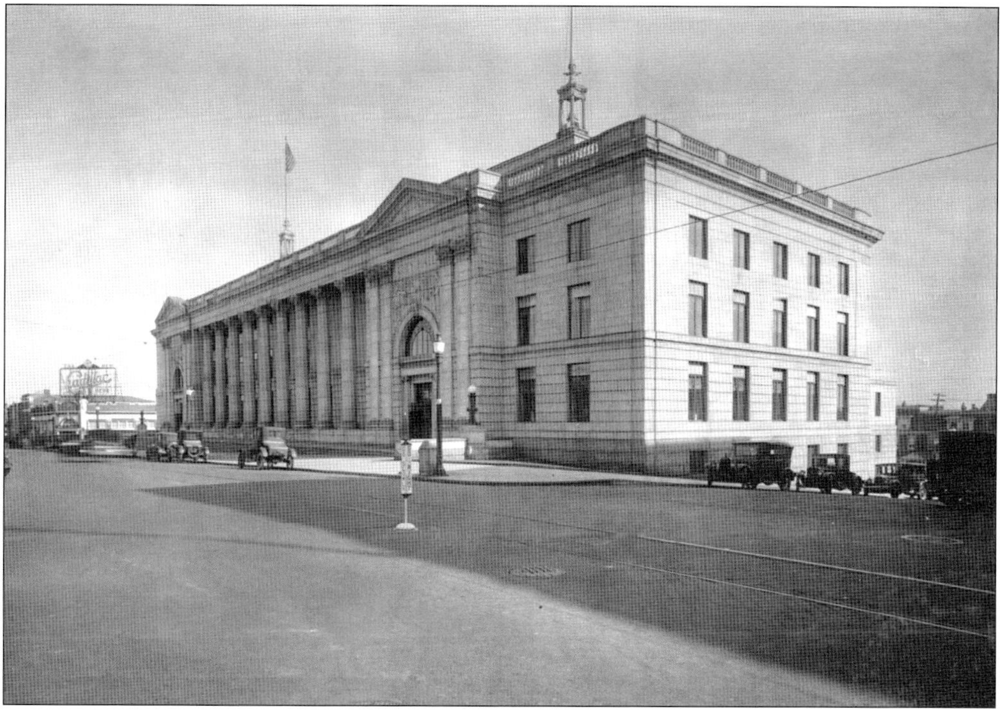

New Castle's County Courthouse/City Hall is seen here in 1925. Philadelphia firm Irwin & Leighton constructed the building, which was dedicated in 1914 and opened three years later. The new county courthouse was built on a 5.3-acre site bordered by Fourth, Sixth, Walnut, and King Streets. This former county courthouse/city hall was renovated into office space.

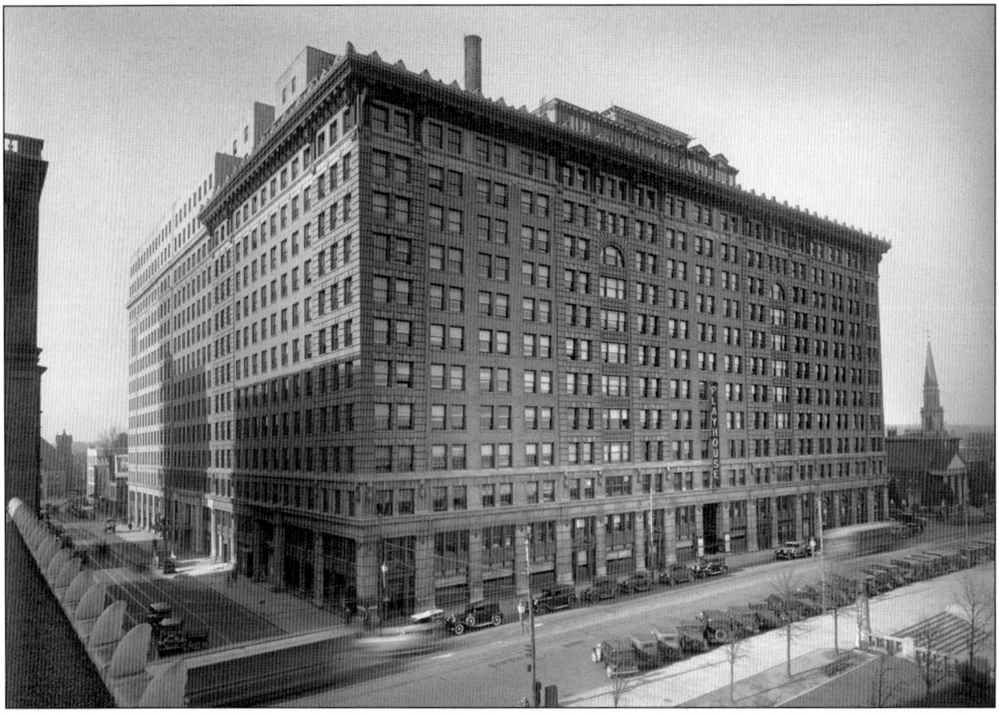

The DuPont Building (pictured above in 1932 and below in 1925) dominates a high point at Rodney Square. The building occupies an entire city block between Tenth, Eleventh, Market, and Orange Streets, and is home to the DuPont Corporation. It also contains the lavish, 150-bedroom Hotel DuPont. The 12-story Italian Renaissance hotel was commissioned by Pierre S. du Pont and opened on January 15, 1913. Also in residence is the 1,256-seat DuPont Theatre, formerly the Playhouse. DuPont executives John J. Raskob, Pierre S. du Pont, and Robert Ruliph Morgan Carpenter (1877–1949) wanted a venue to present "the finest entertainment possible." The theater hosts a variety of live performances, from one-person acts to Broadway shows.

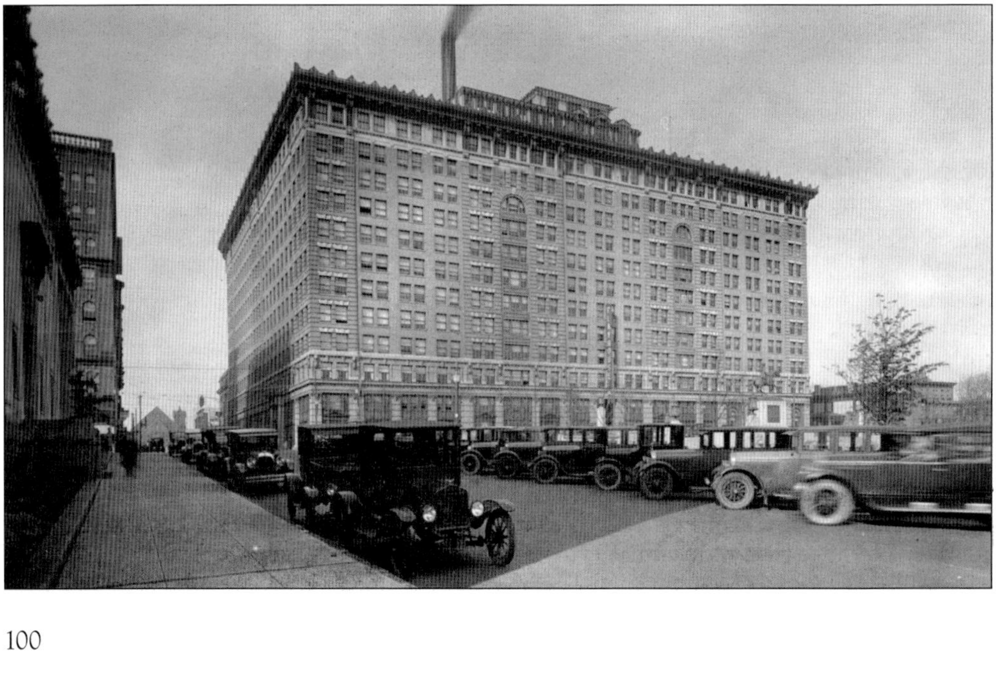

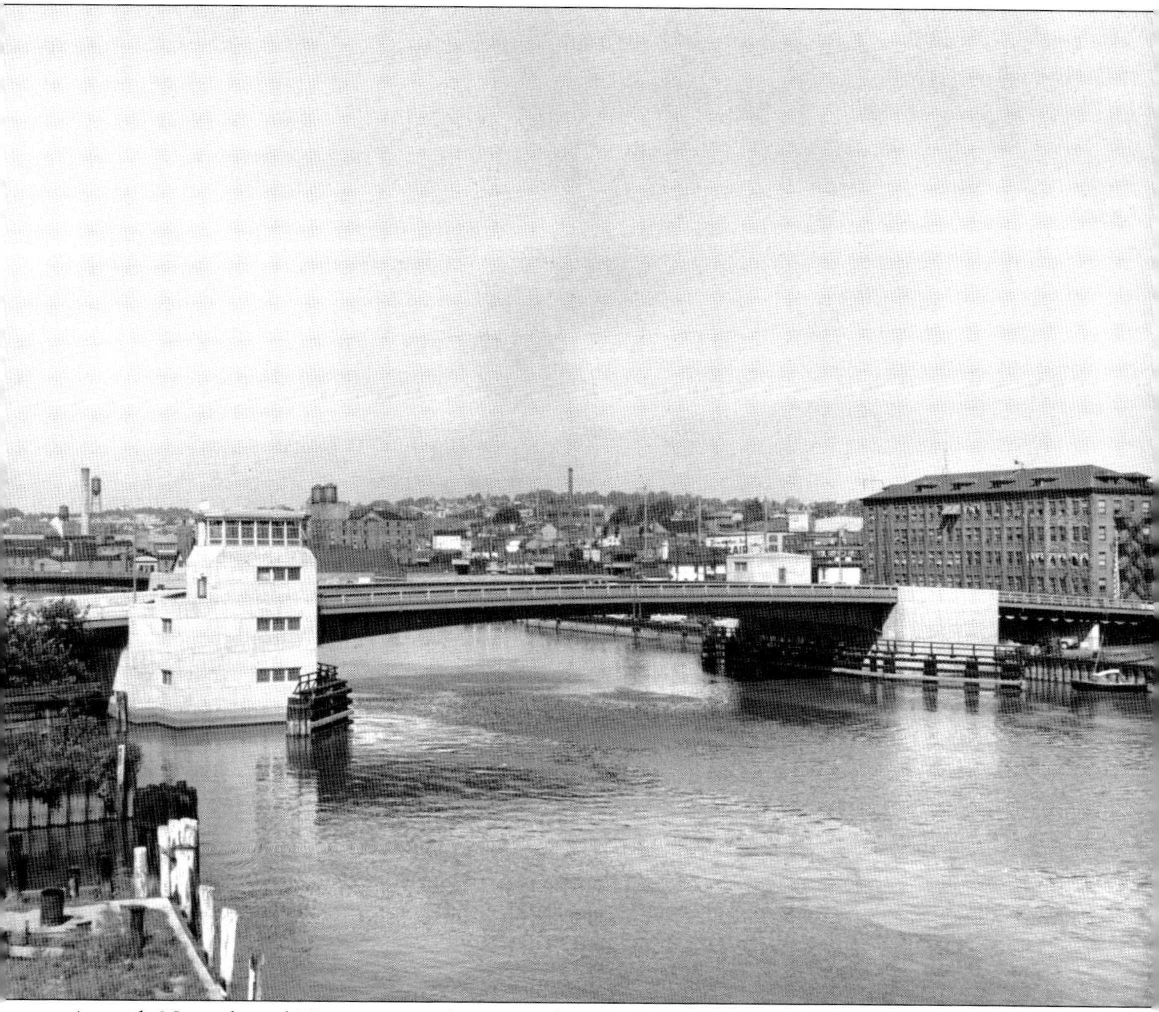

As with Newark and Newport, a solution to downtown traffic congestion was the creation of a one-way-loop route through town. The South Walnut Street Bridge over the Christina River was specifically built for this purpose, and it provided a new southern entrance into the city. Photographed shortly after it opened in 1957, the bridge provided a northbound traffic flow for Walnut Street. Southbound traffic used King Street and exited the city via the South Market Street Bridge. Construction of the South Walnut Street Bridge began in 1955 with required marsh stabilization. The roads leading up to the bridge on both sides of the river were known as the Walnut Street Extension. In addition to the bridge, a major construction project involved the creation of an underpass for the railroad lines while not interrupting service to around 142 trains per day.

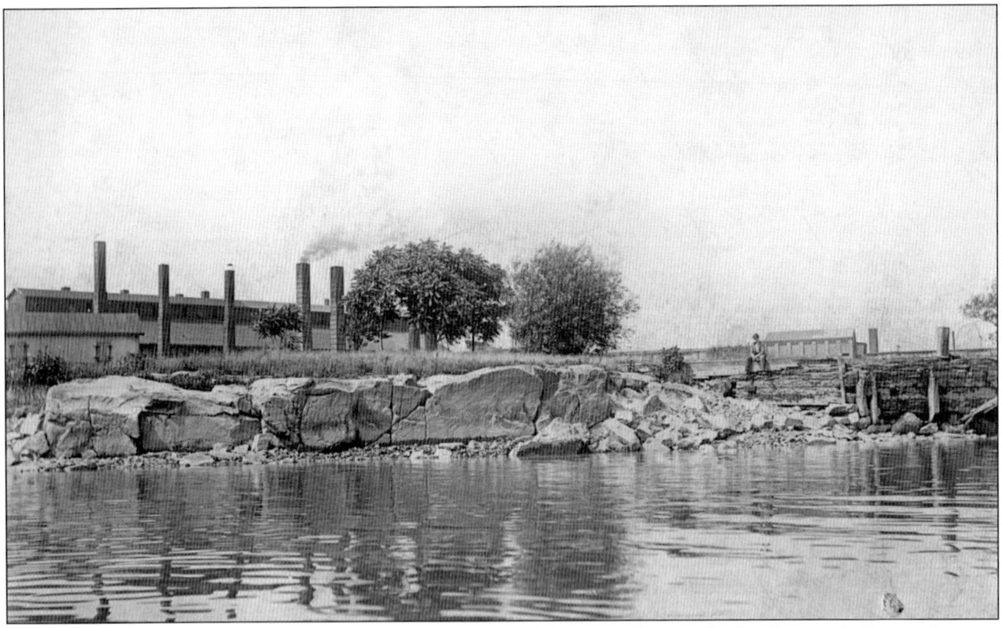

A man sits at "the Rocks," the 1638 landing site of the Swedes, with the Pusey & Jones factory in the background. Pusey & Jones on East Front Street was founded in 1848 by Joshua Pusey and John Jones. The company built general machinery and steam engines, then added shipbuilding in 1853. It would become well known for its pleasure crafts and yachts. (Courtesy of Delaware Historical Society.)

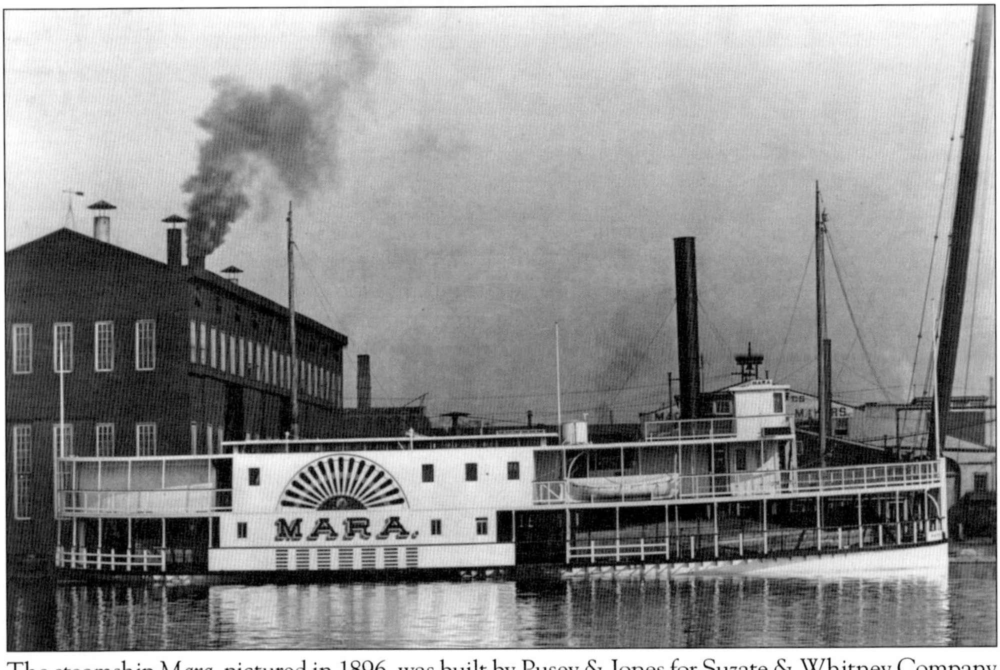

The steamship *Mara*, pictured in 1896, was built by Pusey & Jones for Suzate & Whitney Company for use on Lake Maracaibo, Venezuela. Pusey & Jones also built passenger ships, ferry boats, cargo ships, and dredges, totaling around 500 ships during its lifetime. (Courtesy of Delaware Historical Society.)

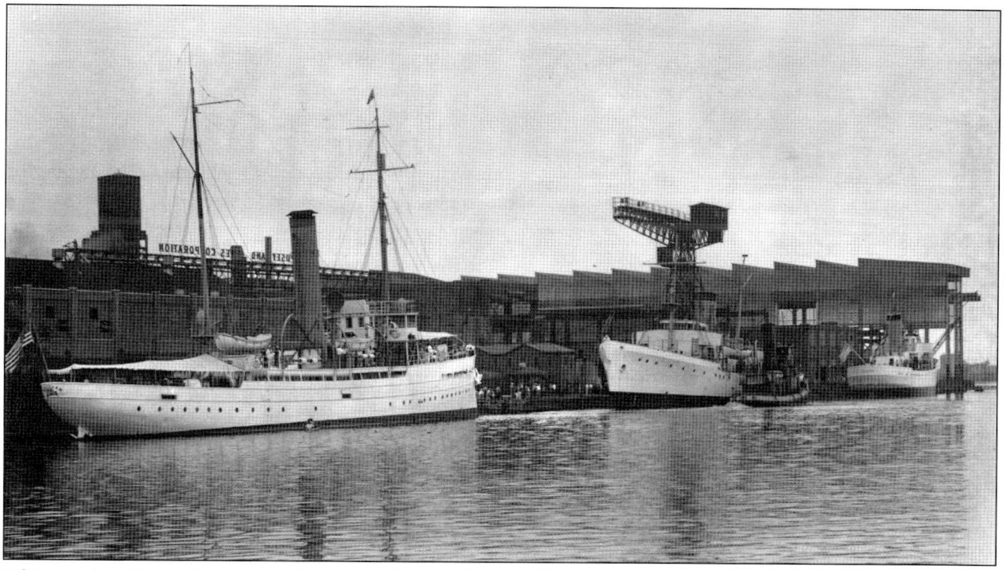

This is the Pusey & Jones plant on September 6, 1934. The company became famous in 1854 with the successful launch of the first iron-hulled sailing vessel, the *Mahlon Betts*. Skeptics had proclaimed that an iron-hulled ship would sink. In 1887, the company built the first steel-hulled yacht to win the America's Cup, *Volunteer*.

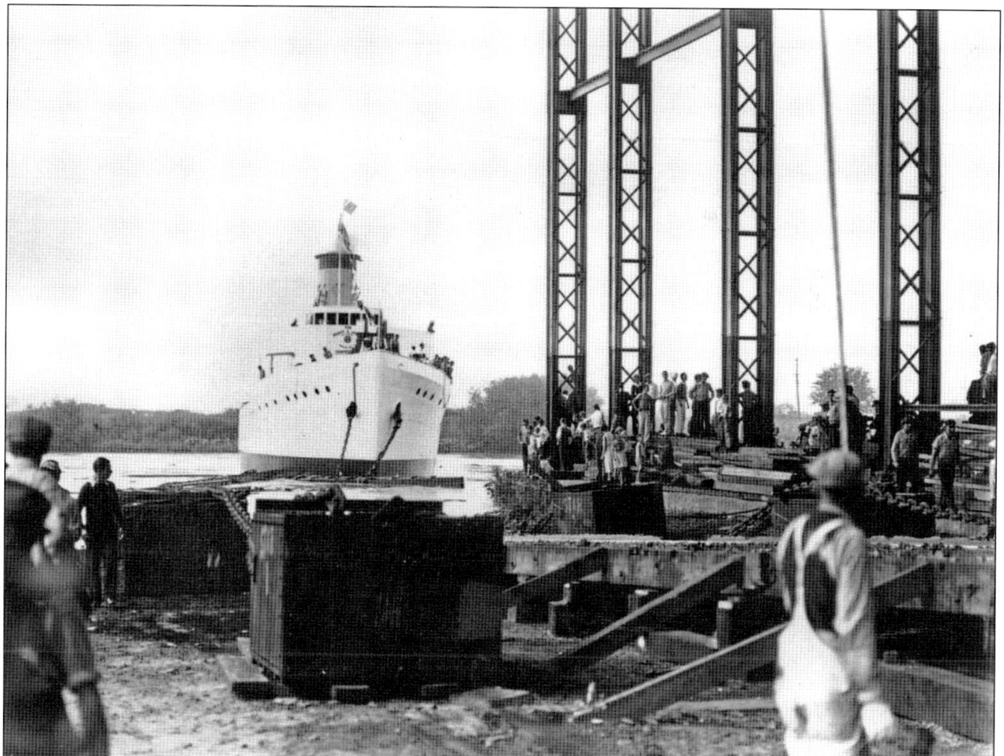

By 1900, the company employed around 900 men and expanded its operations between Lombard Street and between Walnut and Poplar Streets. For World War I production, the workforce increased to 2,000 employees.

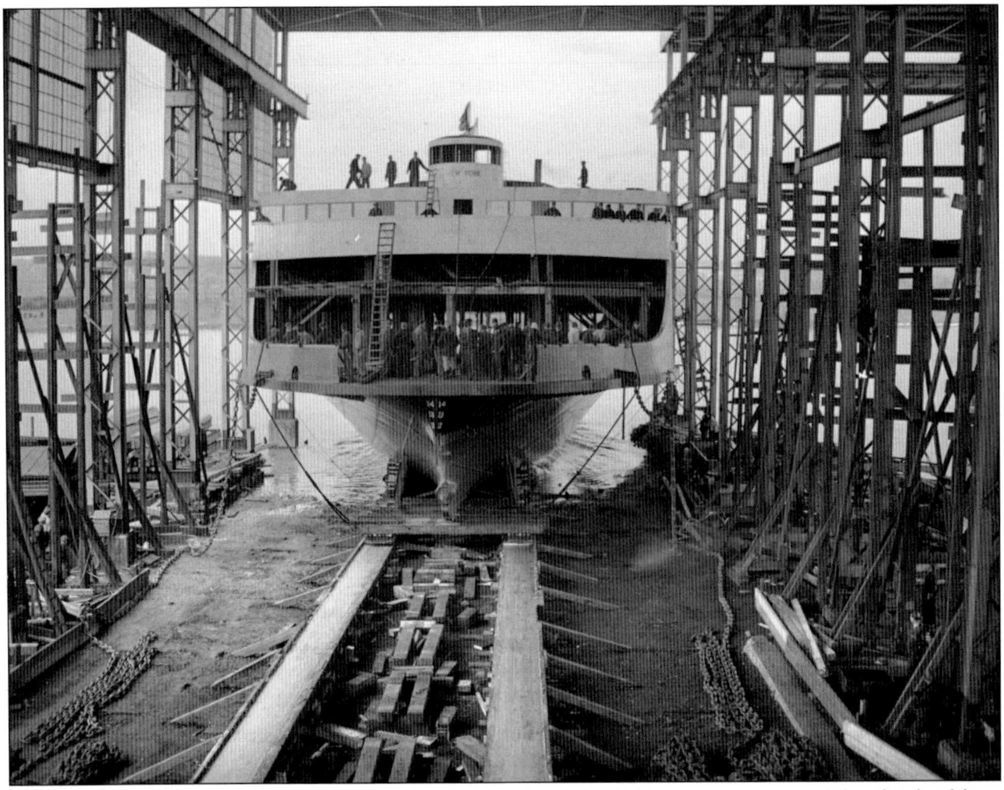

A ferry boat for New York is launched in 1941. After World War II, as demand for shipbuilding declined, Pusey & Jones closed in its two launching bays and converted to full-time papermaking and metal fabrication. The company had been involved with the manufacture of papermaking machines as early as 1867. A 1908 Pusey & Jones machine produced 600 feet of newsprint per minute. The company closed in 1959.

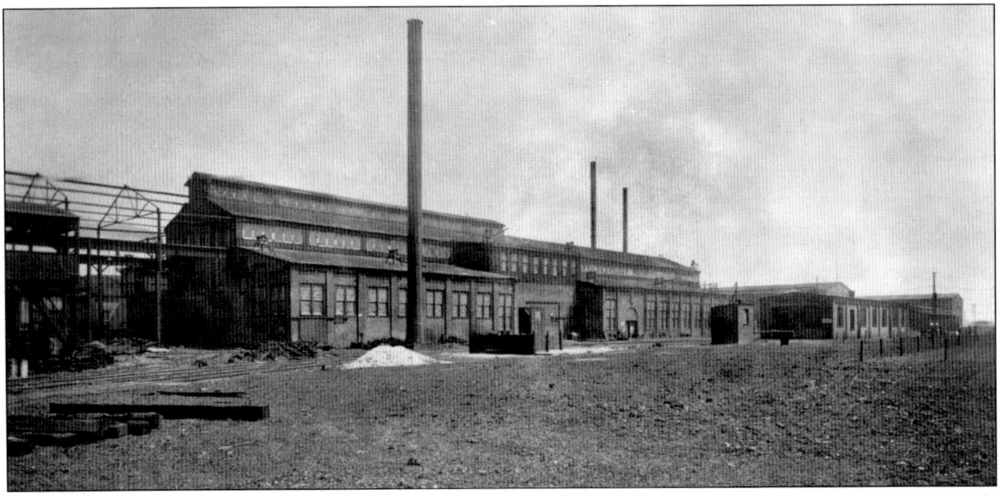

The Lobdell Car Wheel Company was well known for its chilled cast-iron railcar wheels, of which it was once the largest producer in the United States. The company began operations in 1831 at Second and Lombard Streets, land that would eventually be sold to Pusey & Jones when the Lobdell Car Wheel Company moved in 1882 to the present-day site of the Port of Wilmington.

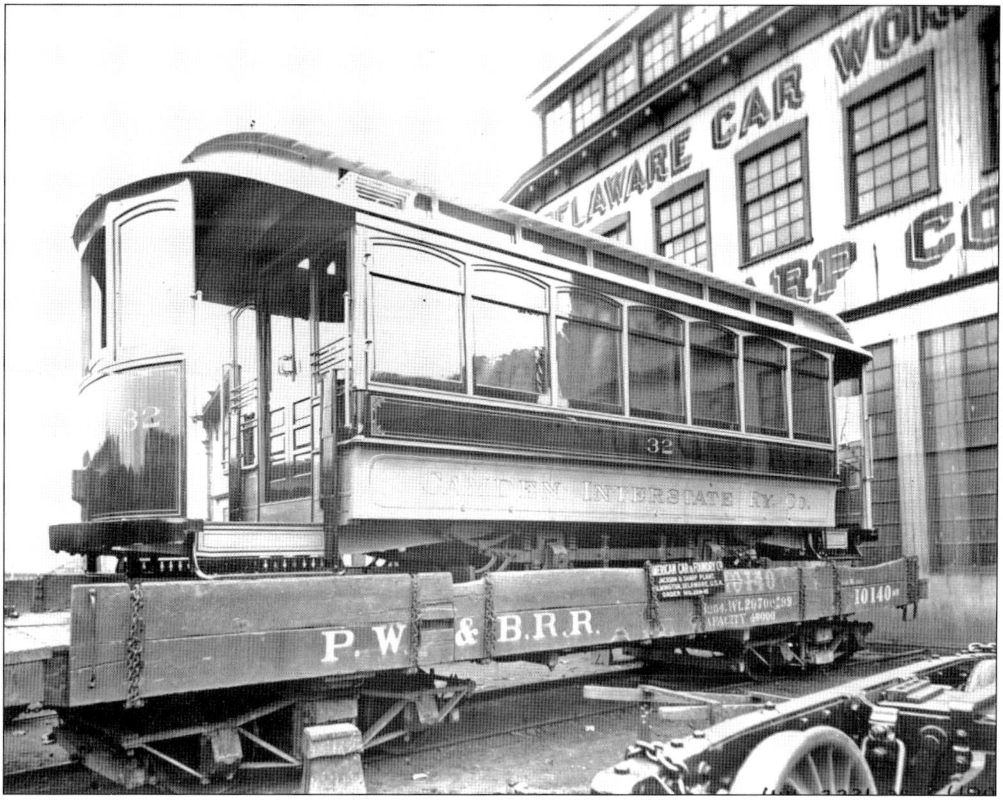

Jackson & Sharp, a manufacturer of railcars and boats, was begun in April 1863 by Job Jackson (1833–1901) and Jacob Sharp (1815–1888). Jackson worked at Harlan & Hollingsworth before teaming up with Sharp to run their own company along the Christina River at the foot of East Eighth Street. Its first cars were produced in 1865 for the Chicago Great Western Railroad.

This is an exterior view of a railcar for the Wilmington, Chester & Philadelphia Railroad. Sharp retired in 1870, but the company continued, building the first narrow-gauge cars in the country for the Denver & Rio Grande Railway in 1871. This innovation put the manufacturer's product in high demand with railroad companies that crossed mountainous terrain. (Courtesy of Delaware Historical Society.)

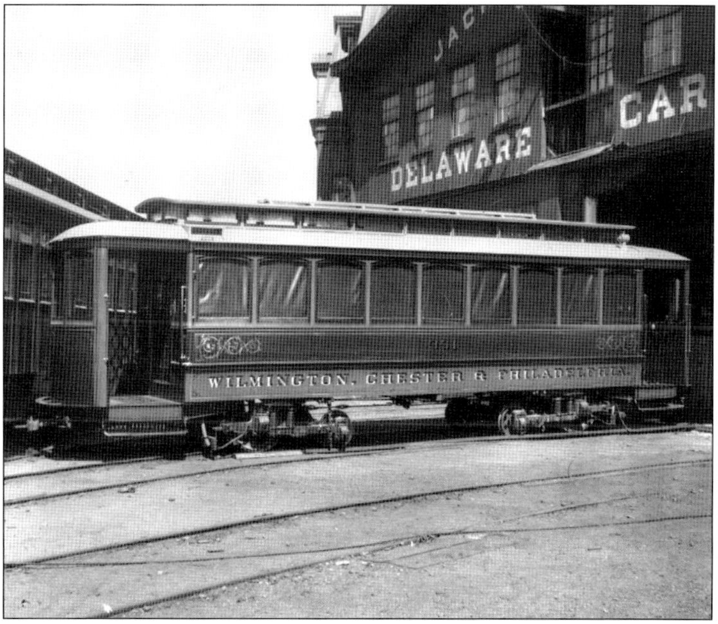

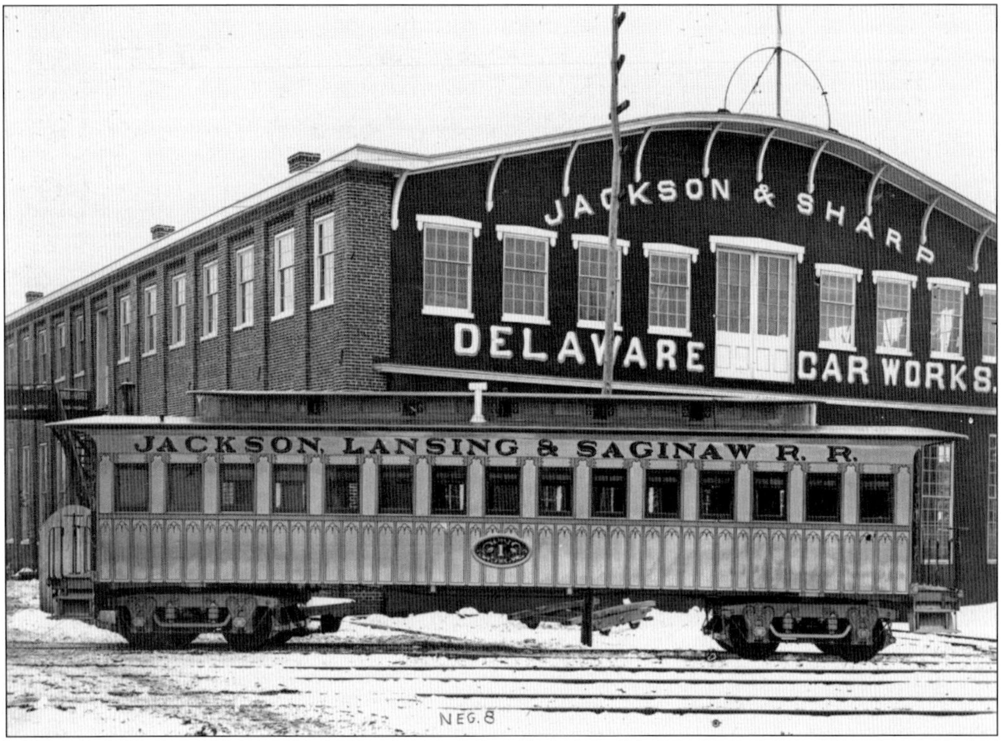

By 1882, Jackson & Sharp covered 25 acres, not counting its shipyard, and called itself "the largest passenger car manufacturer in the country." Its products included diner, freight, mail-baggage, parlor, passenger, private, and sleeper cars, as well as those exported to foreign countries. The company built a variety of ships between 1884 and 1946, including ferry boats, naval vessels (especially during World War I and World War II), yachts and other pleasure craft, schooners, freighters, passenger ships, tanker steamships, barges, dredges, and tugboats. Jackson & Sharp was unique in that it photographed all its trains and ships.

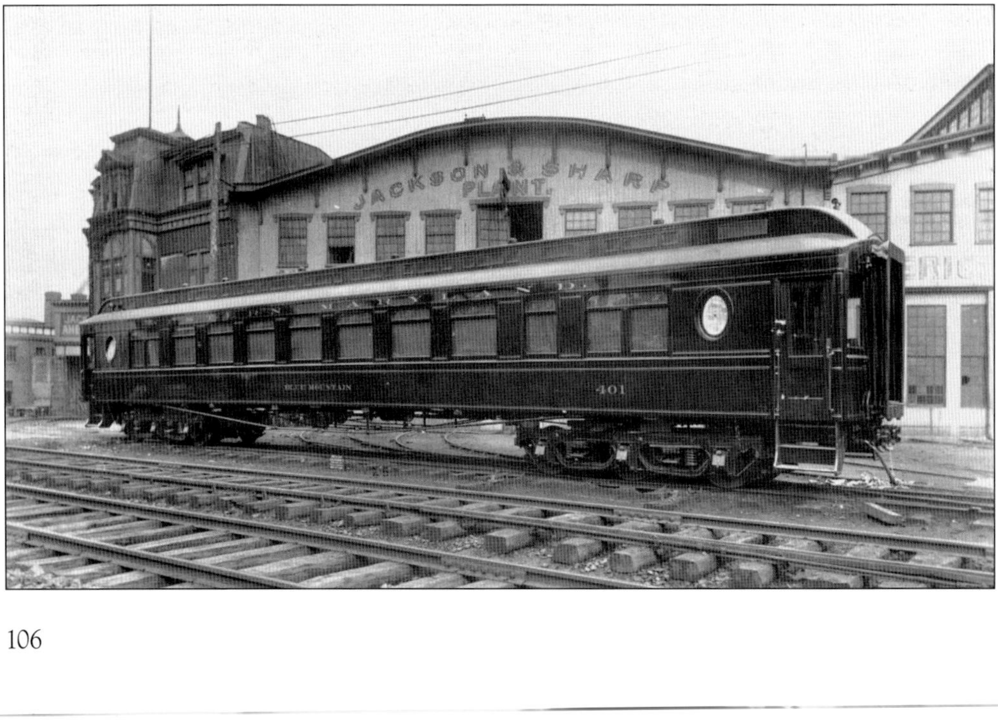

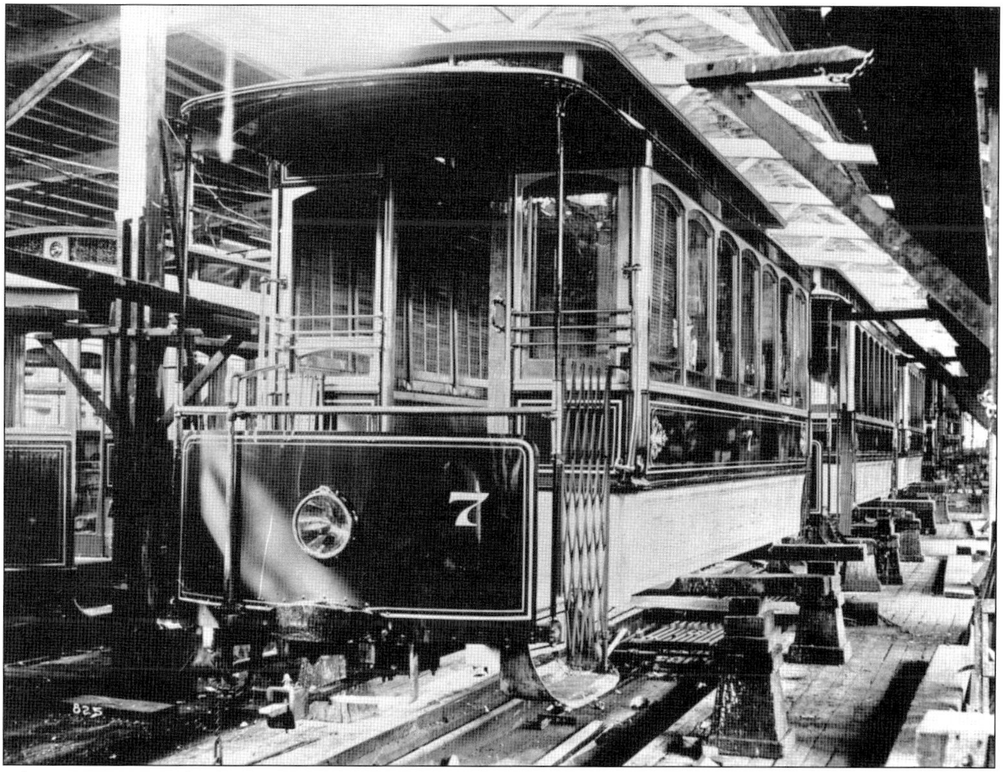

This view is inside the Jackson & Sharp manufacturing facility. During the 1880s, Jackson & Sharp produced around 400 passenger cars per year, employing 1,000 men. The company also built sleeper cars when it acquired the Woodruff Sleeping Car Company. (Courtesy of Delaware Historical Society.)

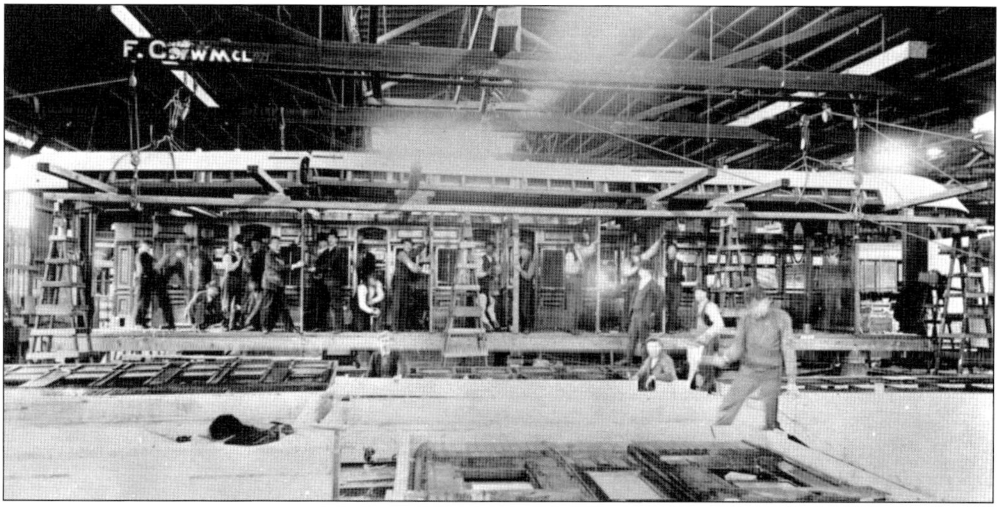

At the 1876 Philadelphia Centennial Exhibition, the company received the Centennial Award for its passenger, boudoir, and library cars. It also received the gold medal for elegance and design and superior workmanship at the 1881 Cotton International Exhibition in Atlanta and another gold medal at the 1883 Chicago Exposition of Railroad Appliances. (Courtesy of Delaware Historical Society.)

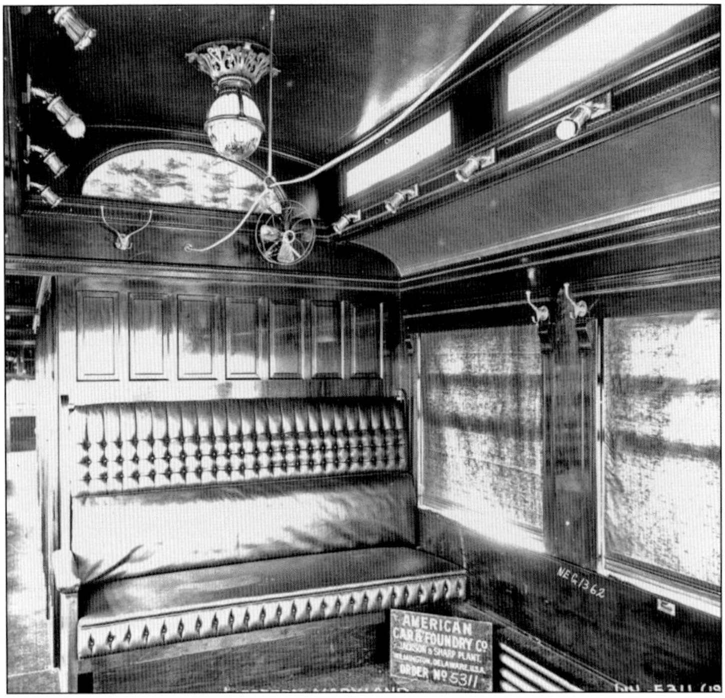

The interior of a Jackson & Sharp car was considered the finest in the country, and the company built many private cars for wealthy Americans and foreign nobility. It was especially known for its interiors that featured cherry, black walnut, and mahogany. Note the little electric fan above the seat—an added feature for comfort—and the ornate lighting. However, in a time of racial segregation, passenger cars were labeled for "white" use only or "colored" use only.

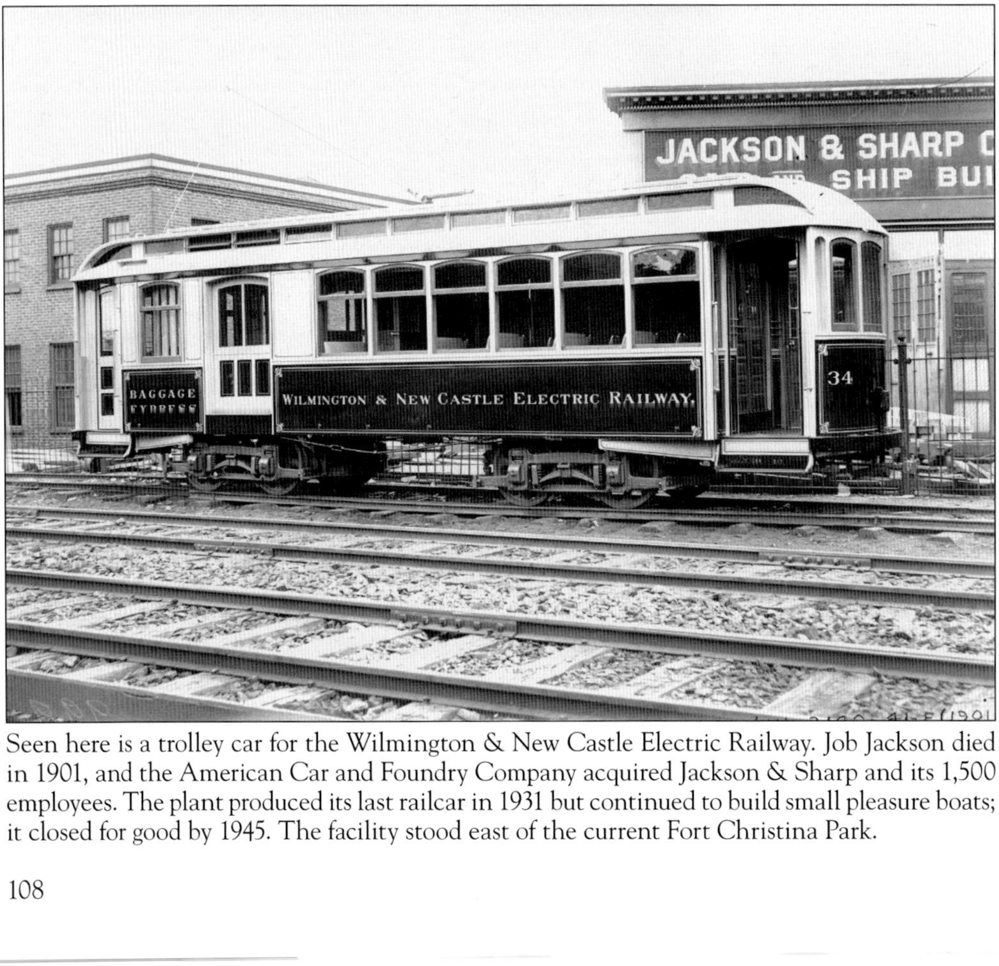

Seen here is a trolley car for the Wilmington & New Castle Electric Railway. Job Jackson died in 1901, and the American Car and Foundry Company acquired Jackson & Sharp and its 1,500 employees. The plant produced its last railcar in 1931 but continued to build small pleasure boats; it closed for good by 1945. The facility stood east of the current Fort Christina Park.

Five

Fort Christina Park

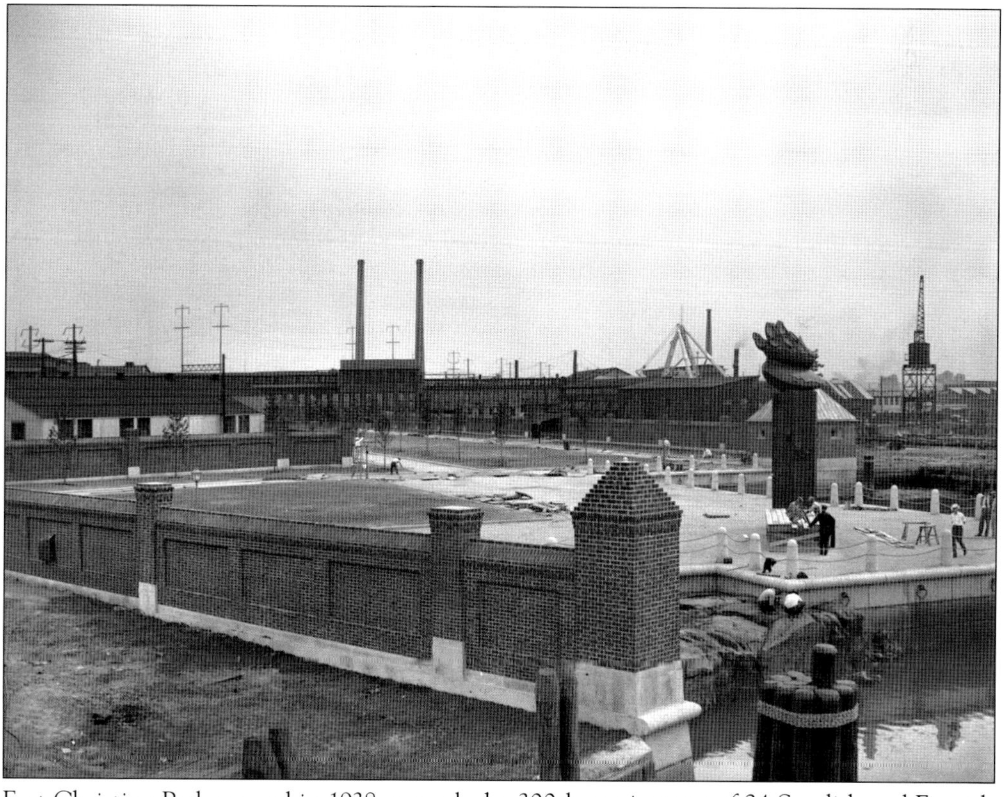

Fort Christina Park opened in 1938 to mark the 300th anniversary of 24 Swedish and Finnish settlers arriving at "the Rocks" on board the *Kalmar Nyckel* and *Fogel Grip* on March 29, 1638. The expedition was led by Peter Minuit (1580–1638), who named the colony Nya Sverige (New Sweden). The settlers' arrival signified Sweden's attempt to colonize the new world, but Sweden's efforts never matched those of Holland, Spain, France, or Great Britain. However, New Sweden is credited with founding Wilmington, Delaware, and with bringing the log cabin to America.

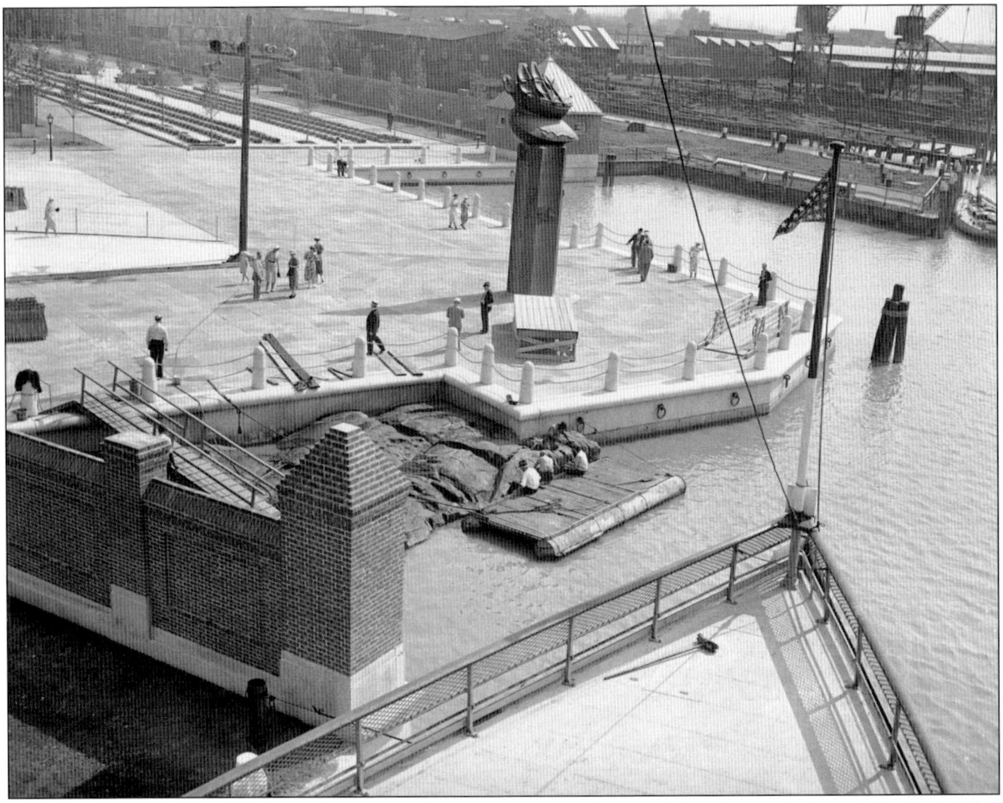

Swedish sculptor Carl Milles (1875–1955) created the 25-foot-tall granite monument seen in the photograph and topped it with a representation of the *Kalmar Nyckel* (Key of Kalmar), one of the settlers' two ships. Peter Minuit named Fort Christina and the Christina River after Sweden's child queen. Queen Christina (1626–1689) had little interest in ruling and stunned her nation when she abdicated the throne and converted to Catholicism in 1654.

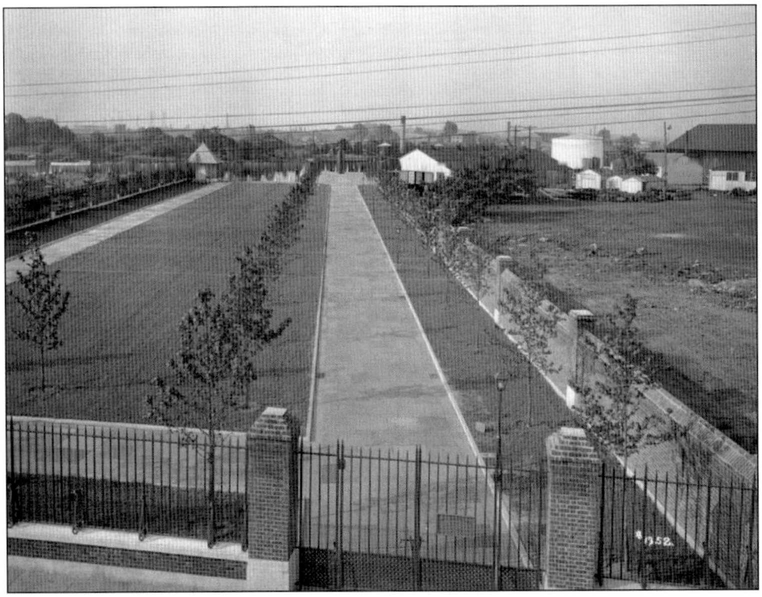

This 1938 view of Fort Christina Park is looking toward the river. The Dutch-built *Kalmar Nyckel* made four trips to the New World, bringing more than 600 Scandinavians. A sister-cities program between Kalmar, Sweden, and Wilmington, Delaware, was established in 1963.

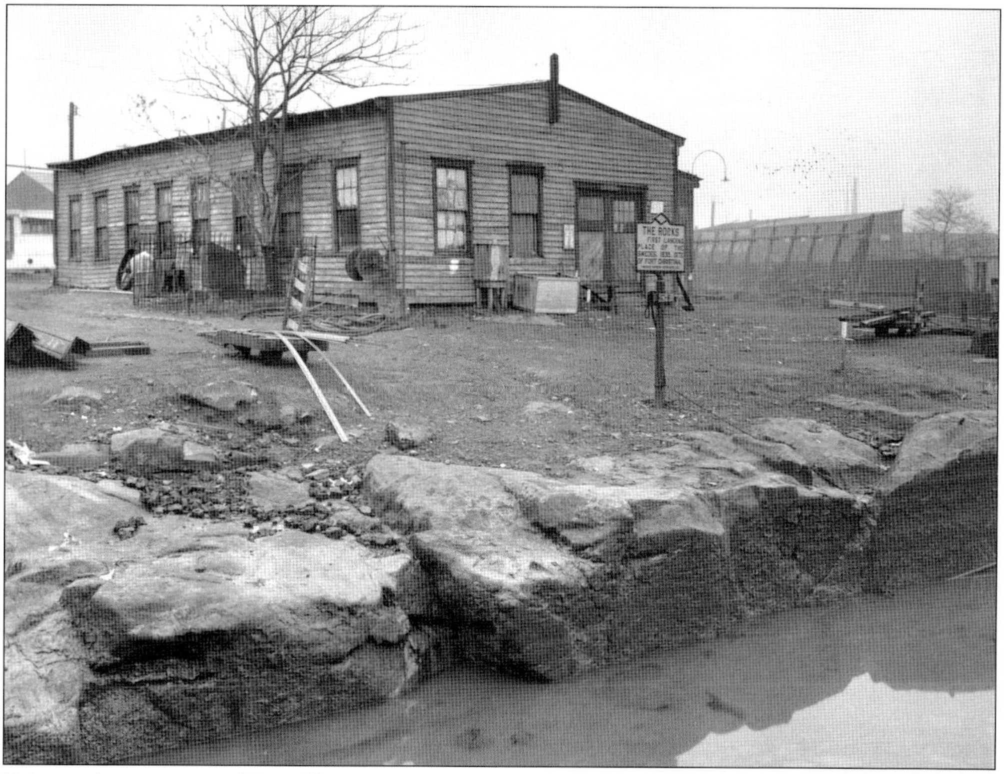

Prior to the creation of Fort Christina Park, the land by "the Rocks" belonged to the defunct McCullough Iron Company. The location's historical significance was then marked by a sign in front of the building and an engraved stone from the Delaware Society of Colonial Dames that stood within a fence next to the building. The Delaware State Highway Department (now DELDOT) cleared the site, built the seawalls and brick enclosure walls, and installed sewers, public walkways, a service building, and landscaping.

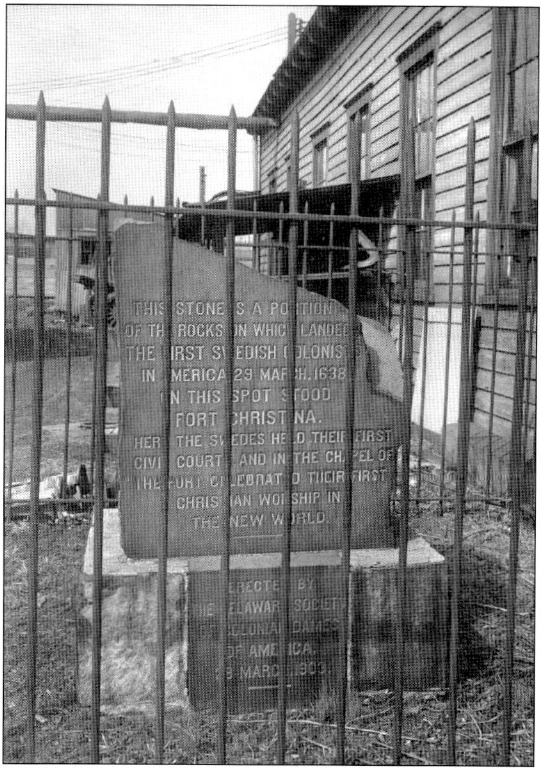

This engraved stone to mark the location of Fort Christina was dedicated on March 25, 1903. The speaker at the event was Delaware chief justice Charles B. Lore (1831–1911), a descendant of the Delaware Swedes. The stone is now part of the brick enclosure wall at Fort Christina Park.

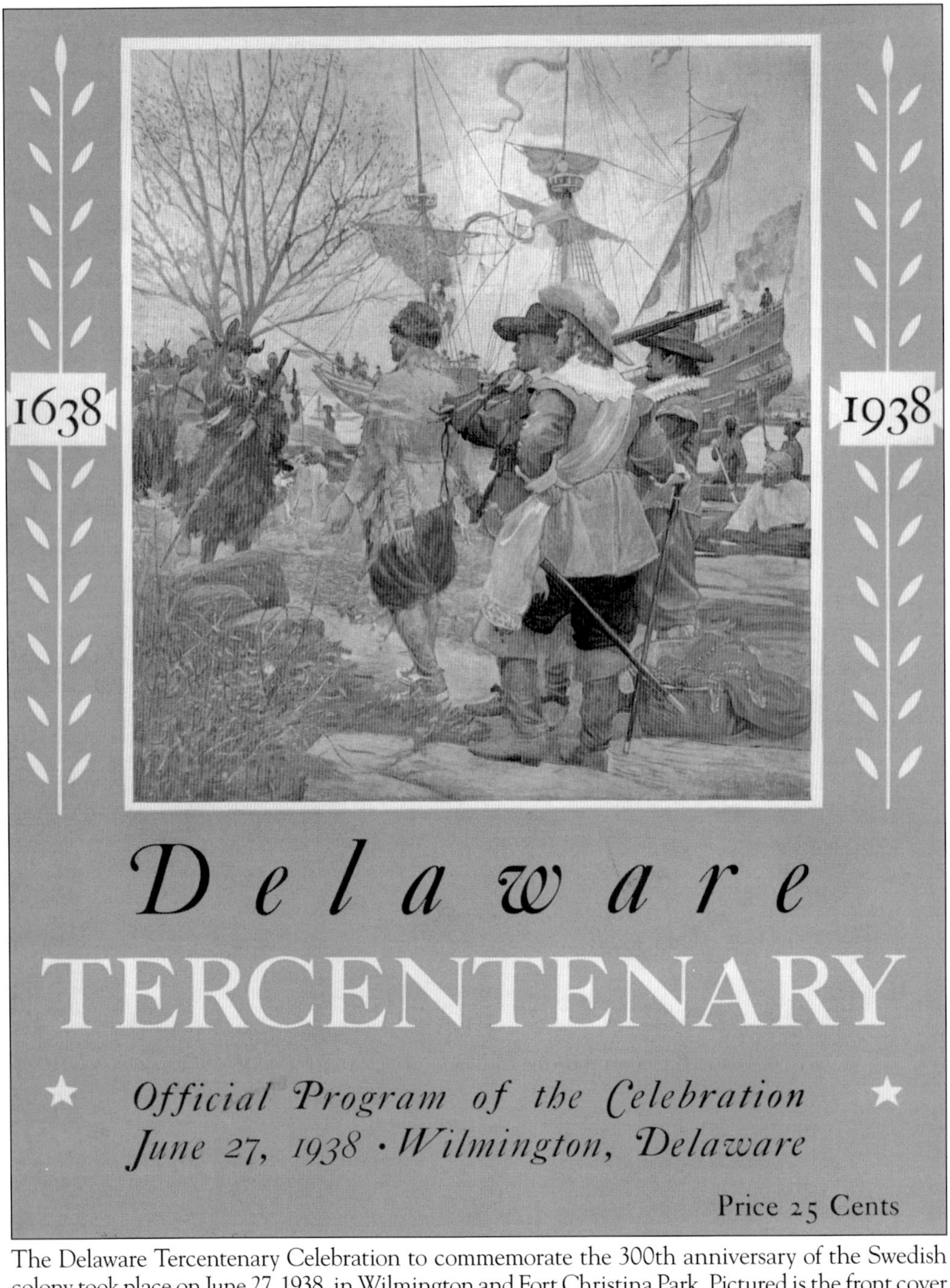

The Delaware Tercentenary Celebration to commemorate the 300th anniversary of the Swedish colony took place on June 27, 1938, in Wilmington and Fort Christina Park. Pictured is the front cover of the official program. It features the Stanley M. Arthurs painting of the Swedish landing, which was also used on a commemorative 3¢ stamp issued by the Post Office Department. The painting depicts the meeting of the Swedes and local natives with whom Peter Minuit made a treaty before firing a two-cannon salute and claiming all the land from the Christina River to Bombay Hook for Sweden. The program gives a brief history of New Sweden, photographs of the expected dignitaries, images of Wilmington in 1938, and a scheduled itinerary of events. (Author's collection.)

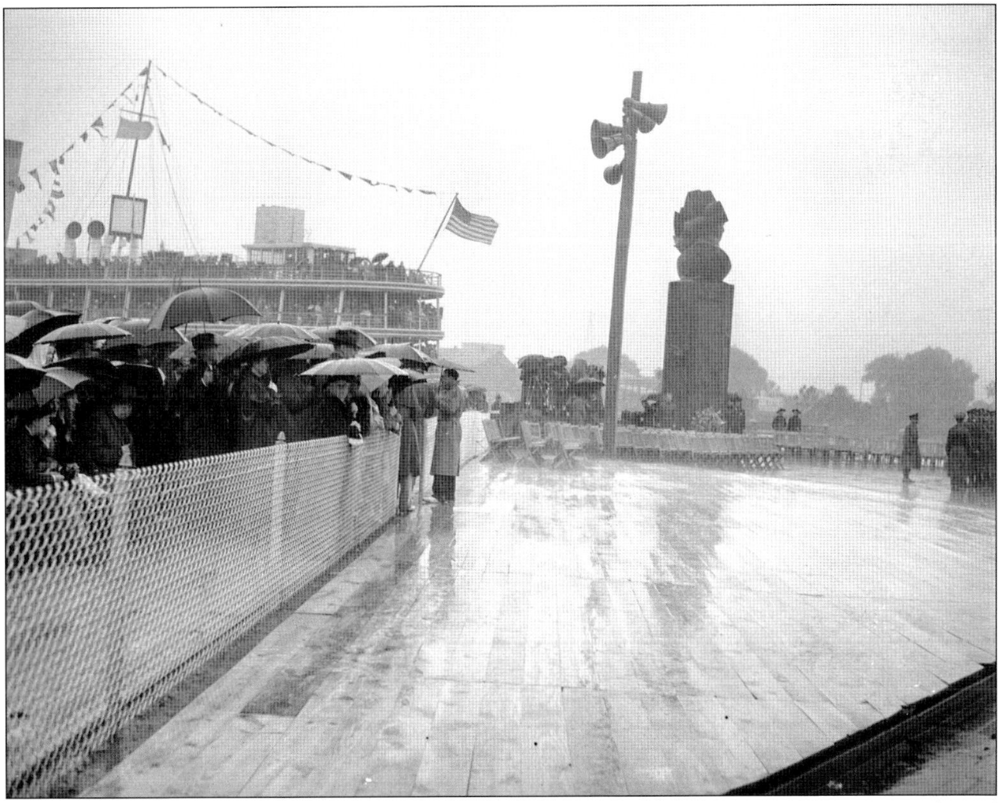

The weather was not ideal for the celebration. People looked on from within the park and from passenger ships. The remembrance of Sweden's lone experiment in the New World can be attributed to a host of people who refused to let it pass into history, particularly Christopher Ward (1868–1943), chairman of the Delaware Tercentenary Commission. After a career as a lawyer, Ward became a civic leader, author, and president of Delaware Historical Society.

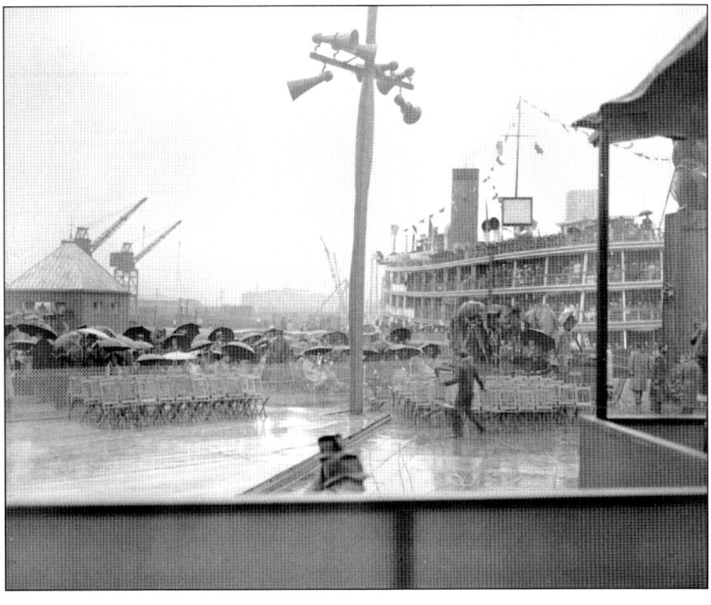

People could only enter the park if they had a ticket. Scheduled at 10:00, the Swedish Royal Commission, headed by Crown Prince Bertil, was presented to Pres. Franklin Roosevelt and to Gov. Richard McMullen.

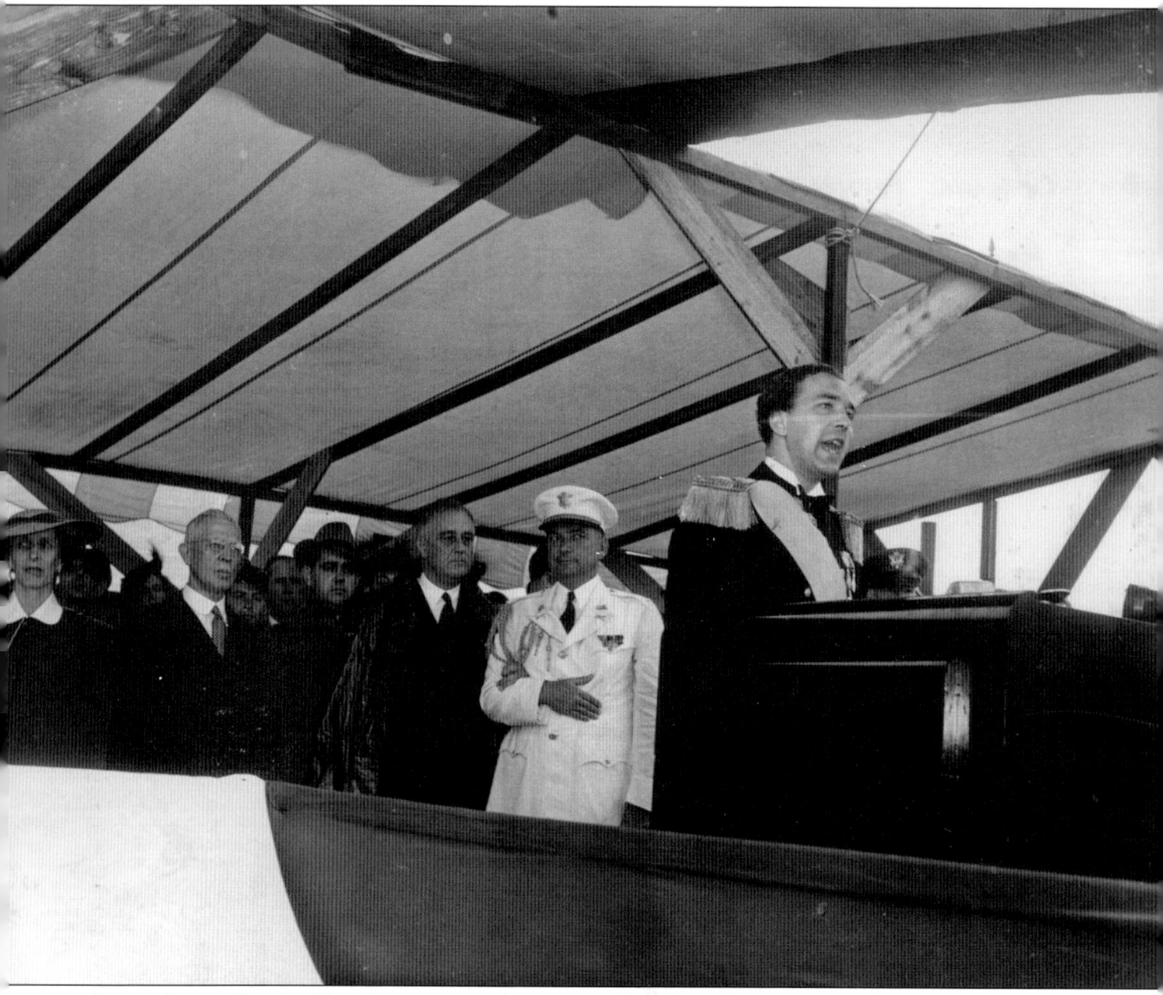

Crown Prince Bertil of Sweden is seen making a speech at Fort Christina Park during the dedication of the Carl Milles monument. Behind him are, from left to right, Sweden's Crown Princess Louise, Delaware governor Richard McMullen, US president Franklin Roosevelt, Roosevelt aide Colonel Watson, and at the podium Sweden's Crown Prince Bertil. Crown Princess Louise's husband, Crown Prince Gustaf Adolf, made the trip to America but was ill and unable to attend. Pres. Franklin Roosevelt accepted the Milles monument on behalf of the American people, saying, "I accept with profound gratitude, in behalf of the people of the United States, this noble monument placed here through the generosity of the people of Sweden. I am confident that to generations yet unborn in Sweden and in the United States it will typify close association and continued good will between our two nations."

At 4:00 p.m., the parade of floats depicting the history of Delaware commenced in downtown Wilmington. Seen here marching past the US Post Office, Courthouse & Customhouse at Rodney Square is a float containing a model of the *Kalmar Nyckel*.

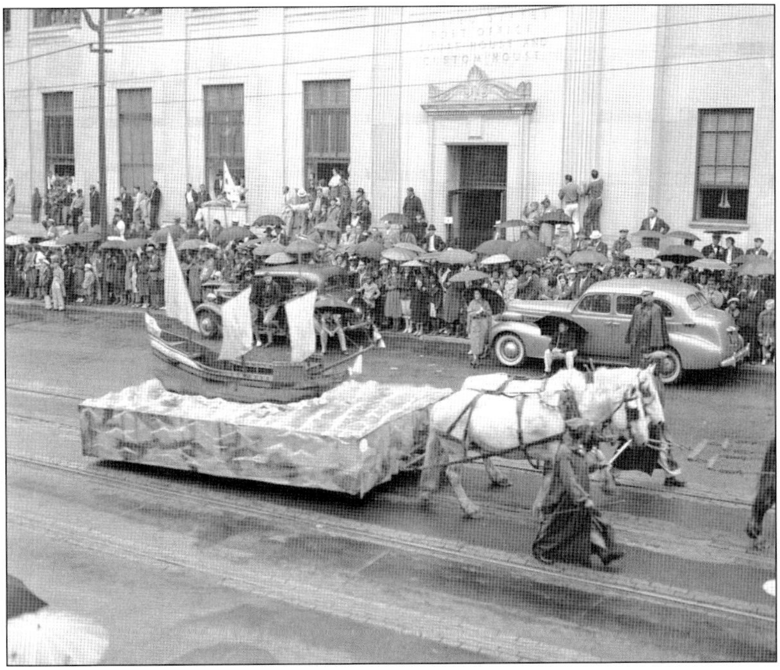

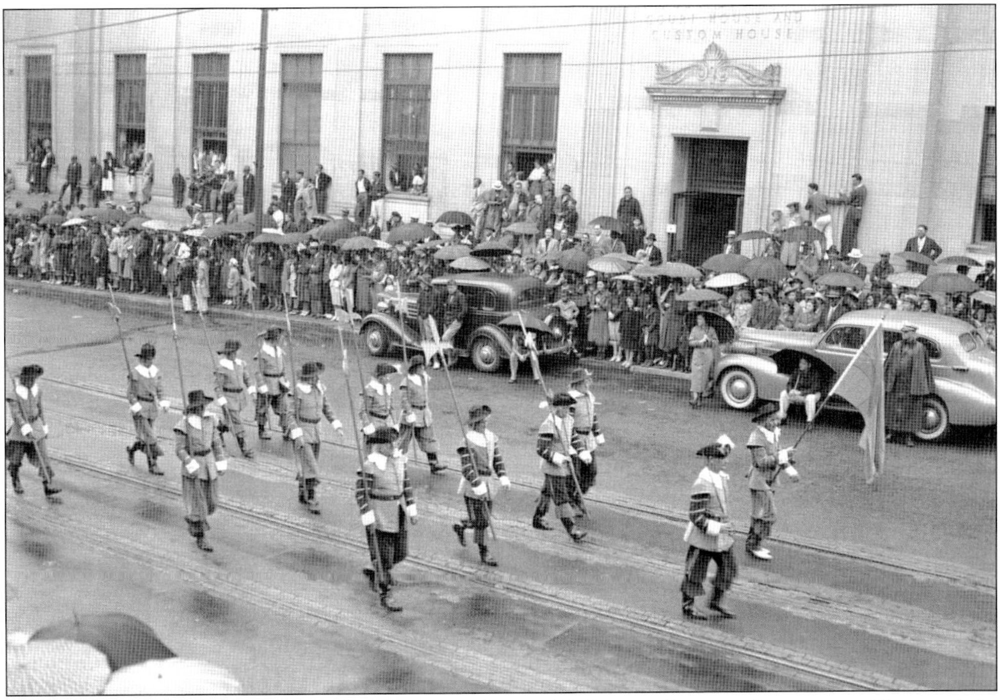

Johan Printz (1592–1663) arrived at New Sweden in 1643 as its first royal governor. He stood six feet tall and weighed 400 pounds. Under his tumultuous 10-year leadership, New Sweden built additional forts and expanded its territory along the Delaware River. Printz built his own manor house on Tinicum Island in 1646. Freemen of the colony complained about his autocratic rule, and with tensions mounting, he returned to Sweden. There is a poem that goes, "No Governor of Delaware / Before or since / Has weighed as much as Johan Printz."

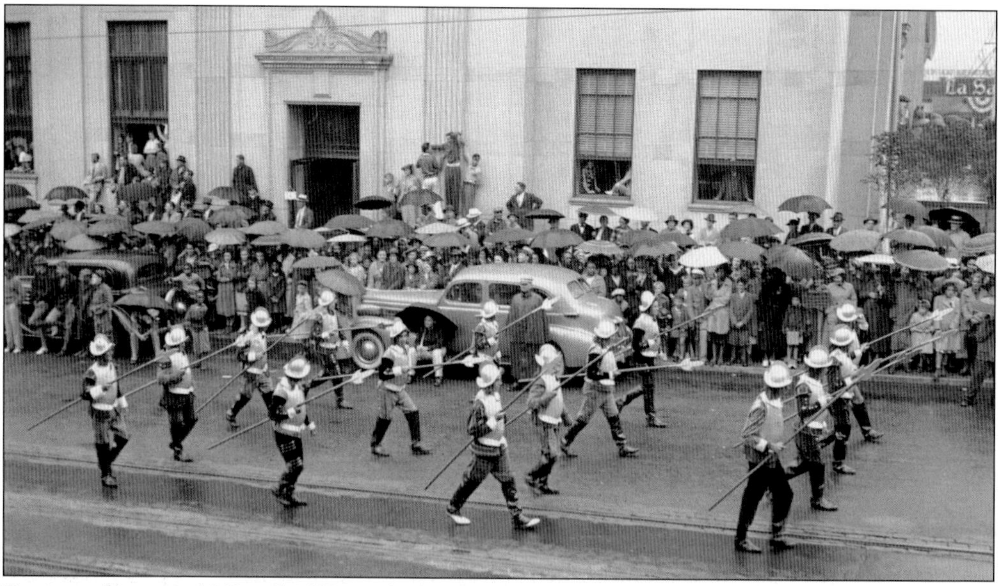

Between the years 1648 and 1653, no ships arrived, and the colony seemed abandoned by its home country. But in 1655, a ship and new governor, Johan Rising, arrived with 300 colonists, and a town with regular streets, called Christinahamn, was created. However, New Sweden would soon surrender to the Dutch without a shot fired.

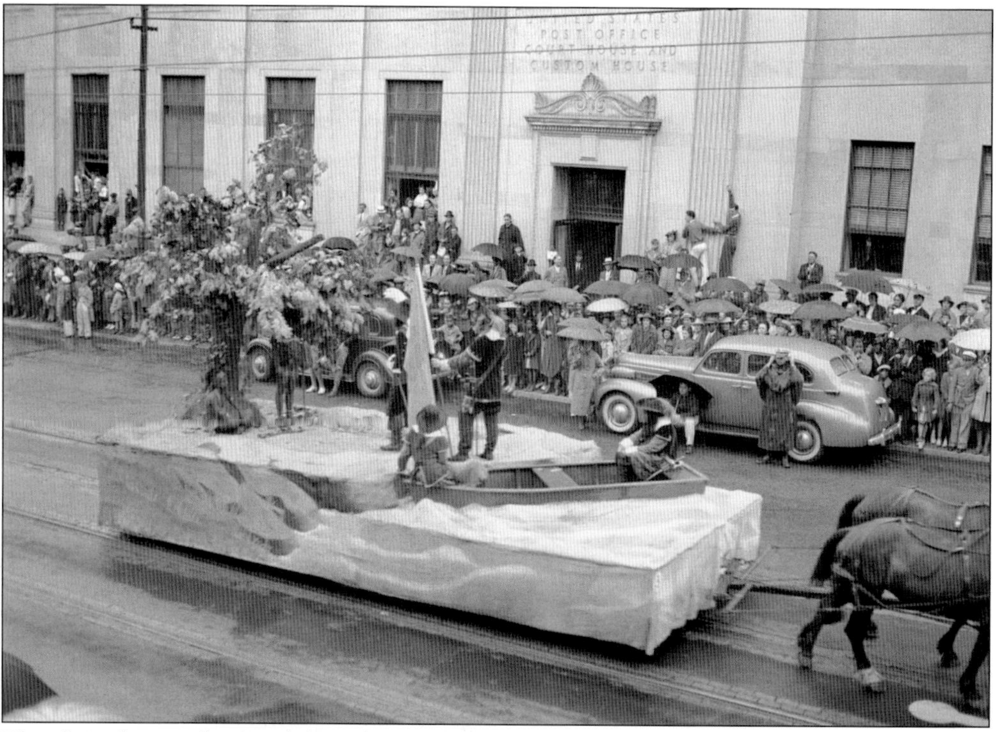

This float depicts the Swedish and Finnish settlers encountering the native population. New Sweden is also credited with the arrival of the first known African settler in Delaware, Antoni "Anthony" Swart. He arrived on the *Fogel Grip* from the West Indies in 1639 and became a freeman and an employee of Governor Printz.

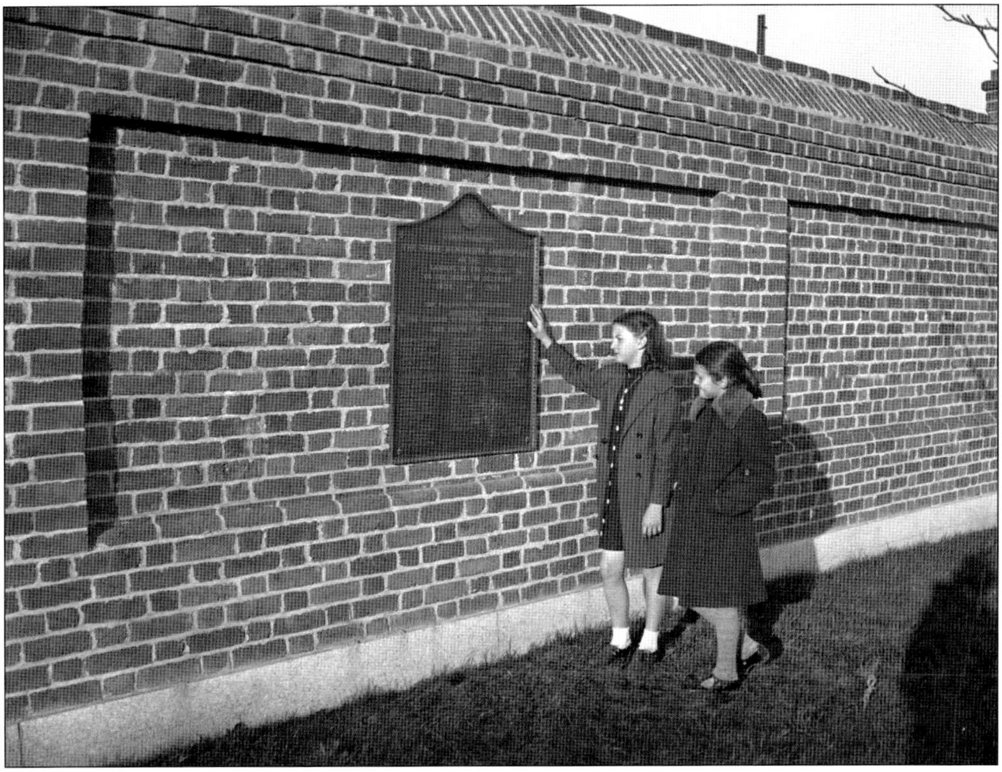

Two unidentified girls read a commemorative plaque from the State of California that hung on part of the brick enclosure wall. The park opened to visitors and tourists after the celebration and remains a historic landmark at the foot of Seventh Street in Wilmington.

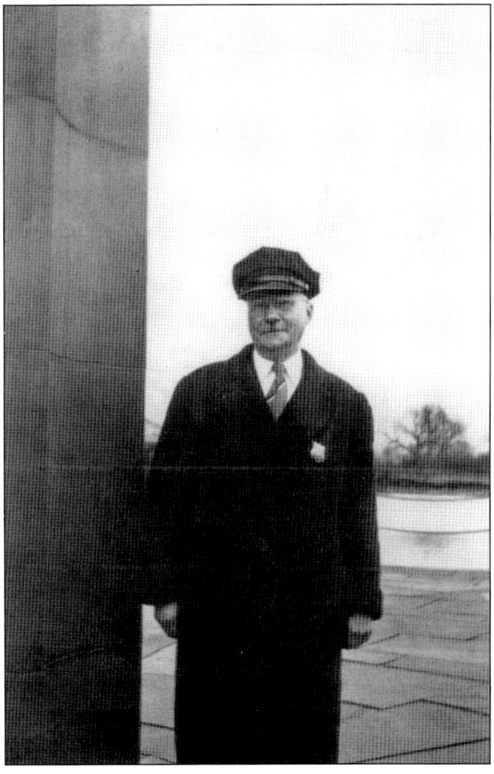

August Martin Anderson (1877–1957), photographed here by his daughter on April 6, 1941, came to the United States in 1903 from Ystad, Sweden. A machinist by trade, he was the only full-time guard at Fort Christina Park from 1941 to 1948. He was also secretary of the Vasa Order District Lodge of Pennsylvania and presented a lithograph by artist David Reyam showing the development of Old Swedes Church to Crown Prince Bertil. (Photograph by Thelma Knight, courtesy of Bruce D. Knight.)

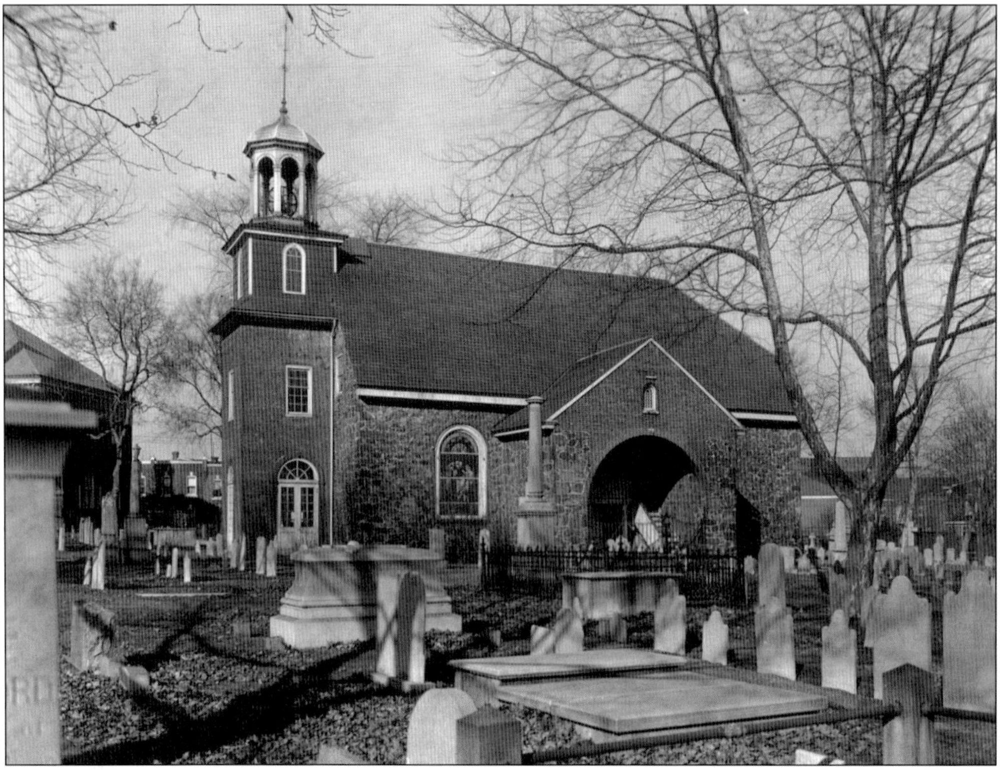

A short walk up Seventh Street from Fort Christina Park is the Old Swedes Holy Trinity Church, built of Brandywine River stones and bricks from Sweden in 1698 and dedicated on Holy Trinity Sunday, July 4, 1699. Holy Trinity is the oldest Christian congregation in the Delaware Valley, tracing its origins to 1640. Eric Björk led the Christina congregation to build the church at the old burial grounds of Fort Christina. Below is the church's interior. Also on the grounds, but not pictured, is the stone Hendrickson House from 1690, now a museum of the New Sweden colony. The Henrickson House was moved here in 1959, having been built originally in 1690 on Crum Creek in Ridley Township, Pennsylvania. (Both, courtesy of Delaware Historical Society.)

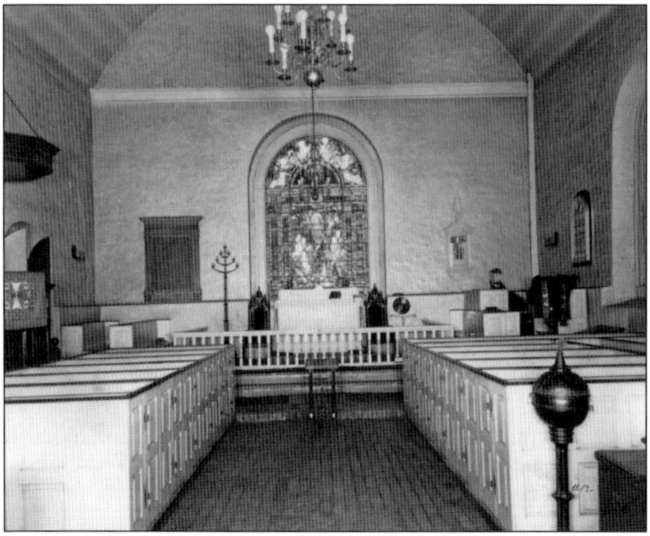

Six

Port of Wilmington

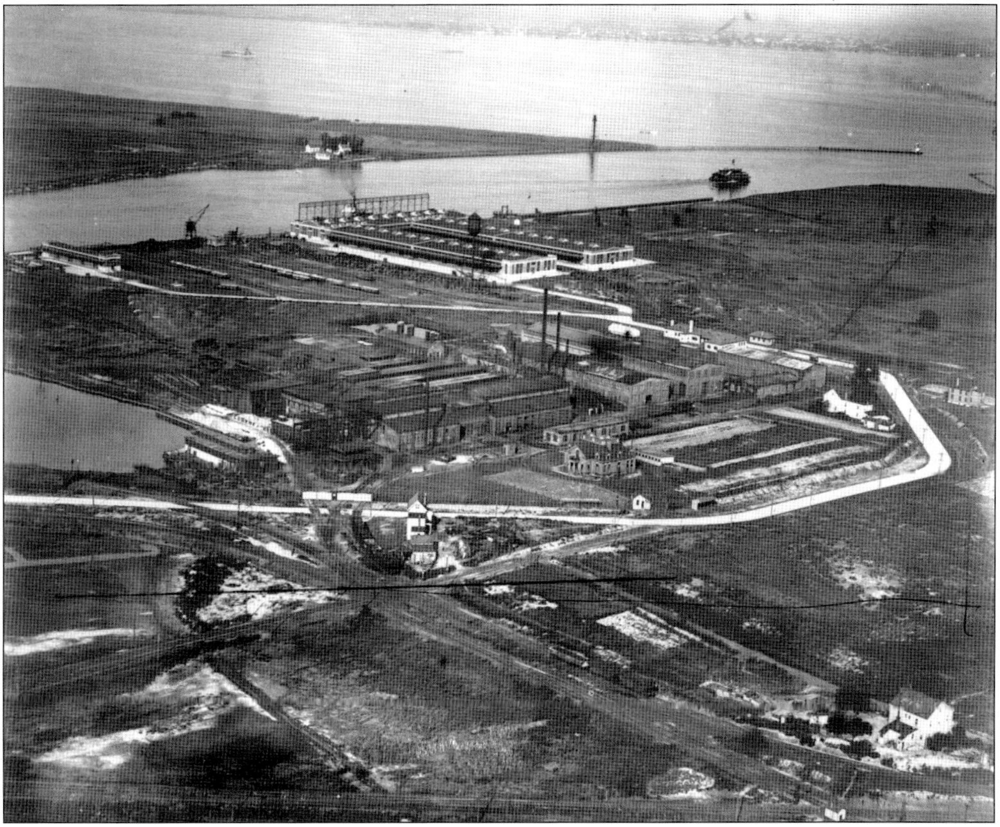

In 1913, the citizens of Wilmington voted in favor of constructing a deepwater port at the mouth of the Christina River to give Wilmington an international seaport that would support the local shipbuilders and railcar manufacturers. Seven years later, the city purchased 101 acres from the Lobdell Car Wheel Company for $2.5 million. The Lobdell Car Wheel Company, seen in the foreground of this 1926 aerial shot, produced its last wheel in 1940. (Courtesy of the Hagley Museum and Library.)

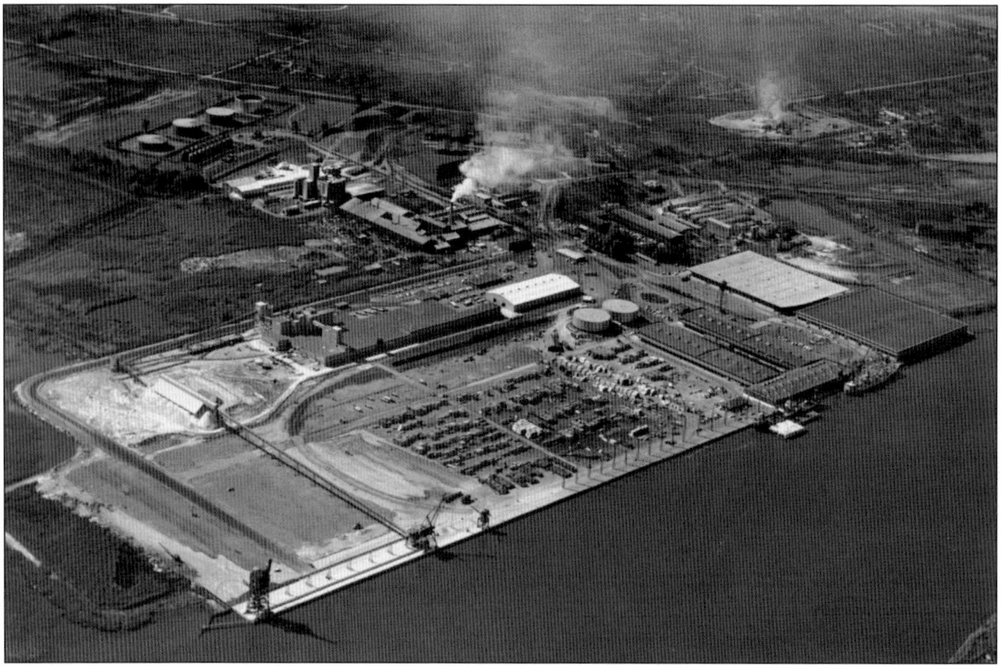

Then called the Wilmington Marine Terminal and owned by the City of Wilmington, the port opened for business in 1923 with three cranes of five- to thirty-ton capacity, able to handle shipments of lumber and wood pulp, lead, ore, fertilizer, and petroleum products.

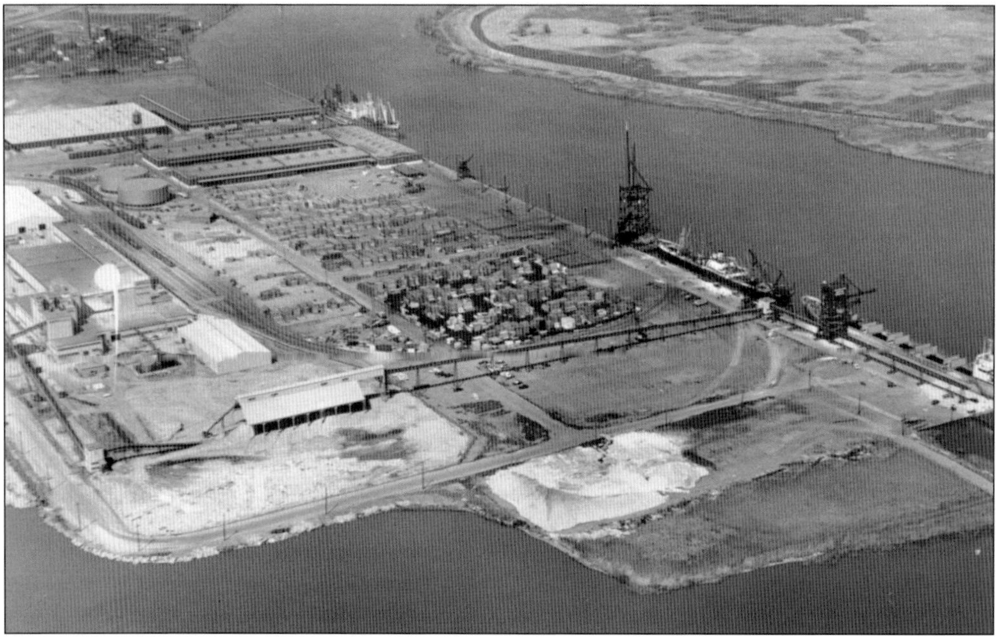

The aerial photograph shows the marine terminal in 1966. Five years earlier, the dock had been extended from 1,000 feet to 3,060 feet to increase its receiving capacity up to seven ships at a time. A gantry crane with a 55-ton capacity had also been added. Also in 1961, the Christina River channel was deepened from 30 feet to 37 feet and widened from 450 feet to 650. (Courtesy of Delaware Historical Society.)

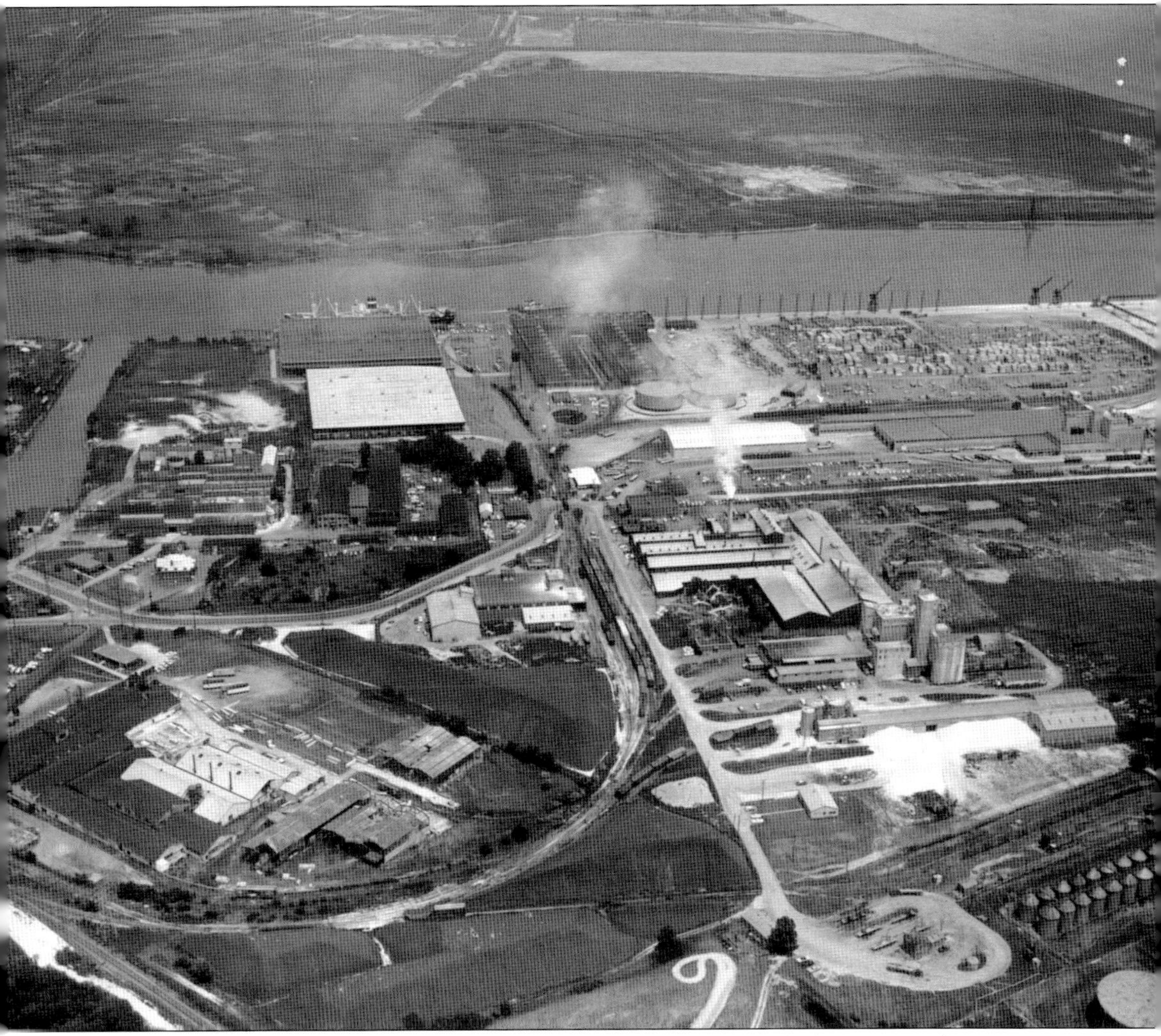

The State of Delaware took ownership of the port in 1995 through the Diamond State Port Corporation. The corporate entity assumed operations of the Port of Wilmington and its related facilities and acquired its obligations from the City of Wilmington. Additionally, the corporation has all the power and authority necessary to maintain and expand the business as necessary. Currently, the port is a full-service deepwater marine terminal that averages 400 vessels annually and an import/export cargo tonnage of more than five million. It has the largest cold-storage warehouse in the nation and is the prime hub for Dole Fresh Fruit Company and Chiquita Fresh North America. Also a major automobile-shipping facility, the Port of Wilmington is the busiest terminal on the Delaware River.

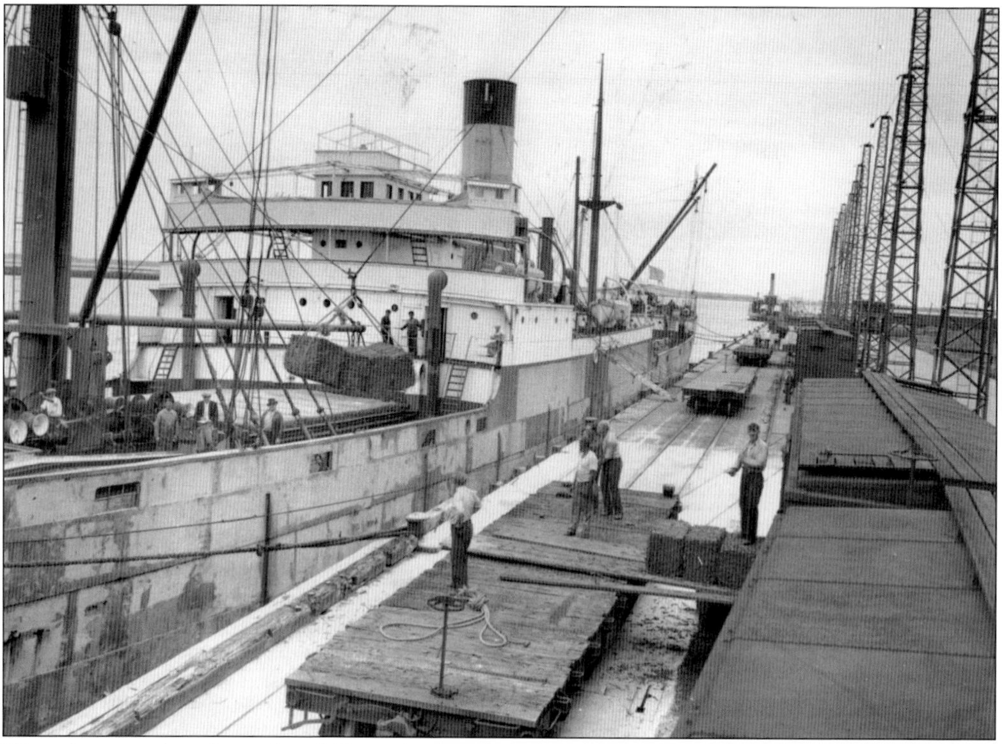

This photograph is from the 1920s and was taken shortly after the marine terminal opened for business. In the 1930s, when the Great Depression hit, the terminal actually saw a rise in tonnage processed—from 230,163 in 1931 to 269,000 in 1934. Also during that period, there was a rise of 39 percent in the number of inbound ships processed, and 52 percent in the number of outbound ships. (Courtesy of Delaware Historical Society.)

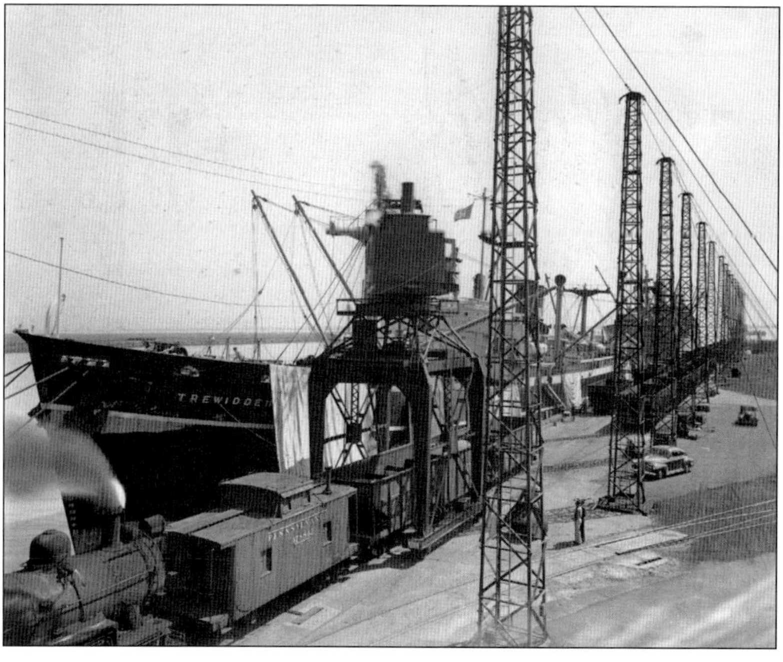

The port has an automobile and Ro-Ro hub berth along the Delaware River. Ro-Ro refers to vessels designed to carry wheeled cargo—such as cars, trucks, and trailers—that are driven on or off the ship on their own wheels. The term is in contrast to Lo-Lo, meaning lift on/lift off and referring to items needing a crane to load and unload.

A busy Wilmington Marine Terminal also involved trains. The Pennsylvania Railroad, the Baltimore & Ohio Railroad, and the Reading Railroad had access to the Wilmington Marine Terminal. The Reading Railroad primarily delivered coal trains and shipped anthracite from Pennsylvania mines.

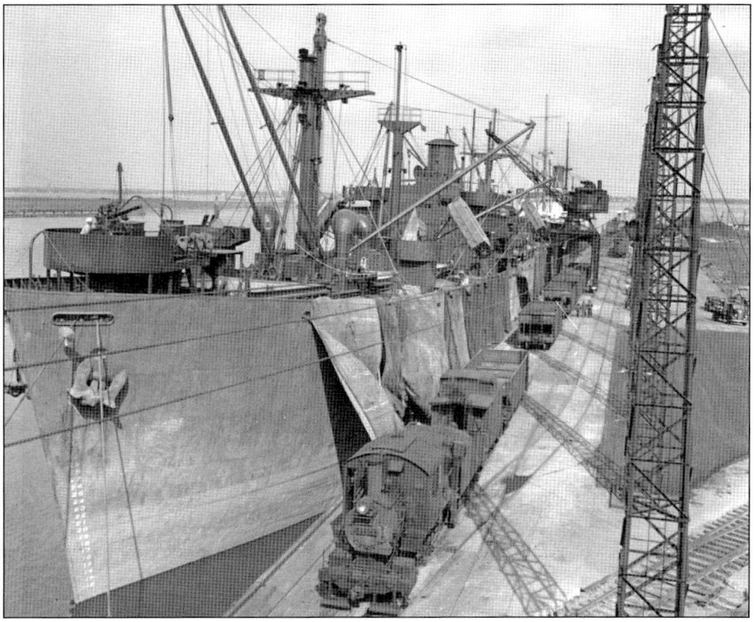

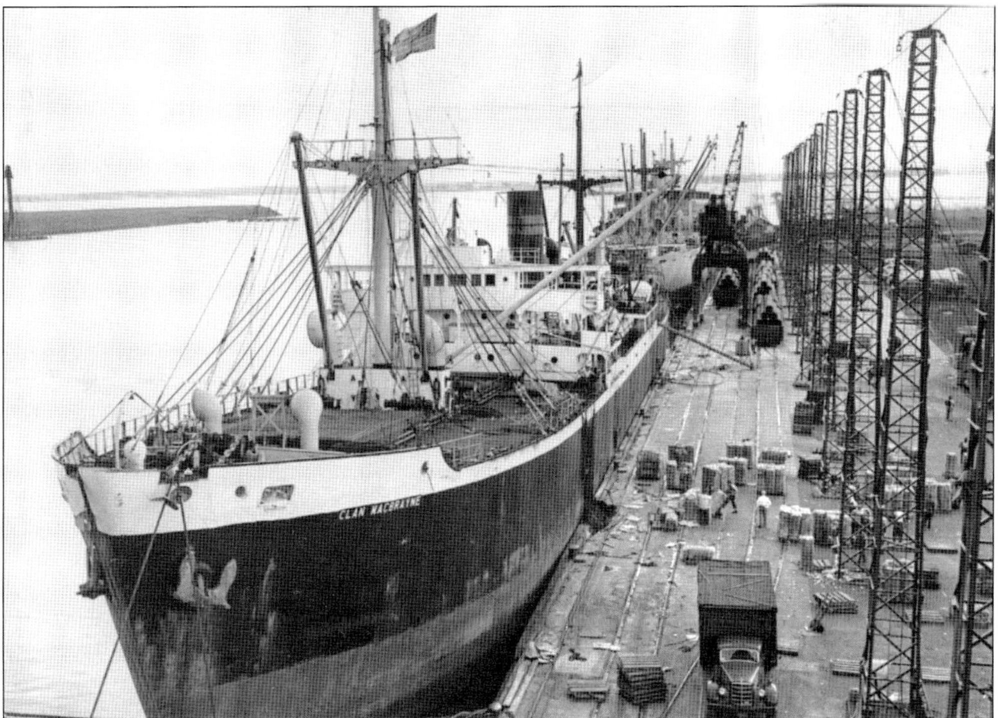

The Wilmington Marine Terminal is seen here in 1950. By 1953, shipments topped 850,000 tons, and two years later, an additional 400-by-420-foot warehouse and new lumber-storage shed opened. Philadelphia has a busy port, but the Port of Wilmington is the busiest on the Delaware because of its service and its proximity to the Atlantic Ocean and the Chesapeake and Delaware Canal, making it a prime location for international trade.

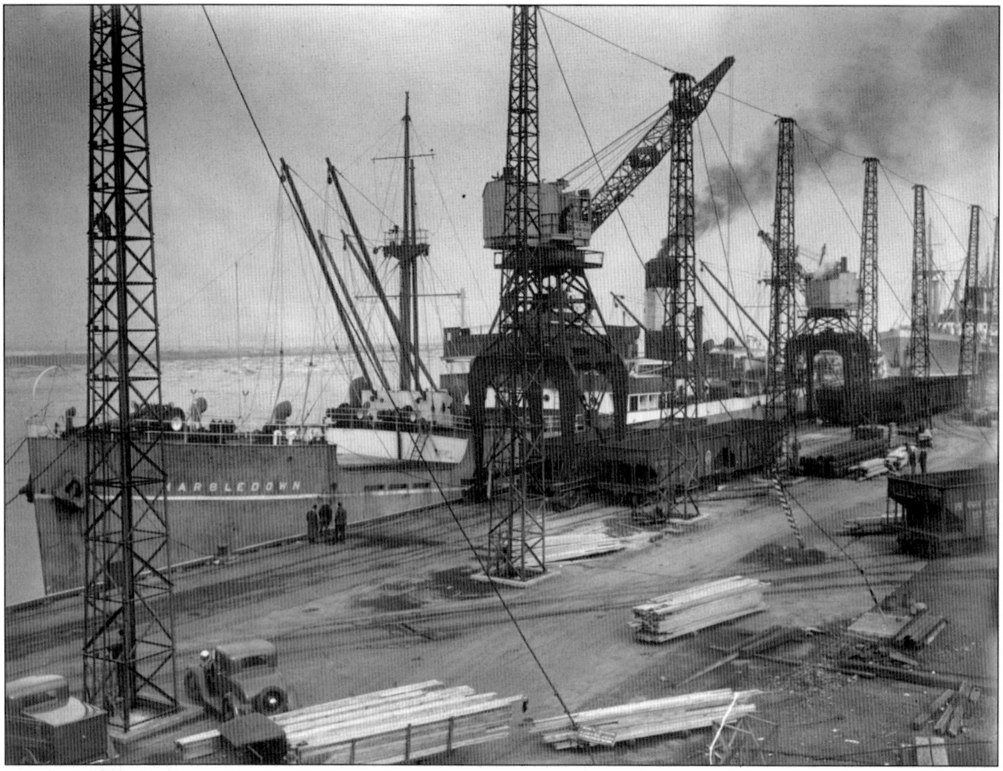

The SS *Harbledown* docked at the Wilmington Marine Terminal in 1936. The British cargo steamer was built in 1933 and was owned by J&C Harrison Limited of London. On April 4, 1941, while en route from Portland, Maine, to London, and carrying 94,157 bushels of wheat, the ship was torpedoed and sunk by a German submarine southwest of Ireland. The attack killed 16 crew members and the master; 23 crew members and one passenger were picked up by the HMS *Veteran* and landed at Liverpool.

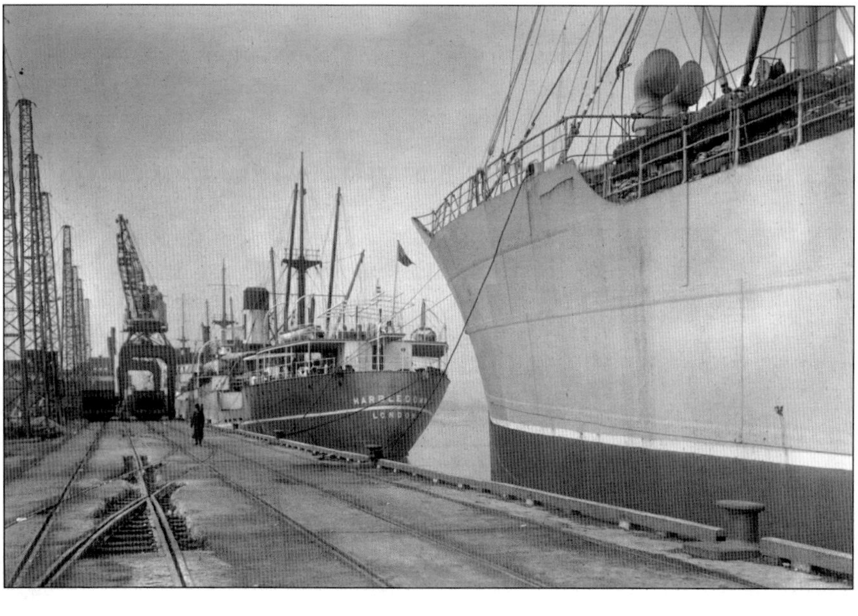

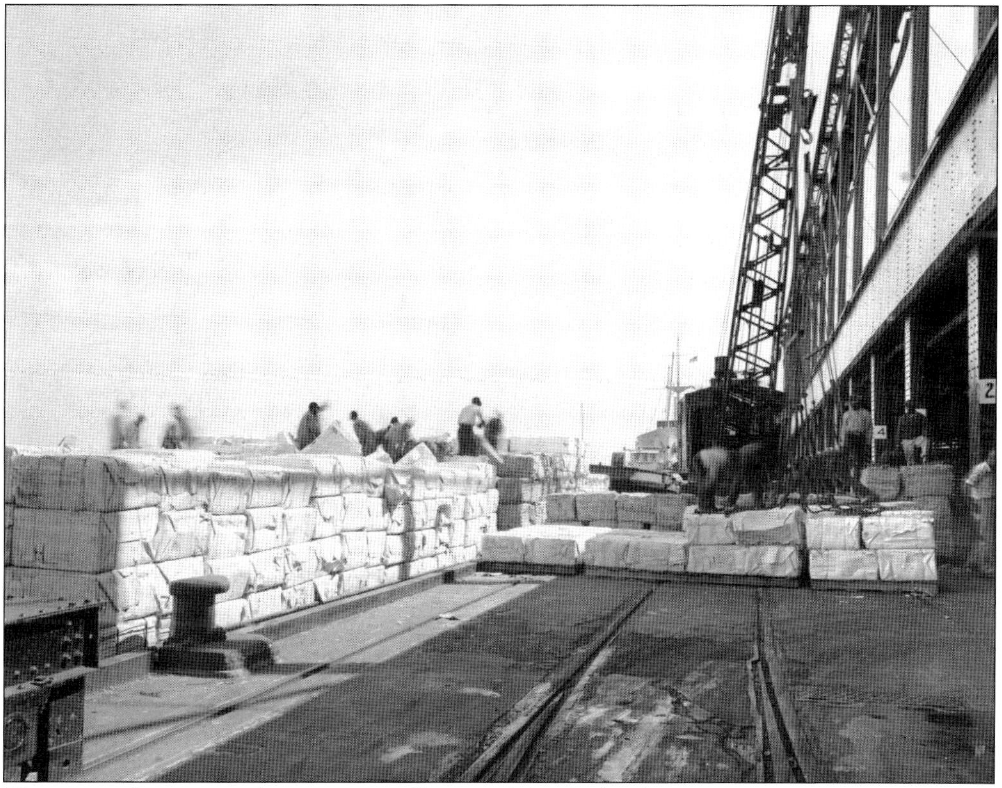

The terminal imports and exports virtually around the clock. The port encompasses over 308 acres and is responsible for 14,600 direct, indirect, and related jobs. It currently produces an annual gross revenue of between $28 million and $32 million, and its busiest season is mid-October through early May, primarily because it handles the winter fruit season from South America. It is the world's largest banana port and the number one gateway for perishable cargo and juice concentrates.

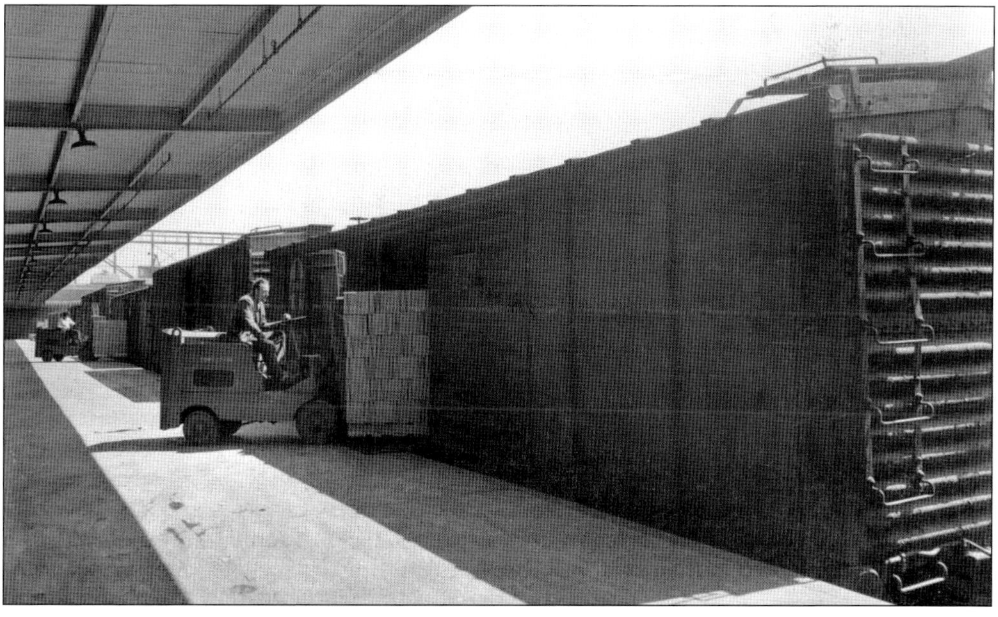

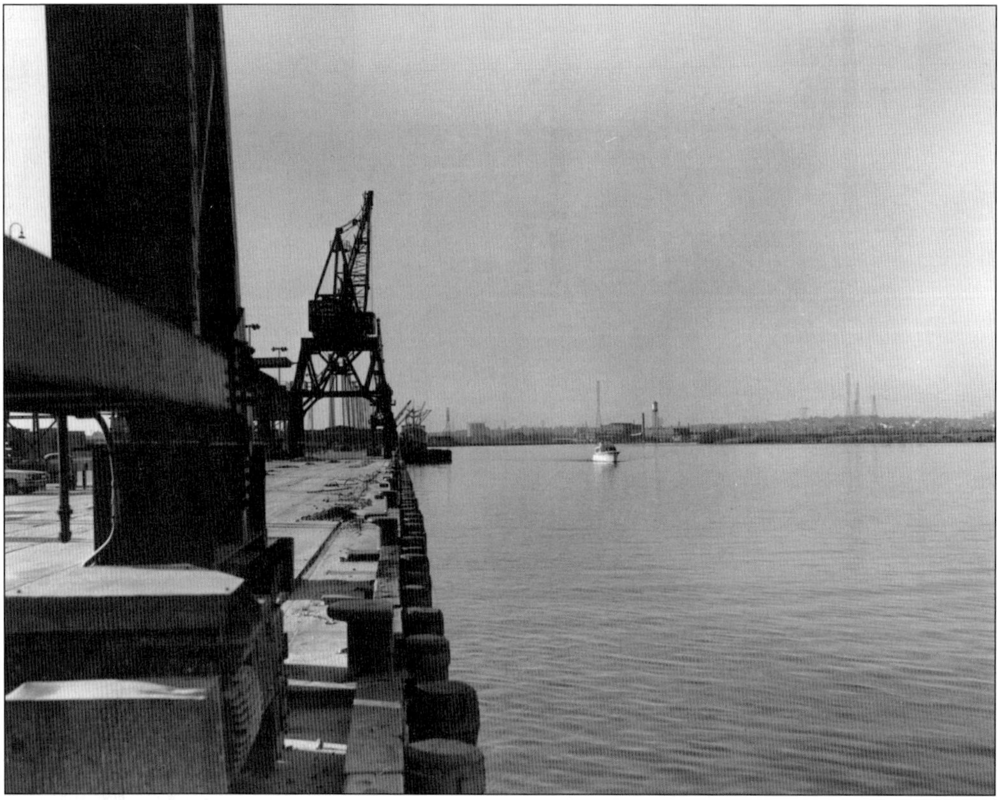

Between Fort Christina Park and the Port of Wilmington, the Brandywine River joins the Christina. The Brandywine's elevation falls from about 160 feet above sea level in Chadds Ford, Pennsylvania, to just a few feet above sea level in Wilmington, and this steep descent provided excellent waterpower for flour milling that put Wilmington flour in high demand before and after the American Revolution; it was also beneficial for the establishment of the original DuPont gunpowder mills.

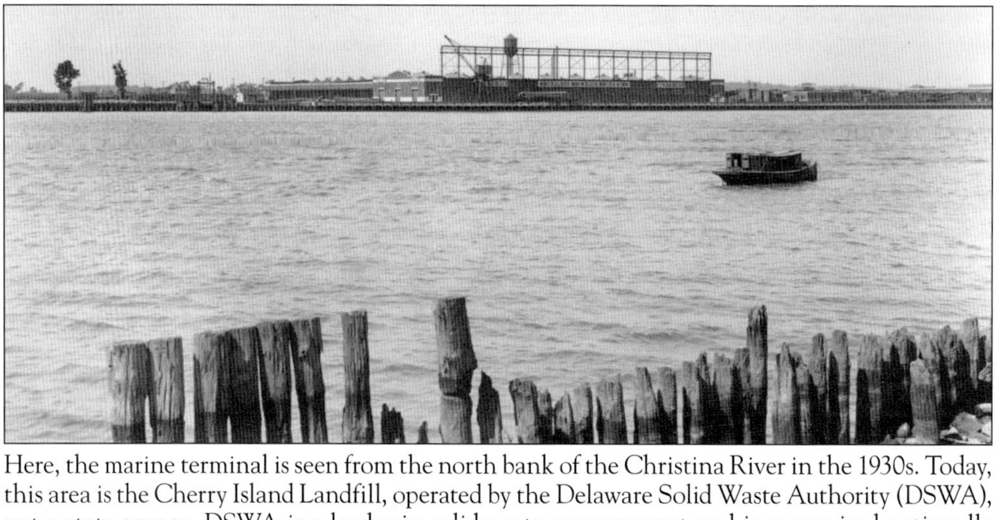

Here, the marine terminal is seen from the north bank of the Christina River in the 1930s. Today, this area is the Cherry Island Landfill, operated by the Delaware Solid Waste Authority (DSWA), not a state agency. DSWA is a leader in solid-waste management and is recognized nationally and internationally for its standard of excellence.

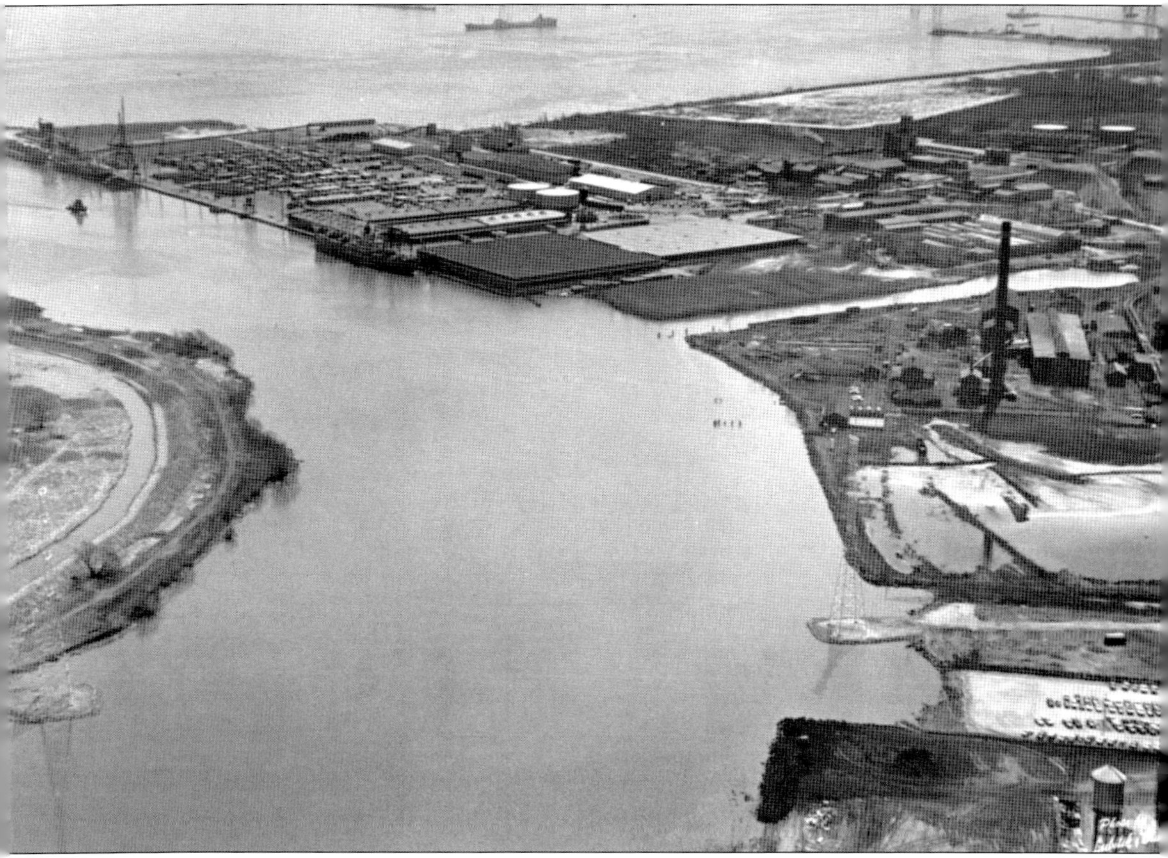

This aerial view of the Christina River as it empties into the Delaware River was taken in 1966, a dozen years before the opening of Interstate 495 and Bridge 1-813 that would cross above the Christina in this area. The Panama Canal is currently being widened to allow for larger ships through from the Pacific Ocean, and this project would double the capacity of the canal by 2015. In order to accommodate the larger ships and the expected increase in business, the Port of Wilmington needs to create a deepwater terminal on the Delaware River. To this end, the State of Delaware is attempting to attract private investment. Dredging work is necessary to increase the depth of the Delaware River from its current 40 feet to 45 feet. The very future of the port may depend on how well it improves its facilities to meet the expected growth in worldwide commerce. (Courtesy of Delaware Historical Society.)